ROSES *Love* GARLIC

COMPANION
PLANTING AND
OTHER SECRETS
OF FLOWERS

LOUISE RIOTTE

STOREY
BOOKS

*The mission of Storey Publishing is to serve our customers
by publishing practical information that encourages personal independence
in harmony with the environment.*

Edited by Julia Needham and Deborah Burns
Cover design by Meredith Maker
Cover illustration by Linda Devito Soltis
Text design by Cynthia N. McFarland
Text production by Eileen M. Clawson
Line drawings by the author
Indexed by Susan Olason, Indexes & Knowledge Maps

The information in this book is true and complete to the best of our knowledge. All recommendations are made without guarantee on the part of the author or Storey Publishing. The author and publisher disclaim any liability in connection with the use of this information. For additional information please contact Storey Books, 210 MASS MoCA Way, North Adams, MA 01247.

Storey books are available for special premium and promotional uses and for customized editions. For further information, please call the Custom Publishing Department at 1-800-793-9396.

Printed in the United States by R. R. Donnelley
10 9 8 7 6

Library of Congress Cataloging-in-Publication Data

Riotte, Louise.
    Roses love garlic : companion planting and other secrets of flowers / Louise Riotte. — [2nd ed.]
        p. cm.
    Includes bibliographical references (p.) and index.
    ISBN 1-58017-028-5 (pbk. : alk. paper)
    1. Companion planting. 2. Organic gardening. 3. Companion crops.
    4. Plants, Useful. I. Title.
SB453.6.R56 1998
  635—dc21   97-42029
                                                              CIP

Table of Contents

The Wide World of Flowers

Flowers, from wildflowers to the finest cultivars, are beloved in every part of the world. Most are used as decorations, but many are also used for medicinal purposes, or to help other flowers grow or resist disease. What is a flower? The word may mean either the blossom or the whole plant. Botanists use the word flower to mean only the blossom of a plant. They call the whole plant — blossom, stem, leaves, and roots — a flowering plant. Any plant that produces some sort of flowers, even a tiny, colorless one, is a flowering plant. Thus, grasses, roses, lilies, apple trees, and oaks are all flowering plants.

Herbaceous (nonwoody) flowering plants are generally classified by the length of time that the plant normally lives. Annuals live only one year. Biennials live for two years, blooming well only the second year. Perennials live for more than two years; they bloom the year after they are planted. Woody flowering plants — trees and shrubs — usually live for a number of years.

By any definition, flowers and flowering plants are essential to life on earth. We depend on them for our food. Flowering plants include almost all of our grains, fruits, and vegetables. We eat the roots of beets and carrots, the leaves of lettuce, the seeds of beans and peas, the fruits of apples and peaches, and the young stems of asparagus, all of which are parts of blooming plants. And artichokes, broccoli, and cauliflower are undeveloped flower clusters. Even the animals that we eat — cattle, sheep, and hogs — live on flowering plants.

We have learned many different ways in which to use plants. Dandelion and elderberry blossoms are used to make wine. Cloves, the flower buds of the tropical clove tree, are used to flavor many foods. Pickled flower buds of the caper bush are used as a relish.

Many flowers are known by their scent, which may range from pleasant to unpleasant, from the delightful fragrance of the rose to the reek of the pelican flower of South America, which smells like carrion. Scent, whether appealing to humans or not, is a key way that flowers attract pollinators.

Most flowers need soil to grow, but some can grow on tree branches, taking their sustenance from the air, while others float on lakes and streams.

Even hot, dry deserts have many lovely blossoms. During and after the rainy season, they spring up as if by magic to bloom quickly and set seed so another generation will be there to rise again when the season is right. Just about the only places flowers do not grow are in the ice-covered parts of the Arctic and Antarctic.

Some water blossoms are so small they can be seen only under a microscope; others, like the giant rafflesia, the largest flower in the world, which grows wild in Malaya and Indonesia, may measure three feet across!

A fascinating aspect of flowering plants, and one with practical value to the gardener, is how the different kinds interact when planted together. This is a subject that we will be looking at closely in this book.

Companion Flowers

Companion planting is not a form of magic. It is simple and practical, making use of known factors in planning a flower or vegetable garden. Companion plantings of some kind have been practiced throughout most of agricultural history.

Early settlers from Europe found the Native Americans planting corn and pumpkins together. In Holland in the 1800s a border of hemp (cannabis) was often planted around a cabbage field to keep away the white cabbage butterflies. Nature herself grows many different kinds of plants successfully as "companions." Furthermore, her plants, in most instances, grow very closely together. Instead of isolating particular kinds or varieties, she often places them shoulder to shoulder. Thus they become a source of needed shade, a climbing support, or a provider of mulch and soil-conditioning food. They may even repel other plants, preventing a sturdy, too-aggressive species from completely taking over.

Legumes such as clover and alfalfa have long been used as companion crops by farmers who have grown them to add nitrogen to the soil. The nitrogen "fixed" by legumes and other plants is not immediately available to neighboring plants but is released when the legume, or a portion of it, dies and becomes incorporated in the soil. In the flower garden lupines and other plants belonging to the Bean family perform the same function.

Some companion plants offer mechanical benefits; roots of large plants may break up the soil for smaller ones and make root penetration easier, especially in tight soil. Deep taproots of dandelions and other plants bring up minerals and make them available to plants growing nearer the surface.

Large plants (hollyhocks, sunflowers) may provide shade, wind protection, or higher humidity for small plants near them. In nature, shrubs growing around the trunk of a tree may protect it from animals. At the same time the tree, because of the shade it provides, protects the shrubs from being overwhelmed by weeds.

Another key to companion planting is controlled competition. A gardener growing a perennial flower border is engaging in one of the most complex forms of companion planting. The garden is designed not only for color, texture, height, and bloom sequence but also for controlled competition through proper spacing and varying heights. Smaller plants are protected by larger ones, but thought must also be given to the aggressive plants that will crowd out slower-growing ones if they are not kept within bounds.

We have also learned that it is unwise to plant together those plants that are susceptible to the same insects and diseases. Columbines, which are very attractive to red spiders, should not be planted near other flowers, or tomatoes, that the spider mites also find tasty.

We know, too, that certain trees exude toxic substances through their roots to inhibit germination of their own seedlings beneath them. This is their natural way to reduce or eliminate competition. On the other hand, the root exudates of dahlias are helpful against certain kinds of nematodes, and they are protective to other flowers growing nearby.

Many rock-garden plants also could be considered companions because they all do well in somewhat dry, sunny sites. Environmental factors make these plants companions.

Pumpkins and corn, as the Indians knew, grow well together because they are suited to the same conditions and their growing rates let them compete favorably for light, water, and nutrients. Plants that like the same growing conditions but occupy different soil strata make good companions — African marigolds and narcissus, for example — and the marigolds also repel certain nematodes that attack the bulbs.

We find many other unusual examples of "togetherness." Hawkweed or Indian paintbrush, a beautiful flower and a great attractant for hummingbirds, will not grow from seed (in cultivation) unless another plant is sown in the same pot with its seeds. The usual practice is to use blue grama (*Bouteloua gracilis*).

So now let's look at some of the flowers and plants, both cultivated and wild, familiar and unusual, that I hope you will find beautiful and useful.

Flower Lore

Adonis, Flower of Adonis *(Adonis)*

This flower is named for Adonis, the beloved of Venus. According to legend, the flower sprang from the blood of Adonis after he was killed by a wild boar.

Adonis plants belong to the Buttercup family, Ranunculaceae. The flowers are yellow or red and have 5 to 16 petals. Use annual and perennial varieties for the front border and rock garden.

African Marigold *(Tagetes erecta)*

"African" is a misnomer, for these plants hail from Mexico. To defeat nematodes that attack narcissus, nurserymen often plant African marigolds as a cover crop before planting the bulbs. To achieve satisfactory control, they plant the marigolds at least three months before planting the bulb crop.

African marigolds are also planted around apple trees or nursery stock used in grafting and budding to discourage pests. Planted near roses damaged by certain nematodes, they restore vigorous growth.

African Violet *(Saintpaulia)*

This is a great favorite of indoor gardeners for its beauty. To propagate, plant the leaves in slightly moistened potting soil in a margarine tub. Slip the tub in a plastic bag and close. New plants will grow quickly and form roots.

Ajuga *(Ajuga)*

Ajuga is a delightful ground cover. *A. reptans* var. *metallica crispa* is especially lovely planted in small patches between the green varieties. It has deep purple foliage and deep blue flowers. Although it can grow in shade, it does best in full sun. *A. reptans* 'Pink Beauty' has whorls of delicate pink flowers in May and June. *A. pyramidalis,* which is larger than the others, has deep green foliage and blue flowers with purple bracts.

Alkanet, Bugloss *(Anchusa)*

This genus name is derived from the Greek *anchousa,* a cosmetic plant or stain; it may possibly have been a coloring from the blue flowers used by the ancient Greek women for eye shadow. However, a red infusion may be prepared from the roots and, as John Gerard says in his *Herball,* "The Gentelwomen of France do paint their faces with these roots as it is said." The genus also provides showy biennials and perennials for borders.

Allheal, Amantilla, Jacob's Ladder, Setwell, Valerian *(Polemonium)*

The common perennial border plant allheal *(Polemonium caeruleum),* also known as Jacob's ladder or green valerian, reaches a height of 18 to 25 inches and bears beautiful blue flowers in June; the variety *album* has white flowers.

The value of allheal lies in its roots, which are dug in spring before the plant has begun its growth. Dry, then pulverize the roots; store the powder in an airtight container. Valerian tea is useful for many nervous disorders such as cramps, headaches, and stomach gases. The flavor is not particularly pleasant, but it is sleep-inducing and tranquilizing. Use a teaspoon of root per cup and steep in boiling water. As an herbal sedative, it is very calming.

Dried valerian added to bathwater helps with skin troubles and has a soothing effect on the nervous system. Because of its sleep-inducing quality, a small amount is beneficial when added to herbal cushions or pillows. Pillows may also contain a mixture of dried peppermint, sage, lemon balm, and lavender with small additions of dill, marjoram, thyme, tarragon, woodruff, angelica, rosemary, lemon verbena, and red bergamot. (See the chapter on Cosmetics and Fragrances for directions.)

Aloe *(Aloe vera)*

The flower of this, nature's own medicine plant, is very undistinguished, having an extremely long stem and very small blossoms. The plant, with more than 200 species, is a vegetable belonging to the Lily family.

Cut leaves exude a juice useful as a wound dressing on a tree limb after it has been cut. The healing qualities of aloe are now widely recognized and the extracts are used in various cosmetics. It is best known for its use on burns. The juice taken internally is also healing.

Alpine Flowers

These flowers know so precisely when spring is coming that they bore their way up through lingering snowbanks, developing their own heat with which to melt the snow. One, *Stellaria decumbens,* is found at 20,130 feet in the Himalayas.

Alyssum *(Lobularia maritima)*

The white, honey-smelling alyssums are charming with 'Martha Washington' geraniums. Or try the 'Violet Queen' variety with a 'Cecile Brunner' rose. Sow outdoors in early spring. Do not cover; the seed needs light to germinate. Pot up alyssum in August for indoor bloom in November.

Amaranth *(Amaranthus)*

This is the common name of a family that includes both weeds and garden plants. The family is mostly herbs. The name comes from a Greek word meaning "unfading," and is appropriate because the amaranth flowers remain colored even when dried.

A member of the Amaranth family, cockscomb *(Celosia),* is very often grown as a garden flower. *Celosia cristata* bears flattish, dense heads of crimson, yellow, orange, or pink flowers and is an excellent pot plant. Another type, *C. plumosa,* grows in the form of a feather plume and comes in scarlet, crimson, and gold. These plants add brilliant color to the garden.

Amaryllis *(Amaryllis)*

This is a genus of beautiful, lilylike plants that are usually grown indoors. Pot an amaryllis in a container only slightly larger than the bulb. Cover about one-third of the bulb with soil. For best bloom, the amaryllis should be potbound.

Potting up amaryllis

Amsonia, Willow Amsonia *(A. salicifolia, A. tabernae-montana)*

This unusual and little-known perennial may be used as a specimen or toward the front of the herbaceous border. Its arching, willowy stems display narrow, glossy leaves and, during May and June, clusters of small star-shaped flowers of a strange steel blue color. The plant grows in sun but prefers part shade, particularly in warm climates. Because it is highly resistant to wind, it grows well in the Southwest and in coastal areas. Amsonias grow slowly, are never troubled by insects or diseases, and rarely need division or staking.

Angelica *(Angelica archangelica)*

This decorative, broad-spreading plant is the largest garden herb. Although a biennial, it will live many years if you keep the flowers cut, but once seed develops, the plant will die. The roots and leaves have medicinal properties. The candied stems are used in confectionery, the fruits have flavoring properties, and an oil of medicinal value is derived from the roots and seeds. Dry seeds do not germinate well.

Anise *(Pimpinella anisum)*

This is a white-flowered annual belonging to the Carrot family. When thoroughly dry, the seed germinates with difficulty. Therefore, you will get better plants from your own fresh seed, and it will add more potent flavoring to bread, cakes, and cookies. Use the green leaves in salads as a garnish.

Aniseed germinates better, grows more vigorously, and forms better heads when sown with coriander. Anise oil attracts fish.

Anthemis *(Anthemis)*

The name comes from the Greek *anthemon,* a flower, and refers to the plant's profuse blooming. Use these aromatic perennials for the border or rock garden. Chamomile tea is made from *A. nobilis,* and a nonflowering variety of this species is sometimes used for lawns, particularly in very dry areas. It is said also to improve the health of other plants when grown close to them.

Anthurium *(Anthurium)*

These greenhouse plants, chiefly from tropical America, belong to the Arum family. They are grown for their brilliantly colored flower spathes that appear in spring and summer, or their ornamental leaves. The name refers to the tail-like flower in the center of the spathe and is derived from *anthos,* a flower, and *oura,* a tail. However, the tail always reminds me of Pinocchio's nose!

One of the most magnificent anthuriums is *A. veitchi,* which has metallic green leaves two to four feet long.

Asparagus Fern *(Asparagus plumosus)*
The plant, a member of the Lily family, is slender, with fernlike foliage on climbing stems. The fronds are very popular for floral arrangements. *A. sprengeri,* an ideal plant for pots, has long branched stems clothed in narrow leaves and bears small white flowers followed by small red berries. *A. medeoloides,* the smilax of the florist, has dense minute foliage.

Aspidistra, Parlor Palm, Cast-Iron Plant *(Aspidistra elatior)*
Gracie Fields made this plant famous in the song "The Biggest Aspidistra in the World." During Victorian times it was probably the most popular houseplant, gradually giving way to the philodendron, dracaena, and ivy. However, it is becoming popular again, perhaps because it is the most easily managed of all houseplants and may be kept healthy and vigorous for years with a minimum of attention.

Aspidistras are shade plants with a low respiration level. Even with little sunlight, the leaves can support a steady growth of all parts of the plant. Flowers come in winter, December to March, and arise at soil level. With their magenta and gold colors, they are reminiscent of sea anemones or tiny exotic lilies, to which they are related. In their native forests of the Himalayan or Japanese foothills, the flowers are pollinated by a tiny snail crawling over them. As "potted captives" the plants seldom produce seeds but may be increased by root division. The types with variegated leaves of cream and green are especially attractive.

Aster *(Aster frikartii)*
The plant sends up an abundance of flowers from June to November, even after a frost or two, and deserves to be seen more often in gardens. Asters are an immense group with about 160 species native to North America. On moist, low soil or by roadsides we find bushy aster *(Boltonia steroides);* New England aster; *Aster tradescanti;* and willow-leaved aster; and on banks of streams and in swamps, purple-stemmed aster *(A. puniceus).* If asters invade pastures or fields, it indicates a need for drainage.

Astilbe *(Astilbe)*
The name is thought to be derived from the Greek word for "not shining," a reference to the leaflets. Perennials are useful for border and rock gardens; the many modern cultivars are generally the most handsome, and are known as *Spiraea.*

Auricula *(Primula auricula)*

The name comes from the Latin *auricula,* an ear, and is a reference to the shape of the leaves, which resemble the ear of an animal. Auricula itself is one of the 30 or so classes into which botanists now divide the genus *Primula.* So-called Alpine auriculas are probably derived from *Primula pubescens* and what are known as florist auriculas from *Primula auricula.*

Baby Blue-Eyes *(Nemophila menziesii)*

This plant shares honors with catnip as a feline attractant. In her book *The Fragrant Garden,* Louise Beebe Wilder says cats "will even dig the plants out of the ground." Baby blue-eyes, however, deserves to be more widely planted, as it makes a colorful ground cover from June to frost.

Baby's Breath, Chalk Plant *(Gypsophila)*

Baby's breath is a must for dainty bouquets. In early summer these plants bear a profusion of feathery panicles of small, starry white or pink flowers on threadlike stems, creating a delicate and beautiful veil-like effect. The plant withstands cutting well and succeeds in any well-drained, not-too-heavy soil, but mix some lime into the soil before planting. *G. paniculata* 'Bristol Fairy' has large panicles of pure white, double flowers. 'Pink Fairy' produces double flowers on strong, wiry stems from June to September and adds an airy, graceful touch when placed with larger cut flowers.

Bachelor's-Button, Cornflower, Blue Bonnet, Bluebottle *(Centaurea cyanus)*

Actually a beautiful weed, the cornflower is of value in supplying bees with honey, even in the driest weather. On limestone soils the cornflowers are blue; on acid soil they frequently develop rose and pink flowers, sometimes both colors on the same plant. The more inclined toward red, the more acid is the soil.

Balm, Lemon *(Melissa officinalis aurea)*

The flowers, which are salvia-shaped, are white, small, and inconspicuous; the heart-shaped leaves are sometimes variegated green and cream. When crushed in the hand, the leaf emits a delicious odor, suggestive of lemon-scented verbena. *Melissa* is Greek for bee, and bees obtain large quantities of

honey from the flowers. The plant will flourish in
ordinary garden soil but needs a sunny, well-drained
location. Balm *(Melissa)* was used by ancient Arabs as
an ingredient in a cordial. Many home remedies call
for it to treat vertigo, migraine, lack of appetite, and
indigestion.

Lemon balm

Bat Flower *(Tacca chantrieri)*

The bat plant is said to have "the blackest flower in the
world." It hails from Malaya and Burma. Some call it
the devil's flower, and the many strange stories told about it probably originate
from the malevolent way in which the eyes in the bloom seem to follow your
every move. Sometimes its curious influorescence looks batlike. To some it
resembles an aerial jellyfish. It is indeed an awesome flower and a prize for
those who want to grow something different.

Balsamroot *(Balsamorhiza sagittata)*

A powder of stems and leaves is somewhat toxic to pea aphids. The seeds
are edible and may be roasted, ground, and mixed with flour to make a
bread, according to author Nelson Coon.

Begonia *(Begonia)*

There are many varieties of begonias — tuberous begonias, wax or fibrous-
rooted types, and those grown for their ornamental leaves such as *Begonia
massoniana* 'Iron Cross', as well as less well-known types.

All begonias grow well in pots, porch boxes, or hanging baskets. The
best potting compost consists of two parts fibrous loam; one part leaf mold
or peat moss; half a part well-decomposed manure; and a sprinkling of
sand. Add ¼ ounce of bonemeal to each quart of compost. Keep the
atmosphere moist and shade the plants from hot sunshine. Begonias do well
planted with *Achimenes* (a gesneriad) in pots or boxes, as both take the same
culture and will bloom well in shade.

Belladonna Lily *(Amaryllis belladonna)*

The common garden amaryllis may be grown permanently outdoors in
California and Florida, but in most places the large tuberous bulbs are
taken up and stored during the winter. Store them with caution because the
alkaloids present in the bitter-tasting bulb cause trembling and vomiting if

inadvertently eaten. The showy, sweet-scented flowers are typically rosy pink and trumpet-shaped, which makes for a beautiful pot plant. Some members of the Amaryllis family, such as the century plant and the Cuban and Mauritian hemp, are sources of useful fibers.

Bergenia *(Saxifraga* or *Megasea)*

These handsome plants, about one foot tall, have masses of decorative broad, deep green foliage and clusters of pink flowers that appear in early spring from March to May. They are fine for the front of the border, to "face down" shrubs, as an informal ground cover, and for the rock garden.

Bible Leaf, Costmary, Alecost *(Chrysanthemum balsamita)*

Used as a bookmark, the bible leaf provided some distraction for children to smell during long church services in colonial days. The plant will grow in some shade but will not bloom there. The flower heads are golden yellow, small, buttonlike, and in loose clusters.

Bleeding Heart *(Dicentra)*

This old-time favorite is still very popular. It may have red, pink, or white flowers. *D. spectabilis* is the old-fashioned showy bleeding heart with long, graceful, pendulous racemes covered with heart-shaped pink flowers on plants about two feet in height. Of easy culture, these plants increase in size but do not need transplanting or dividing very often. However, since they do go dormant early in the fall, it is wise to set another plant close by as a filler; *Anemone vitifolia* is recommended for this purpose.

Blue False Indigo *(Baptisia australis)*

This perennial of unique appeal makes an outstanding cornerstone in the perennial border. Its blue-green leaves stay handsome all season and its nine- to twelve-inch spikes of intense blue, pealike flowers bloom in late spring and summer. It is splendid as a companion for Oriental poppies, and grows best in a lime-free soil in a sunny location.

Borage *(Borago officinalis)*

Borage is the common name of a familiar herb whose leaves and flowers have traditionally been used in claret cup and other beverages, to which it imparts a cucumber-like fragrance and refreshing flavor. The blue flowers are also dried for use in potpourri. It is an annual and easily raised from seed sown in spring in ordinary garden soil.

For many centuries, borage has been used medicinally; in the preparation of various cordials and cups, it is believed to have an exhilarating effect. Pliny had a high opinion of its virtues "because it maketh a man merry and joyful." However, present-day herbalists advise against using borage for long periods.

The plants require a sunny position, but the blue coloring of the flowers is finest when the plants are grow in poor soil.

Bouncing Bet, Soapwort *(Saponaria officinalis)*

Bouncing Bet

This showy flowering plant grows almost too readily. Its great virtue lies in its sudsing quality, the bruised leaves acting as a soap when agitated in water. The lather may be used as a shampoo. When decomposed, the lathering substance (saponin) helps to retain soil moisture. (See also *Cuckoo Flower,* page 20).

Bouncing Bet was brought to the New World more than 300 years ago for its valuable lathering qualities. It was once used extensively for washing fine silks and woolens. The carnation-like pink and white flowers cover the plant during its long blooming season.

Bromeliads

Did you know that you can force a bromeliad to bloom by covering it for five days with a plastic bag that has an apple inside? A bromeliad is any plant belonging to the Pineapple family. Typical bromeliads are aechmea, billbergia, cryptanthus, nidularium, tillandsia, and vriesia.

If you're cramped for space indoors, try miniatures. Among my favorites are the little bromeliads, specifically those known as *Cryptanthus,* or earth-stars. The species known as *C. vivittatus minor,* for example, forms a rosette three to four inches across. It hugs the ground and is composed of leathery-stiff leaves, the edges of which have tiny spines. If you run your index finger lightly along one, it will remind you of a cat's tongue.

The leaves are striped lengthwise in color that varies depending on age and growing conditions. Usually they are a combination of green with red or pink suffusion. The flowers, which are white and typical of cryptanthus, grow from the center of a mature plant; hence the name of the plant.

Buckbean, Bogbean, Marsh Trefoil
(Menyanthes trifoliata L.)

Buckbean

This perennial plant found in marshes and bogs has white flowers tinged with rose borne in a terminal cluster on a stalk four to twelve inches long. Rootstalks used as an emergency food must be dried, ground, then washed several times to leach out the bitter principle, and then dried again. Fernald describes the bread made from such flour as "thoroughly unpalatable but nutritious." In Europe the roots have been used to replace hops in making beer.

Bulbs

You can have bulbs flower in succession, from snowdrops in early spring to lilies in late summer. There are bulbs for every purpose:

Beds and borders. Try hyacinth with English daisies in pink or white, pansies in selected colors, or forget-me-nots for color combinations. Tulips give a medley of color in a good-sized tulip bed edged with pansies.

Rock gardens. Small bulbs bring color and early-season interest. Snowdrops lead off; then come the crocus species in white, yellow, and lilac shades; followed closely by little *Iris reticulata* in very dark purple with orange veinings. Other suggestions include grape hyacinth *(Muscari)*, glory-of-the-snow *(Chionodoxa)*, spring glory *(Scilla)*, small narcissus *(Narcissus minimus)*, hoop-petticoat daffodil *(N. bulbocodium)*, and angel's-tears *(N. triandrus)*, to name but a few possibilities that do well together.

Forcing bulbs for winter bloom. Narcissus, such as paper-whites and Chinese sacred lily, are the easiest and earliest to bloom. Set them in bowls of pebbles and water in September and they'll bloom for Thanksgiving. Later starts will prolong the season. Hyacinths, white Roman and the miniatures in yellow, pink, and blue, grow well in bowls of vermiculite or the special bulb fiber obtainable from dealers. Daffodils and tulips are mostly grown in standard pots or bulb pans in a good soil mixture. Use precooled daffodil bulbs or cover pots outside until after a heavy freeze before trying to force them.

After blooming, spring bulbs should have the dying flowers cut off, though not the whole stem, so that the plant's strength is not wasted in seed production. Work the soil lightly between the bulbs with a hand fork or hoe before planting with annual bedding plants for summer display.

Naturalizing bulbs. Some bulbs grow and flower for many years under natural or "wild" conditions; their only need is good soil. Snowdrops often grow and flower on the north side of a slope for generations. Grape hyacinths grow and spread. So will Siberian squill and glory-of-the-snow. Crocuses bring color and interest to bare ground. Plant poet's narcissus *(Narcissus poeticus)* near water. Spanish bluebells *(Scilla hispanica),* in delicate shades of white, pink, and blue, enliven the somber green of ferns in a moist, shady spot. Daffodils naturalize readily although they will not increase as rapidly in grass as under cultivation. Trumpet or large-cupped daffodils look enchanting on a grassy slope.

Cactus

The origin of the bizarre Cactus family is shrouded in mystery. Botanists theorize that the first cacti evolved from roses because their lavish, showy flowers closely resemble roses in shape and structure. Cactus blossoms are unbelievably beautiful, especially the fragrant flowers that bloom at night.

Native Americans and other southwesterners find a variety of uses for cacti. Many species have delicious edible parts: The pads of opuntia taste like green beans, and the flowers may be used in the same way as squash blossoms. The fruits of some species taste like strawberries. The pulp of the barrel cactus is used to make cactus candy.

Some of the giant cacti are used as lumber, to roof houses and to make cradles. Peyote cactus buttons have been used for centuries for medicinal and religious purposes. Many cacti are beautiful and interesting even when not in bloom and are widely used in the Southwest for landscaping. Many cactus fanciers in more northern climates enjoy potted cactus or indoor cactus gardens.

Cacti comprise a perennial family of herbs and shrubs equipped with areoles. No other plants have these unique organs of growth. From them spring branches, flowers, glochids, spines, and, when present, leaves. If areoles are removed, the cactus will die.

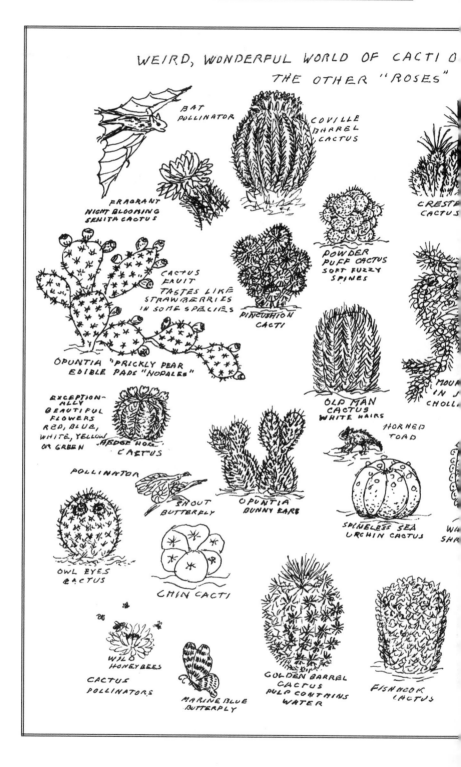

WEIRD, WONDERFUL WORLD OF CACTI O...
THE OTHER "ROSES"

BAT POLLINATOR

COVILLE BARREL CACTUS

FRAGRANT NIGHT BLOOMING SENITA CACTUS

CRESTE... CACTUS

POWDER PUFF CACTUS SOFT FUZZY SPINES

CACTUS FRUIT TASTES LIKE STRAWBERRIES IN SOME SPECIES

PINCUSHION CACTI

OPUNTIA "PRICKLY PEAR EDIBLE PADS "NOPALES"

OLD MAN CACTUS WHITE HAIRS

MOUN... IN S... CHOLL...

EXCEPTIONALLY BEAUTIFUL FLOWERS RED, BLUE, WHITE, YELLOW OR GREEN
HEDGE HOG CACTUS

HORNED TOAD

POLLINATOR

SNOUT BUTTERFLY

OPUNTIA BUNNY EARS

SPINELESS SEA URCHIN CACTUS

WI... SHR...

OWL EYES CACTUS

CHIN CACTI

WILD HONEY BEES
CACTUS POLLINATORS

MARINE BLUE BUTTERFLY

GOLDEN BARREL CACTUS PULP CONTAINS WATER

FISHHOOK CACTUS

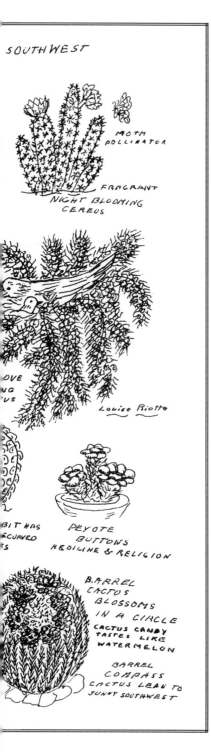

SOUTHWEST

MOTH POLLINATOR

FRAGRANT NIGHT BLOOMING CEREUS

Louise Riotte

OVE NG US

BIT HAS ECURVED S

PEYOTE BUTTONS MEDICINE & RELIGION

B. BARREL CACTUS BLOSSOMS IN A CIRCLE CACTUS CANDY TASTES LIKE WATERMELON

BARREL COMPASS CACTUS LEAN TO SUNNY SOUTHWEST

Cacti: The "Other Roses" and Some Pollinators

Bat (pollinator)
Coville barrel cactus
Fragrant night-blooming senita cactus
Opuntia (edible pads; fruits of some species
   taste like strawberries)
Hedgehog cactus (exceptionally beautiful
   flowers)
Snout butterfly (pollinator)
Owl eyes cactus
Chin cacti
Wild honeybee (pollinator)
Marine blue butterfly
Pincushion cacti
Opuntia 'Bunny Ears'
Golden barrel cactus (pulp contains water)
Powder puff cactus (soft fuzzy spines)
Old man cactus (white hairs)
Horned toad
Spineless sea urchin cactus
Fishhook cactus
Crested cactus
Mourning dove family in jumping cholla cactus
Wait-a-bit (sharply recurved spines)
Moth (pollinator)
Fragrant night-blooming cereus cactus
Peyote buttons (used in medicine and religion)
Barrel cactus (tastes like watermelon)

Calla Lily, Arum Lily *(Zantedeschia)*

This plant is easily grown in mild climates such as in California, where it sometimes "escapes" and grows wild. The most popular kind is the common calla, which has handsome green leaves and bears large white flower spathes. It is cultivated in large quantities by market growers for the spathes, which are in great demand for decorative purposes, particularly at Easter.

The common calla and its varieties are moisture-loving plants and must be grown in rich, loamy soil that does not dry out quickly. In parts of North America where the winters are mild, the common calla and its varieties may be grown outdoors. They thrive in moist or wet soil on the edge of a pool or pond, or may even be planted in shallow water.

Calla lily

The chief kinds of yellow or golden calla are *Z. elliottiana* and *Z. angustiloba.* The pink calla, *Z. rehmannii,* is a smaller and much lower plant than the white or yellow-flowered kinds. There is also a spotted calla, *Z. albomaculata,* and a black-throated calla, *Z. melanoleuca.* This last has yellow spathes with a conspicuous black-purple spot at the base inside.

In Lapland, people grind the root of the marsh calla into flour for bread.

Candytuft *(Iberis)*

This plant is practically foolproof even for "purple thumbers," and does well in any soil in sun or light shade. To extend the blooming period, shear off the spent blossoms. Use this evergreen subshrub for edging borders and garden walks, in the rockery, or for mass plantings. Most candytufts have white flowers; *I. jucunda* is noted for its dense pink flowers and blue-green foliage.

Canna, Indian Shot *(Canna)*

These tender herbaceous perennial plants from South America and the West Indies have unbranched, stately stems springing from a fleshy rootstock. During the summer they have large, ornamental foliage and brilliant, showy, gladiolus-like flowers in dense terminal clusters.

The leaves and stems of cannas have insecticidal properties. They are particularly useful as a greenhouse fumigant to control aphids, ants, and mites. Place newspapers in the bottom of a pail with a metal grating on top of them. Above the grating put a layer of straw to act as a buffer; then place leaves and stems on top. Light the newspapers; the leaves will smolder rather than burn, producing thick smoke. Close the greenhouse door tightly and smoke the leaves for about 30 minutes.

Carnation *(Dianthus)*

These charming plants of cheerful colors and spicy fragrance have attractive, often bluish green foliage. They are fine for borders, edging, and rock gardens. The hardy border carnation, *D. caryophyllus,* blooms almost perpetually. Grow it in well-drained soil with lime added and protect it in winter with a dry mulch. Cut back the plants after blooming.

Carnations are very popular for Mother's Day.

Carpetweed *(Mollugo verticillata)*

This is a low-growing weed that forms mats in gardens and on paths. It thrives well on lighter, sandy soils, but will not resist hoeing and cultivation.

Charles Harris in his book *Eat the Weeds* states that carpetweed is good steamed or boiled, or used as a potherb.

Carrion Cactus *(Stapelia)*

This cactus looks and smells like carrion and attracts carrion flies from a long distance. Bluebottle flies also seek it out and have been known to lay their eggs on the leathery petals, as they do on another foul-smelling plant, *Amorphophallus rivieri,* or devil's-tongue.

Carrot, Wild

See *Queen Anne's Lace.*

Catchfly *(Silene)*

This group of plants often infests dry meadows, clover, and alfalfa fields. It may become a pest if not controlled by early cutting. The sleepy catchfly, forked or hairy catchfly, and night-flowering catchfly are all annuals and propagate by seed. The sleepy catchfly opens its flower only to bright sunshine. The name catchfly is derived from a gluelike substance on the stem, which does catch flies.

Celandine, Great *(Chelidonium majus)*

This plant grows here and there in barnyards, pastures, and roadsides. It contains a yellow, slightly poisonous juice, which was once used against warts (hence the popular names wortweed, killwort, and devil's milk). It has also been recommended that the freshly oozing juice be applied daily to corns until cured, or used on sores of horses. There is a caustic quality in the juice (even more in the roots than the upper parts) that could be of medicinal value for skin conditions. Cultivation and early cutting before it goes to seed will keep celandine from spreading.

Ceratostigma *(Plumbago larpentiae)*

This plant is truly one of the most rewarding of all perennials. Growing only six to eight inches high, it forms mats twelve to eighteen inches across, solidly covered with clusters of intense peacock blue flowers in late summer and fall. Simultaneously the interesting leathery foliage turns deep mahogany red. Use the plant for ground cover or for underplanting shrubs. It will grow virtually anywhere, good soil or bad, well drained or poorly drained, in heat or cold, sun or shade!

Cherokee Rose *(Rosa laevigata)*

This charming decoration of our southern states originally came from China, but is now widely and permanently naturalized. The foliage is evergreen and shining and the immense white single blooms have the rich fragrance of the gardenia.

Chickweed *(Cerastium arvense)*

The field-mouse-ear chickweed is a beautiful flowering native plant used in gardens. It derives its name mouse-ear from the shape of its leaves. The blossom is large, white, and star-shaped. Because of its creeping rootstock (every joint can produce a new plant), it can become troublesome in pastures. Plow and cultivate to control it. In *Gardening Without Poisons,* Beatrice Trum Hunter says that "rye overpowers chickweed." Chickweed likes roadsides, sunny hills, and even grows way up on high mountains.

Common mouse-ear chickweed *(Cerastium vulgatum),* which propagates only by seed, has smaller leaves and blossoms than the field mouse-ear. It likes to grow in fields and on roadsides. Early cultivation in grainfields will lift up the shallow roots and so eradicate this perennial.

Chinese Lantern *(Physalis alkekengi)*

Chinese lantern is often grown for its large, showy calyxes, which are attractive as winter decorations. The white flowers are followed by dense clusters of bright orange-scarlet, lanternlike husks enclosing scarlet berries. Cut the stems in autumn and dry to preserve. Chinese lantern is an aggressive plant that will rapidly take over, so grow it in a waste spot to prevent crowding other flowers.

Chocolate Flower *(Berlandiera lyrata)*

This branched perennial has pale yellow, daisylike flowers that smell like chocolate. The underside of the "petals" have brown veins. The large green bracts below the flower are attractive for dried arrangements.

Christmas Rose *(Helleborus niger)*

This perennial herb is often cultivated in gardens for its midwinter bloom. Because it blooms in early spring in some regions, it is often incorrectly called the Lenten rose. The white or pink-white flowers, about two inches across, become purplish with age. The thick but fibrous rootstalk, which is blackish brown, yields drugs for commercial use. However, the rootstalk is violently poisonous if eaten and, as a warning, emits an unpleasant odor when cut or broken. It has a bitter, slightly acrid taste. The poisonous leaves may cause dermatitis on contact.

Chrysanthemum

See the chapter on Companion Planting with Flowers and Herbs.

Clove *(Syzygium aromaticum)*

This is the name given to the flower buds of a tropical tree that grows wild in the Moluccas, or Spice Islands, and in Sumatra, Jamaica, the West Indies, and Brazil. The tree's purplish flowers grow on jointed stalks and are picked before they open. Reddish when first picked, they turn dark brown when dried. The dried buds are used as a spice. They have a fragrant odor and a warm, sharp taste. Maybe you know them best as decorations for a fine ham.

Clove Pink *(Dianthus caryophyllus)*

This is the gillyflower of medieval Europe, popular for its variety of color and sweet, spicy fragrance. Before oriental spices became available to everyone, the flowers of clove pinks were used with foods and for flavoring wine and vinegar. These lovely old-fashioned pinks bloom from early summer until late fall and keep the air delightfully perfumed — and the plants are winter hardy.

Clover *(Trifolium)*

Like other legumes, clover fixes the nitrogen from the air by means of bacteria growing on its roots. When the clover is plowed under, the nitrogen enriches the soil. Many of the clovers are used for cover crops, including the common red or sweet clover.

There are also bur, crimson, Egyptian, and Persian or Wood's clover, but red clover is the most important member of the family. The flowers of red clover will not be fertilized unless a bee pollinates them. When red clover was first planted in Australia, there were no bumblebees to carry the pollen; not until they were introduced did the red clover produce seed. Crimson clover is much used for soil improvement. Its flowers are often red but may be white or yellow.

Red clover herb tea is especially good for canaries. To make: Steep two teaspoons in ½ cup hot water and allow to stand 15 minutes. Put a few drops a day in the canary's drinking water.

Clover honey is very delicious and one of the best-known flavors.

Coleus *(Coleus)*

These are superb, colorful foliage plants for shady spots in the garden — and they are fine houseplants as well. The luxuriant foliage displays shades of red, green, crimson, yellow, white, pink, and combinations thereof. As exotic in color and form as they are, coleus are probably due for even bigger changes. They react strongly to radioactivity, and many new forms have been seen at the nuclear installation outside Knoxville.

Columbine

Columbine *(Aquilegia)*

These hardy perennial plants bear spurred, beautifully colored flowers from May to July. They grow wild in North America, Siberia, and other north temperate countries and belong to the Buttercup family, Ranunculaceae. The word *Aquilegia* is derived from *aquila,* an eagle, an indication of the spurlike petals.

Columbines will thrive in ordinary garden soil and are easily raised from seed. A sunny or partially shaded location suits them. But keep them to themselves — they do not companion well with other plants and are also very attractive to the red spider. However, the hummingbird finds their red and yellow bells irresistible.

Comfrey, Knitbone *(Symphytum officinale)*

This plant was believed to aid the knitting of fractured and broken bones and has been used for this purpose for centuries. The leaves make a poultice for bruises, swellings, and sprains. It has also been used for lung disorders, internal ulcers, external ruptures, burns, and splinters. However, it has been found to contain compounds that damage the liver and is no longer recommended for internal use.

Grown in the garden, comfrey is beneficial to other plants — a sort of "plant doctor." Because it is deep-rooting, comfrey does not rob minerals in the surface soil from other nearby plants. It keeps the surrounding soil rich and moist and gives protective shade and shelter with its large, rough leaves. Flowers are pale blue pink, bell-form, and borne in drooping clusters.

Compass Plant, Rosinweed, Pilotweed *(Silphium laciniatum)*

The scientific name refers to the resinous juice of these plants. Although the genus includes fifteen species of perennials in North America, only two are likely to be seen in cultivation.

The plant bears yellow flowers that look much like sunflowers. It is a coarse plant and sometimes grows to be 10 feet tall. The leaves are about 1½ feet long and are cut into several lobes. The petioles, or leaf stalks, bend so that the leaves, by pointing in a north–south direction, escape the strong midday sun, but get the full early-morning and late-afternoon light. Frontiersmen and hunters in the prairies of the Mississippi Valley noticed that this plant's leaves, pointing north and south, accurately indicate the points of the compass.

Coriander *(Coriandrum sativum)*

Grown for its savory seed, coriander is not suitable for the flower garden because the foliage and fresh seed have an evil smell. However, the foliage is delicate and lacy and the rosy white flower umbels are beautiful. The ripe seeds are fragrant and the odor increases as they dry. Use them in cooking.

Cotton, Ornamental *(Gossypium)*
These two-foot plants have pink buds and creamy blossoms, followed by big white bolls of cotton.

Creeping Charlie, Ground Ivy, Gill-over-the-Ground, Cat's-foot *(Glechoma hederacea)*
This member of the Mint family is a ground-hugging vine that returns year after year to produce pretty purple flowers and an aroma that protects nearby plants from insects. It spreads rapidly, sending down roots wherever it touches the ground, and likes a partially shaded location. According to some sources, sniffing the crushed foliage relieves headaches, and the roots contain a substance that stops bleeding.

Crown Vetch *(Coronilla)*
Crown vetch is wonderful for preventing soil erosion along steep banks and for choking out unwanted weeds. It increases quickly by sending out roots both above and below ground. The neat, billowy foliage grows no higher than two feet and, in season, is a mass of lovely pink flowers.

Cuckoo Flower, Meadow Pink *(Lychnis floscuculi)*
Originally from Asia Minor and Siberia, this plant prefers moist meadows and has some value for feeding livestock. Its blossoms are bright red. (The familiar garden varieties, pink, white, or blue, are known as phlox.)

The roots of all *Lychnis* species contain saponin, which produces a soapy foam if stirred in water. Before the discovery of soap, it was used along with the true *Saponaria* for washing. To this same group also belong red campion, found on grainfields and in pastures, and white cockle or evening lychnis, so called because its white blossoms open in the evening and close at sunrise.

Cupid's Dart, Love Plant *(Catananche caerulea)*
The flower spikes, springing from silver-green foliage, are an exquisite corn-flower blue and stay in bloom from early June right up to late September. These are superb as cut flowers, either fresh or dried to preserve the glorious color in long-lived arrangements. Plant in full sun in well-drained soil; they will seldom need dividing.

Cup Plant *(Silphium perfoliatum)*
This plant has yellow flowers, and its leaves join together to make a cup around the stem.

Cyclamen *(Cyclamen)*
This is a genus of dwarf tuberous plants from the Mediterranean regions. They are exotically handsome and best grown in a cool temperature. *Cyclamen* is from the Greek *kyklos,* a circle, referring to the coiling of the flower stems in some species after flowering. This is the plant's method of bringing the seed capsules down to soil level.

Do not keep these plants near any orchid plant at any time, as they give off ethylene gases that kill the orchid and its blossoms. However, cyclamen has long been esteemed for killing parasites on fruit trees. The principle, saponin, found in the bulbs, is effective fresh or dried.

Daffodils *(Narcissus)*
Daffodils announce the advent of spring. Their cheerful yellow combines well with the violet-purple of the grape hyacinth, or you might finish the bed off with a ring of crocuses. Daffodils discourage moles. In Europe and England the interest in daffodils has sometimes assumed the proportions of a craze. Rival enthusiasts grow and cross daffodils, getting extravagant prices ($500 to $2,000) for no more than five or six bulbs. In America we have never taken these flowers so seriously, but love them nevertheless and plant them widely in our spring gardens.

Daffodils

Dahlia *(Dahlia)*
If you want an ideal flower, try the vigorously growing dahlia for an abundance of beautiful blooms and, best of all, relative freedom from diseases and pests. They come in many sizes, many colors, and single or double flowered. Cactus varieties are particularly attractive.

Dahlias grow best in deep, fertile, well-drained soil in a sunny location; the plants are easily damaged by cold. Separate root clusters and plants about the time of the last killing frost. Space them three or four feet apart if you want large exhibition flowers. For large blooms, allow only one stalk per root to develop. Remove all small, weak sprouts. When the shoot is about six inches tall, pinch it back to the third set of leaves to promote branching.

Dahlias protect nearby flowers against nematodes.

Daisies, White or Ox-Eye *(Chrysanthemum leucanthemum)*

These are the well-known white flowers with long stems and yellow centers that often infest pastures, hayfields, and lawns. They are frequently planted with grass seed but should be avoided in the lawn. They increase with increasing acidity of the soil, standing surface moisture, and loss of lime. Good neutral compost with lime in it, bonemeal, surface harrowing, or frequent raking of the lawn to break the upper crust and root felt will take care of this problem.

Cultivated daisies are something else again, and there are many beautiful varieties for beds and borders.

Damiana *(Turnera aphrodisiaca)*

This Mexican and African plant has been widely recommended for treating impotency and for its tonic effect on the nervous system. Long ago, the Aztecs used the leaves of damiana as an aphrodisiac. A commercial liqueur made from damiana, called Liqueur for Lovers, can be purchased in the United States.

Datura, Thorn Apple, Jimsonweed *(Datura stramonium)*

Both seeds and leaves yield narcotic drugs used in medicines. The strong odor of the plant causes drowsiness and if used sparingly, smoke from dried datura leaves is calming to honeybees when opening a hive. Sucking nectar from the flowers has poisoned children, and some have died from swallowing the seeds. Even eating the boiled plants produces irrational behavior. Early California Indians knew this and gave their children potions made from the plant to obtain visions especially upon reaching puberty, but expert shamans regulated the dosage.

Datura, though somewhat coarse, is nevertheless a beautiful plant and because of the large white blossoms is also called angel's-trumpet. Datura helps the growth of pumpkins when planted in their vicinity.

Daylily *(Hemerocallis)*

The daylily has long been a mainstay of perennial plantings. The usual method of propagation is by clump division, easily done in autumn, but for best results a clump should not be divided more often than every two or three years.

Another reproduction method is by proliferation. The sturdy little rootless plants that develop along the flower scapes (stalks) in the axil between the rudimentary stem leaves and the stalk eventually die if they do not touch the earth; nature probably intended them to spread the plant when the flower stalk finally breaks and falls to the ground. Give nature an assist. When the flowering period is past and the stalk starts to dry, cut off the pro- liferation by severing the stalk about two inches below. Insert the proliferation in a pot full of good growing mix with the base just below the soil surface. Keep soil moist. Roots will soon develop from the base. After good root development, set the plant out in the garden.

Daylily

If you have a slope or terrace too steep to mow, try planting daylilies and iris together. Their roots will hold the soil, and their blossoms, which arrive successively (the iris blooming first), will delight you all summer. Daylilies are unaffected by the juglone washed from the black walnut's leaves. The flower buds are delicious dipped in batter and fried.

Not generally known is the fact that daylilies are a tasty food. Buds and blossoms can be sautéed in butter with a little salt and used alone or added to a zucchini and tomato dish. They may also be dipped in batter and fried. They may even be dried for later use in soups and stews.

Death Camas *(Zigadenus venenosus)*

Sometimes cultivated in gardens, this bulbous perennial plant is found below 8,200 feet in meadows, pastures, open slopes, and along roadsides from Canada to Florida, Texas, New Mexico, Arizona, and California. All parts of the plant are toxic; poisoning has followed even the eating of the flowers. The onionlike bulb has a dark-colored outer coat but lacks the onion odor.

Another variety of camas, the Indian quamash, Queen of the Bulbs, played a vital role in the history of some Native Americans. With breadroot and cous, camas constituted their basic starch food.

Camas of this type are found as high as the subalpine zones, growing along streams or in moist meadows. They cover vast areas so closely that in springtime the effect is that of lakelets of brilliant blue. Their flowers, grouped on spiny racemes, are spectacular. The ovate bulbs also look like onions. The big blue flowers clearly differentiated this plant, the "bringer of life," from the death camas, the "bringer of death," with its small yellow blossoms.

Delphinium

Delphinium, Larkspur (*Delphinium* spp.)

Widely cultivated for their beauty, many of these plants have escaped to roadsides and fields. One gardening book calls the delphinium "a confused hybrid of uncertain origin." No matter; it's a hardy flower that's easy to grow. The prevailing color is blue, but cultivated forms come in many colors — some even have beautiful double blooms. All species of the plant contain alkaloids of varying quantities. Ingesting young leaves before the flowers appear causes poisoning, but the plants' toxicity decreases as they age. Leaves and seeds may cause dermatitis on contact.

Common field larkspur *(D. consolida)* yields the alkaloids delcosine and delsoline, found effective against aphids and thrips. Powdered roots are toxic to bean leaf roller, cross-striped cabbageworms, cabbage looper, and melonworms.

Dentaria *(Dentaria)*

The name is from the Latin *dens,* a tooth, and refers to the toothlike scales of the roots. The plants are uncommon but useful little perennials for shade. Try them in porch boxes located on the north.

Dittany, Burning Bush *(Dictamnus albus)*

The Greek name, *dictamnos,* refers to Mount Dicte, Greece, where, according to legend, Zeus was born, and where this plant once grew. One species, a curious perennial, gives off a volatile oil from the upper part of its stem that may be ignited in hot weather and will burn without harming the plant.

Dog Fennel *(Anthemis cotula)*

This plant is sometimes mistaken for camomile, but once you know the true camomile fragrance you will never confuse the two; dog fennel has a rank, weedy odor. To tell them apart, cut one of the well-developed little daisylike blossoms vertically through the middle. True camomile has a hollow center; dog fennel is solid.

Dragon's Head *(Dracocephalum)*

From the Greek *drakon,* a dragon, and *kepthale,* head, the name refers to the gaping flower mouth. Both annuals and perennials are useful for the front border.

Dumbcane *(Dieffenbachia)*

These evergreen foliage plants are widely grown in greenhouses, homes, restaurants, and lobbies as potted ornamentals. The two most commonly cultivated species are *D. picta* and *D. seguine.* They thrive planted outdoors in the southern part of the United States. The flowers are tiny; the fruit is fleshy.

All species contain calcium oxalate as needlelike crystals in the stems and leaves. This toxic plant is called dumbcane because chewing on it causes temporary speechlessness. The irritation of the mouth can be fatal if the base of the tongue swells enough to block the throat.

Dutchman's-Breeches *(Dicentra cucullaria)*

This plant is a native of the eastern woods and has a surprisingly sweet scent. But beware: Eating the leaves and roots produces poisoning and such nervous symptoms as trembling, loss of balance, staggering, weakness, difficulty in breathing, and convulsions.

Edelweiss *(Leontopodium alpinum)*

This hardy perennial likes sun and a dry location. Do not cover the seed because light promotes germination, which takes place in 15 to 20 days. The gathering of edelweiss has long been symbolic of daring achievement, since it is native to the high rocky ledges of the Swiss Alps. The plant grows 12 inches high and is a soft gray-green.

Eglantine, Sweetbrier, Wild Rose *(Rosa rubiginosa)*

Eglantine is lovely but can become too much of a good thing. It immigrates from hedgerows to pastures where it shoots up quickly. This indicates that the pasture has not been grazed sufficiently and should be mown and harrowed. The prickly canes can be troublesome to cattle and sheep. If they become established, they will protect the growing and seeding of other weeds. Cut the plants while they are still young and the canes are soft.

Elephant Heads *(Pedicularis groenlandica)*

This large clumping perennial grows to three feet with delicate fernlike leaves. The rose-pink flower resemble an elephant's head with its large floppy ears and long trunk. Flowers in tall spikes emerge from the ferny foliage in August. The plant is nice for naturalizing as it grows well in moist meadows, bogs, streams, and lakeshores from Greenland to Alaska and south to the mountains of New Mexico. Seed should be cold stratified for 30 days before sowing in spring.

Evening Primrose *(Oenothera)*

Oil of evening primrose is said to be the world's richest source of natural, unsaturated fatty acids. It is helpful in cases of obesity, mental illness, heart disease, arthritis, and for relief from postdrinking depression.

The cultivated *O. tetragona* 'Fireworks' is a cheerful plant with dark green dwarf foliage, tinted purple in the spring. The red buds open to profuse silky bright yellow flowers borne during June and July.

Oenothera missouriensis, evening or Missouri primrose, is classed as a wildflower. It has immense four- to five-inch, cup-shaped yellow flowers. A low-growing species, it is ideal for border or rock garden. The winged seedpods are tan, often streaked with crimson, and are excellent for dried arrangements. The plant likes fertile, well-drained soil and a sunny location.

Evening primrose

Everlasting, Fragrant *(Gnaphalium polycephalum)*

This is the fragrant immortelle of the autumn fields, spicy and sweet, often growing in old fields and woods. *G. ramosissium* is a fragrant pink-flowered everlasting.

Everlasting Pea *(Lathyrus grandiflorus)*

Use this plant as a control against field mice.

Eyebright *(Euphrasia officinalis)*

Eyebright is characterized by lovely white flowers, striped violet, that open in summer. The plant was once thought to be effective in treating ophthalmia. Culpeper writes: "If the herb was but as much used as it is neglected, it would half spoil the spectacle makers' trade. The juice or distilled water of eyebright, taken inwardly in white wine or broth or dropped into the eyes for diverse days together helps all infirmities of the eyes that cause dimness of sight. It also helps a weak brain or memory."

Some people smoke dried eyebright as they would tobacco. A kind of wine can be made by cooking it with unfermented wine at harvest time; however, eyebright should not be taken internally because there have been cases of stomach disorders. The juice is acrid and has an unpleasant taste.

False Saffron, Safflower *(Carthamus)*

False saffron is a thistlelike plant with large, attractive flower heads varying from white to brilliant red. It has been grown in dry areas of Asia, Africa, and Europe for hundreds of years. The chief value is in the oil and meal made from the seeds. The oil is used in the diets of persons suffering from heart disease and hypertension, and is a valuable source of linoleic acid. The meal is fed to livestock.

Fennel, Sweet *(Foeniculum officinalis)*

In the garden, fennel is valued for its masses of fringed foliage. In times past the fragrant seeds were made into a tea for babies' colic. Mixed with peppermint leaves they also make a delicious tea, calming to the nerves. The Italians consider fennel valuable as a key to longevity and virility; the Egyptians, Greeks, and Romans all vouched for fennel, using it in salads, fish sauces, and fennel soups. Fennel oil, which contains estrogens, has a reputation as an antiwrinkle agent.

The Florence fennel, prized for its enlarged leaf bases and used like celery, is a close relative and is grown the same way. These fennels are poor companions for bush beans, caraway, kohlrabi, and tomatoes. The black swallowtail butterfly lays its eggs on fennel, dill, and parsley, and its beautiful black and gold caterpillars are ravenous.

Feverfew *(Chrysanthemum parthenium)*

Feverfew, an old favorite for edging, has little white buttons ¾ inch across, and yellow foliage with a characteristic strong, bitter odor.

This little daisylike flower is sometimes incorrectly called pyrethrum. However, like the real thing, it works as a bug chaser and can be planted as a border around roses or scattered throughout the garden. Feverfew grows in tufts, becoming bushlike and occasionally attaining a spread of as much as three feet. The single-flowered form was the feverfew cultivated in old physic gardens. The modern forms, largely used for cutting, are double-flowered. Feverfew is an accommodating flower that will grow in any soil, gives generous bloom all summer, and self-sows readily.

Feverweed
See *Joe-Pye Weed.*

Fig *(Ficus)*
Figs have their flowers inside the fruit. The fig wasp, blastophaga, lays its eggs at the base of the flowers, thus ensuring pollination. Figs have long been considered love food by primitive peoples.

Fingerleaf Weed
This weed lives on acid soil and indicates increasing acidity. Weeds are specialists and close observation tells us a great deal about the soil they grow on.

Fireweed, Great Willow Herb *(Epilobium augustifolium L.)*
The large, showy flowers are borne in terminal spikelike clusters. They have four purplish or rose-colored petals that may be occasionally pink or rarely white. The plants are common along roadsides and on open hillsides from southeast Alaska north to the Arctic and west to the Alaska Peninsula and the Aleutian Islands. They also are found in the mountains, along streams, and in clearings throughout North America and Eurasia. Fireweed was one of the first living plants found after the Mount St. Helens volcanic eruption.

Native Americans collect the young shoots in spring and mix them with other greens; they peel and eat the young stems raw. Like other tender young greens, these are a good source of vitamin C and vitamin A. Fireweed honey is one of the finest.

Flax *(Linum)*
Narbonne flax is an elegant, free-flowering perennial with feathery, blue-green, evergreen foliage, just right for a sunny spot or a rock wall. The

flowers, 1¾ inches across, are sky blue with dainty white eyes. The 1½-foot plants with slender, erect stems bloom generously.

Dwarf golden flax (*L. flavum compactum*) has a myriad of bright yellow translucent flowers one inch across and makes a fine border plant. Give these full sun and a moist but well-drained location.

Fleabane *(Erigeron)*

This weed invades relatively good land, and is one of the few weed "presents" the American continent has given Europe. It was inadvertently introduced about 1655 in a stuffed bird. Its acrid oil is used against mosquitoes, hence the name fleabane. Sensitive people may be allergic to this weed; however, it is still collected for medicinal purposes. Canadian fleabane *(E. canadensis)* can be ground up to make melonworm repellent.

Forget-Me-Not *(Myosotis sylvatica)*

These lovely, dainty plants are most effective in the garden when planted in large drifts. The popular variety 'Blue Bird' is a compact, attractive plant with the bluest of all blue flowers. The flowers are too fragile for indoor arrangements and do not last well when cut. If cut as they fade, the flowers will bloom over a long period of time. The variety *alba* has white flowers.

Botanists say the hairy stems of many forget-me-nots are intended to keep ants and similar insects from stealing the nectar reserved for flying insects that pollinate.

Funkia, Plantain Lily *(Hosta crispula)*

This plant is characterized by its bold, colorful, fragrant flowers that are excellent for cutting and its leaves that are dramatically splendid in cut arrangements. *Hosta crispula,* of Japanese origin, has two-inch flowers of funnel form and lavender color, and each leaf has a serrated look. Protect from strong winds.

Gentian *(Gentiana)*

Ordinarily the gentians are without fragrance, but the rare perennial fringed gentian has a delightful scent suggestive of strawberries.

Septemfida (var. *lagodechiana*) is an enchanting summer-flowering gentian with deep, true blue, one-inch blooms with a white throat. The dense, heart-shaped foliage, which likes summer heat, forms an attractive ground cover.

To sprout gentian seed, get a box about six inches deep, put in two inches of coarse gravel or broken crock pieces, then three inches of fine, porous soil. Plant the seeds in the soil and cover with one inch of peat moss. Sink the box in the garden in filtered shade and keep it moist until the seeds germinate. Treat other hard-to-sprout seeds like cyclamen, smilax, violet, canna, Christmas rose, and nasturtium this way as well.

Geranium *(Pelargonium)*

The hybrid geraniums in scarlet, cherry, salmon, coral, and white are simply gorgeous. In addition to these introductions, geraniums that could only be propagated by cuttings can now be grown from seed.

Geraniums make good companions for roses because they repel Japanese beetles. Geraniums also repel cabbageworms when planted among the brassica, and the white geranium is helpful when planted near corn.

Geranium, Scented-Leaved *(Pelargonium)*

In competition with the gorgeous Zonals, the sweet-leaved geraniums fell out of fashion, but the wheel is turning again. The sweet-leaved geraniums offer the best of scents and immense variety, including the filbert, nutmeg, cinnamon, almond, lemon, orange, apple, anise, rose, pine, musk, violet, lavender, balm-scented, and many more. All of these also bloom but the flowers are inconspicuous.

A leaf of the rose-scented geranium in the bottom of the glass imparts a delicious flavor when making apple jelly. Use the oil of geranium as an insecticide against red spiders and cotton aphids.

Gladiolus *(Gladiolus)*

Thanks to Dr. Forman McLean of the New York Botanical Gardens, we now have sweetglads — scented gladiolus. Gladiolus are gorgeous flowers — tall and dramatically beautiful, coming in many brilliant colors. But keep them away from peas and beans, which dislike their presence.

Globe Artichoke

This elegant perennial dates back to the 16th century and is a form of cardoon, a favorite of the ancients. It prefers cool, often foggy summers and is grown mainly in California. If allowed to blossom, the great thistlelike flowers are gorgeous. The edible buds are a great delicacy and one of our most expensive "vegetables."

Gloxinia *(Gloxinia)*

One of the most popular gift plants, this native of tropical America is remarkable for its richly colored, velvety leaves and large, bell-shaped flowers. It is widely cultivated as a houseplant and in greenhouses.

Goldenrod, Sweet *(Solidago odora)*

There are more than 100 species of goldenrod. It's used for dyeing, giving colors from mustard to brown olive, depending on the strength used. Anise-scented goldenrod is a delightful beverage plant. Collect the leaves when the plant is in bloom and use them fresh or dried, with peppermint leaves, as an after-dinner summer tea.

Goldenrods are also medicinal, for not only did Native Americans employ this common plant as a cure for sore throat and for pain in general, but herbalists also recommend it today as a diaphoretic in colds and coughs, and as an aid in rheumatism. In fact, the generic name, *Solidago,* means "I make whole," that is, heal.

Goldenrod

Goldenrod is incorrectly blamed for hay fever and similar allergies; ragweed, which blooms at the same time, is the real culprit.

Goldenseal, Indian Turmeric, Orangeroot, Yellow Puccoon *(Hydrastis canadensis)*

A perennial flowering forest plant of the eastern United States, goldenseal has showy, eight-inch-wide leaves and greenish white, ¼-inch flowers, followed by large clusters of red fruit. Native Americans dried and ground the thick yellow root for medicinal purposes.

Groundsel *(Senecio vulgaris)*

This common plant of waste places and pastures is of erect growth with grayish green leaves, branching with jagged lobes. Flower heads are in close terminal clusters, the individual flowers being of tubular shape, solid, and yellow, like minute candles, and possessing no ray petals. This herb is particularly

Groundsel, or ragwort, is a favorite of caged birds, which seem to understand the value of this mineral-rich herb.

rich in minerals, especially iron. Animals seek it out as a tonic, especially poultry, and it is relished by caged birds kept as pets. The herb has powerful drawing and antiseptic properties. Mixed with ground ivy it makes an important poultice. It strengthens the eyes and reduces inflammation.

Gunnera *(Gunnera insignia)*

These ornamental perennials are mostly from the southern hemisphere. They prefer to live on the inaccessible mountainsides of Guatemala and Panama. The huge leaves measure from four to five feet across and resemble our common pot geranium. Gunnera is of such massive proportions that usually it is only planted in public grounds for landscape effect.

One leaf is capable of serving several people as an umbrella. Gunnera bears a large stalk covered with thousands of small, brownish, wind-pollinated flowers. A similar species of gunnera is found in the mountains of Hawaii.

Hen and Chickens, Houseleeks *(Sempervivum tectorum)*

These plants grow without care in a sunny spot. There are 60 or more varieties, from tiny green cobwebby ones to sturdy copper-colored ones like 'Heuffell'. They need little soil and are fine for covering walls, rocky hillsides, or small pockets in rocks or paving. They are hardy and colorful in late winter. The Romans thought they would protect a house from lightning if they grew on the roof.

Hepatica *(Hepatica acutiloba)*

These perennials bloom in early spring. Their soft-pink flowers resemble anemones and are surrounded by sharply pointed leaves that often persist through winter. Just six inches tall, these wildflowers are fine for naturalizing.

Hollyhock *(Althaea rosea)*

This native of China is a tall perennial herb that is usually treated as a biennial in our gardens. The roots are demulcent and emollient, thus of good use as cold and diuretic remedies. The generic name, *Althaea,* is derived from the Greek *althainein,* meaning "to heal." Hollyhock is good to rub on bee stings if the leaves are bruised in oil and made into an ointment.

Holy Herb, Yerba Santa *(Eriodictyon californicum)*

The small white and lilac flowers are fragrant. The leaves are strongly aromatic when crushed and were used medicinally by Native Americans for colds.

Hops, Bear Hops (*Humulus lupulus*)

Prepare the young sprout like asparagus or use as a potherb for soup. At one time ground hops were a substitute for baking soda. The greenish yellow flowers are used commercially in the preparation of beer and ales.

A pillow of hops, instead of feathers, will induce sound, refreshing sleep. Powdered hop leaves are toxic to southern armyworms and melonworms.

Horehound (*Marrubium vulgare*)

The wild and woolly horehound is not a very decorative herb; the flowers are small, mintlike, and white, while the leaves are covered with a dense, felted wool that gives the whole plant a downy, whitish appearance. Unlike most mints, the flavor and medicinal properties of horehound are not volatile or easily lost, so the plant can be used fresh or dried or boiled without driving off the flavor. Horehound tea is good for colds and horehound candy is good for coughs.

To make horehound candy, prepare a small decoction by boiling 2 ounces of the dried herb in 1½ pints of water for about 30 minutes; strain this and add 3½ pounds of brown sugar. Boil over a hot fire until it reaches the requisite degree of hardness (testing from time to time in a cup of cold water). Then pour into flat tin trays, previously well greased. Mark into sticks or squares with a knife as it becomes cool enough to retain its shape.

Hyacinth (*Hyacinthus orientalis*)

These fragrant flowers are natives of eastern Mediterranean lands and western Asia. The plant has a large bulb with a purple or white scaly covering and from four to six linear-lanceolate, hooded, bright green leaves. The flowers are produced in spring on a terminal cylindrical cluster on a central stem from six to twelve inches high. In cultivated varieties the flowers are white or various shades of red and blue. The white and blue companion well with tulips by offsetting their flashing, brilliant colors.

Hyssop (*Hyssopus officinalis*)

This plant, with its dark blue blossoms, neat linear leaves, and bushy growth, is attractive in the flower garden. It may be clipped like boxwood to make a low hedge, although this will be at the expense of the blossoms. There are also white and pink varieties. Hyssop is good to plant with grapevines. Planted with cabbage, it will deter white cabbage butterflies.

Ice Plant *(Mesembryanthemum crystallinum)*

This one is a little trailer and creeper grown for its thick, succulent foliage and tiny, white blossoms. The fat, fleshy leaves are covered with glistening dots that have the appearance of ice, thus the popular name. The plant may be started from cuttings and does well in the driest and thinnest of soils. Try it in hanging baskets, window boxes, and rock gardens.

Identifying Specimens

To identify poisonous plants, contact your local Poison Control Center. New York State College of Agriculture offers a mail-order service to identify plants for people with no local means of assistance. Packaged plants may be sent to Extension Specialist, D.H. Bailey Hortorium, Ithaca, NY 14850, with an accompanying letter explaining exactly where the plant was found and the date it was collected.

Indian Blanket *(Gaillardia)*

Our native gaillardias have been developed into a variety of horticultural forms. The rich yellow and red daisies thrive in hot, dry places and bloom all summer long. They are fine as cut flowers and are easy to grow. Plant Indian blanket with calendula, Iceland poppy, and Maltese cross.

Indian Licorice *(Arbrus precatorius)*

Also known as rosary pea, this plant is a native of India. Generally the seeds are brought into the United States by tourists who have visited tropical areas. The hard, attractive, bright scarlet or orange seeds hold abrin, one of the most deadly poisons known, but they have been used for rosaries, necklaces, bracelets, and toys.

Indian Paintbrush *(Catilleja)*

These perennials grow to 1½ feet tall. Their large, showy, brilliant red to orange, leaflike bracts surround the tiny, inconspicuous flowers.

Indian paintbrush is thought to be parasitic on other plant roots. It is difficult to transplant, but it can be grown from seed if seed of another plant is grown in the same pot. Blue grama *(Bouteloua gracilis),* a grass, will encourage the seed to sprout.

Indian paintbrush

Seed may be sown outdoors on bare ground around sage or clumps of native grasses. The plant has a long period of bloom and is attractive to hummingbirds.

Indian Pipe *(Monotropa uniflora)*

These strange parasitic ghost flowers never fail to shock when we unexpectedly come upon them, clustered in seemingly sinister closeness, deep in some somber woodland. At certain periods of their development the waxen white or flushed flowers give forth a "delicate and wholly sweet scent." They are often found in dry woods, usually under pine or beech trees, and get their food from decaying plants in the soil.

Iris, Fleur-de-lis *(Iris)*

The name comes from the Greek word for "rainbow." These perennial plants in many attractive colors grow throughout the temperate region, blooming in spring, summer, and a few in autumn. Many of the tall bearded varieties are gorgeous, earning for themselves the name poor man's orchid.

Iris

Their worst enemy is the iris borer. If you find these, dig up the plants, clean out the borers, and dip the rhizomes (roots) in diluted chlorine bleach (one part bleach to ten of water) before replanting.

Iris is one of the earliest plants to bloom in the garden and teams well with grape hyacinth and daylilies. The dried root of the Florentine iris is called orrisroot. It is used in perfumes, powders, and medicines.

Ismene *(Hymenocallis)*

Ismene is a real treasure for southern gardens, where the bulbs are hardy. In June four to five giant funnel-shaped flowers are borne on each stem. The flowers are richly perfumed and uniquely shaped, having a delicately fringed cup framed by five long sepals, and come in shades of white and yellow. This exquisitely different flower may be grown as a pot plant in the North.

Ixia *(Ixia hybrida)*

Ixia, boasting the greatest range of color of any bulb, is cool-loving, which makes it very desirable for indoor cultivation. The stems are slender and graceful; the flowers offer white, yellow, purple, ruby, blue, and green, in many shades and variations, usually with a black eye. The flower spikes contain 6 to 12 flowers, each one to two inches in diameter. Pot the bulbs in late autumn in a mixture of loam, leaf compost, and sand, placing eight or nine in a six-inch pot. Keep cool and dark until growth starts, then bring into light and warmth.

Jade Plant (Crassula)

Jade plants have been popular for a long time, and are favorites with plant lovers in North America. Some advanced growers are even treating it as a tropical bonsai, yet the jade plant is easy for beginners to grow as well. Common jade, *Crassula argentea,* has dark green leaves that become red-edged in sufficient sun. Mature plants bear clusters of star-shaped white or pale pink flowers at the branch tips in winter or spring. Its dwarf form, *C. argentea minima,* is simply smaller in all its parts.

Jade is virtually trouble-free. Mealybugs are the chief insect pest; eradicate them by using a cotton swab dipped in alcohol. Malathion should not be used on jade or other crassulas.

Jewels-of-Opar (Talinum paniculatum)

This garden treasure has bright, waxy green foliage with a myriad of cameo-pink flowers that open every afternoon. It is 1½ feet tall and good to use for borders and rock gardens. It is heat resistant and naturalizes well.

Jewelweed (Impatiens biflora or I. pallida)

This tender, succulent, tall-growing annual is often found in extensive patches in damp woods. The expressed juice is a light orange color and is an antidote for poison ivy, which it often grows near.

The jewelweed has pretty flowers, butter yellow in color, followed by slipper-shaped seedpods about ¾ inch long. When ripe they will suddenly split, the two sides curling back into tight spirals with an audible snap, and throw their seeds in all directions.

Jewelweed is so called because its leaves are unwettable; rain will stand on the leaves in round drops, shining like jewels, without ever wetting the leaf surface.

Jimsonweed (Datura stramonium)

This weed spreads usually by having its seed carried by birds. It is very poisonous, causing a kind of intoxicated state, but has some medicinal value. It is helpful when grown with pumpkins. See *Datura*.

Job's Tears *(Coix lacryma)*

This three-foot ornamental grass bears hard, pearly white seeds that make distinctive necklaces.

Joe-Pye Weed *(Eupatorium purpureum)*

The joe-pye weed grows mostly in moist damp thickets, ditches, and streams, invading only badly drained meadows. The plant is named for a Native American herb doctor, but is also called feverweed. The juice is said to heal open sores and bruises; hunters have observed that wounded deer will search for it and eat it. (Early peoples learned much about the medicinal qualities of plants by watching animals when they were sick or injured.) Feverweed is closely related to thoroughwort *(E. perfoliatum)*.

Jungle Cacti *(Epiphyllum)*

These strange flowering plants are almost unbelievably beautiful. Somewhat resembling orchids in their delicate loveliness, they include both day- and night-blooming varieties. They are every color of the rainbow except blue. If you are a cactus lover, these will delight you.

To grow these, begin with the right potting mix: four parts leaf mold, one part fine redwood bark, one part well-aged steer manure, one part perlite, one part horticultural charcoal. (If you cannot obtain leaf mold, commercially packaged camellia-azalea mix is a good substitute.) For each cubic foot of mix, add ½ cup bonemeal. If you live in an area that has alkaline water, add ½ cup garden sulphur per cubic foot of mix.

Keep the plant in a pot a bit small for the size of the plant, and do not make the soil too firm. During November and December, keep the soil nearly dry (but do not let the skins shrivel); at other times keep it moderately moist. Grow in a temperature of 60° to 70°F except when resting the plant (when it should be kept at 50° to 55°). Give all light possible in winter, but from March through September shade it lightly from strong sun. It may be put outside in summer.

Kalanchoe *(Kalanchoe)*

These showy, winter-blooming plants make long-lived pot plants. Tender succulents with attractive flowers, they are chiefly natives of the tropics and

South Africa and belong to the Crassula family. Sow in spring for winter and spring bloom. The flowers are orange-scarlet, pink, orange-red, and white.

Kiss-Me-over-the-Garden-Gate *(Viola tricolor)*
This is the wild pansy sometimes called Johnny-jump-up. It is a hardy perennial, but rather short-lived. Sow the seeds of this charming little flower outdoors; it will need no special care.

Kitaibelia *(Kitaibelia vitifolia)*
This hardy perennial flowering plant with ornamental foliage is a native of eastern Europe and belongs to the hollyhock family, Malvaceae. The stems, which grow about eight feet in height, have large, vinelike leaves; the large pink flowers open in summer.

This plant thrives in a sunny position and is fine for planting at the back of the herbaceous border. It prefers light, well-drained soil, and may be planted in autumn or spring. Propagation is by division of the roots at planting time or by seeds sown outdoors in summer.

Kniphofia *(Kniphofia)*
This member of the Lily family is sometimes called torch lily or red-hot poker. Hailing from Africa and Madagascar, these perennials are also called tritoma. They are very showy plants for borders, mostly in the red and yellow color range. In cold areas they will need winter protection.

Lady's Slipper *(Cypripedium)*
These beautiful orchids are found in swamps and wet woodlands, most numerous in the eastern and southeastern states. The flowers that grow on straight stems have a pouchlike lip, hence the name lady's slipper. They are beautiful, but be careful in handling; all species contain a poisonous substance in the stalks and leaves that frequently causes dermatitis.

Lavender *(Lavendula)*
Lavender has a long and creditable history as a stimulating or medicinal plant. Among its many virtues are its soothing effect on the stomach, its use as a disinfectant, and its power to relieve sprains, headaches, and toothaches. Flies steer clear of it and, according to the old demonologists, the fragrant odor of lavender is guaranteed to ward off evil spirits. The essential oil of lavender is produced from the leaves and has been an ingredient of love

philtres from earliest times. The oil also stimulates the generation of new cells and in so doing helps to preserve the health and youth of the skin.

Three varieties, used in industry, medicine, and household preparations, are beautiful additions to the garden. These are spike *(L. spica)*, true or English *(L. vera),* and French lavender *(L. stoechas).* Both flowers and leaves are fragrant. Plants must be grown in poor soil to produce the most fragrance; in good soil they grow more luxuriantly but fragrant essential oils are lacking.

Licorice *(Glycyrrhiza glabra)*
The wild licorice of North America is *G. lepidota.* From licorice roots we get a valuable flavoring material that is fifty times as sweet as sugar. But oddly, although sweeter than sugar, licorice has the power to quench thirst. In 1951 it was discovered that licorice root contains the female sex hormone estrogen, used in the treatment of menopausal problems.

Chewing a licorice stick helps those who wish to stop smoking.

Even the fibers that remain after the licorice is extracted from the roots are valuable. They are used in making fire-fighting foam, boxboard, insulation board, and other products.

Ligularia *(Ligularia dentata)*
This bold perennial has large, heart-shaped leaves, bronzy green on the upper surface and a rich mahogany-red below. In July and August, orange daisy flowers brighten the plant. It does best in a constantly moist soil in a partially shaded location.

Lily *(Lilium)*
This perennial comes in many colors and is lovely used with delphinium, aster, and marigold. It grows well in raised beds and is ideal for mass plantings along a wall. *L. longiflorum,* the Easter lily, is pure white with a powerful fragrance, and is a very popular gift at Easter time. Easter lilies should be watered regularly through their flowering period. They've been cultivated for more than 3,000 years.

Lily

Lily of the Valley *(Convallaria majalis)*
Lily of the valley, a single species, is a lovely, fragrant spring-blooming herb. It is commonly cultivated in the partial

shade of gardens everywhere and is a great favorite. It looks best in mass plantings but makes a fine ground cover for narcissus. However, if narcissus and lily of the valley flowers are put together in the same vase, they will soon wither.

To get flowers by Christmas, professional Dutch growers of the 1870s planted moss-wrapped pips (rooted buds arising from the rootstalk) in sand about a month before the holiday, giving them bottom heat and liberal watering until sprouts appeared.

The leaves, flowers, berries, and rootstalk are well known for their toxicity. They contain dangerous amounts of cardiac glycosides (convallarin and convallamarin). Children have lost their lives just by drinking the water from a vase containing a bouquet of lily of the valley.

Live Forever (Sedum spectabile)
This hardy succulent lives up to its name. It displays heads of pinkish bloom above gray-green foliage in late summer. The plant will tolerate poor growing conditions, is transplantable at almost any season, and propagates readily by leaf cuttings. Recently developed varieties have flower colors ranging from ivory to rosy red.

Lobelia, Blue Cardinal Flower (Lobelia inflata)
This field plant of North America is commonly called Indian tobacco. The leaves are pointed and yellowish green with hooded flowers of a brilliant blue. This was one of the most important herbs of Native Americans but can be harmful in internal use.

Since the lobelia blossom is such a lovely blue, it combines well with white alyssum and red rosebuds for bouquets or tiny place markers. And lobelia, like alyssum, is an excellent plant for "clothing" a pot, planter, or window box planted with larger plants. Keep well pinched to promote shapeliness and persistent bloom.

Love-in-a-Mist (Nigella)
Whether you think of it as love-in-a-mist or devil-in-a-bush, its other name, this charming blue, purple-blue, or white annual makes a hardy plant for the border, where it is very beautiful for several weeks. Well-grown plants bear finer blooms and remain in flower longer than those that are crowded.

Love-Lies-Bleeding, Tassel Flower *(Amaranthus caudatus)*
This native of India, the Philippines, and other warm countries has
drooping stems bearing dark, reddish purple blooms.

Lupine *(Lupinus)*
There are about 100 species of lupines found in the United States. They are
showy, hardy, and grow profusely in fields, on ranges, and on mountainsides. The pealike blossoms, in loose clusters at the ends of the branches,
may be blue, purple, yellow, pink, or white. Some but not all species of
lupine hold toxic alkaloids throughout the entire plant and are a common
cause of stock poisoning.

Lupine, which is a legume, is helpful to the growth of corn as well as
most cultivated crops. Plant in full sun or light shade.

Cultivated lupines come in a gorgeous assortment of colors — blues,
pinks, reds, purples, maroons, and many striking bicolor
combinations. The individual flowers are large, with
some standards up to an inch across.

Marigold *(Tagetes)*
The marigold, "herb of the sun," is as
helpful in the flower garden as in the vegetable garden, serving the same purpose of
driving away nematodes. They are particularly useful with chrysanthemums, calendulas, and dahlias. Brown areas on lower
leaves signal the underground feeding of
the foliar nematodes.

Marigold

Martynia, Devil's Claw, Unicorn Plant *(Martynia)*
Sonoran tribes domesticated this plant for the long black fibers of the
"claws" on the fruit. They were used in basket weaving. The seeds may be
eaten like sunflower seeds or pressed for oil. The fuzzy green seedpods are
picked when half-grown if wanted for pickling. The strange mature pods
are often used for decorations.

Meadow Saffron *(Colchicum autumnale)*

This plant blooms in fall, and will do so even without soil around its poisonous bulbs. Colchicum, derived from the bulbs, is the source of a present-day drug used to treat gout and also has been used to produce doubling of chromosomes in plants.

Meadowsweet *(Filipendula ulmaria, Spiraea)*

Meadowsweet is perhaps the most important of all nature's remedies. Chemists discovered acetylsalicylic acid in this plant, synthesized it, and called it aspirin. But the dried leaf in its natural form can be ground with mortar and pestle and used wherever aspirin is recommended without aspirin's side effects. Meadowsweet is particularly recommended by herbalists as an antidote for rheumatism, arthritis, gout, and all kidney and bladder complaints, particularly gravel and cystitis.

Mescal Bean *(Sophora secundiflora)*

The beautiful green glossy leaves and the display of fragrant sweet-pea-like lilac flowers, borne in a drooping inflorescence, are very impressive. This excellent landscape plant is particularly good for poor alkaline soils, and tolerates heat and drought well.

The beautiful seeds are large, brilliant, and coral, and even though they are very poisonous, the Mexicans use them for necklaces. Powdered seeds of this flowering shrub are toxic to armyworms.

Mexican Hat *(Ratibida columnifera* var. *pulcherrima)*

This flower, dark mahogany-red or yellow with a red blotch, is a form of the prairie coneflower, the dramatic yellow daisy with cone-shaped brown center. The perennial plant is about one foot tall, and given full sun it will bloom continuously from summer to fall. Grow it with the purple coneflower *(Echinacea purpurea)*, which is taller (three to five feet) and also flowers from summer to fall. The lavender-purple daisies make excellent cut flowers.

Mignonette, Little Darling *(Reseda odorata)*

The mignonette has a low bushy mass of smooth, soft green leaves. The tiny flowers, growing on tall spikes, are yellowish white with reddish pollen stalks inside. The larger-flowered varieties are prettier but less fragrant. The mignonette is a good border plant that grows best in cool temperatures and light soil. If the seed fails to sprout, check for ants; they have been known to carry off the seed.

Milkweed *(Asclepias)*

These rather coarse erect plants grow in dry fields, on hillsides, in woods, and along roadsides. Their profuse milky juice accounts for their name. Milkweed juice is said to remove warts.

There are about 60 species distributed throughout the United States but only a few are cultivated. The white, pink, or rose-colored flowers develop in round clusters. The large, rough-surfaced, flat seedpods are filled with many seeds, each with a tuft of long, silky hairs. Divested of the seeds, the silky hairs are sometimes used as background for pictures made with butterflies and dried flowers.

An old-time method of trapping cutworms consisted of placing compact handfuls of milkweed in every fifth row or hill of cultivation and tamping them down. Cutworms gathered in this trap material where they could be easily collected. Clover and mullein were also used for this purpose.

Some species of milkweed have medicinal value, but all are known for their content of resins and most of them are exceedingly poisonous to humans and livestock. The poison is concentrated in the stout stem and in the leaves.

Mimosa, Humble Plant, Touch-Me-Not, Hairy Sensitive Plant *(Mimosa pudica)*

The sensitive plant is so called because its leaves will fold together with sufficient irritation or cloudy weather, representing one of the most remarkable cases of physiological response in the plant kingdom. The timorous plant has a mechanism that reacts whenever a beetle, ant, or worm crawls up its stem toward its delicate leaves; as the intruder touches a spur, the stem raises, the leaves fold up, and the assailant is either rolled off the branch by the unexpected movement or is obliged to draw back in fright.

Mint *(Mentha)*

Many delightful mints are used medicinally, for cooking, and for fragrance. These seven are among the most frequently grown:

Apple mint (M. rotundifolia) has stiff stems growing 20 to 30 inches tall. The rounded leaves are slightly hairy and gray green, about ¼ inch long. This mint has purplish white flowers and is not good for culinary use, but American apple mint *(M. gentilis* var. *variegata)* has a fruity, refreshing odor and taste.

Corsican mint (M. requienii) is a creeping sort that grows only about one inch high. The tiny, round leaves form a mosslike mat. Small, light purple flowers appear in summer. When bruised or crushed underfoot, the foliage has a delightful minty or sagelike fragrance. Plant it between stepping stones.

Golden apple mint (M. gentilis) has smooth, deep green leaves, variegated with yellow. It grows about two feet high and makes an attractive ground cover where taller, spring-flowering bulbs are planted.

Orange mint or bergamot mint (M. citrata) has lavender blossoms in dense flower spikes and a characteristic minty odor.

Pennyroyal (M. pulegium) is an attractive plant with small, rosy lilac flowers, blooming late in the summer and early autumn. Pennyroyal is believed to repel insects in the garden and is good to rub on a cat's collar to repel fleas.

Peppermint (M. piperita) or its flavor is familiar to many people. It has strongly scented small purple flowers and three-inch leaves with toothed edges. Peppermint grows to about three feet.

The plant produces many creeping stolons (runners) that spread quickly in favorable environments. It is propagated by pieces of the runners and, like many of the mints, can be increased from slips (clones) planted in moist, sandy places.

Leaves are darker than those of the spearmint, larger, and not so crinkly. The plant has a reddish tone. Even the small leaves near the rosy lavender flower spikes have red on their margins.

A medicinal oil is expressed from the dried leaves of the flowering plants and is considered a

Mint

powerful analgesic. The oil is also used to flavor tooth powders, pastes, and washes. The leaves of peppermint make a wonderful tea, reputed to be good for the nerves. One author has called this tea one of nature's best tranquilizers. Peppermint is used in cooking and for flavoring candy.

Spearmint (M. spicata) is another familiar species. It is usually used in mint jelly. The leaves are dark green; the mature plant is 1½ to 2 feet tall.

Mints have been used medicinally since ancient times and modern commerce still makes use of them. Spearmint and peppermint are two of the most common flavorings for everything from chewing gum to toothpaste.

Most mints do best in light, moist, moderately rich soil, and in shade or partial shade. They spread underground by means of stems and runners. Use the leaves fresh or dried; add them to potpourris, lamb, and jelly. Spearmint is the best for garnishing iced drinks (the mint juleps of the South). Add fresh leaves of peppermint, pineapple, apple, and orange mints to fruit cocktails or sprinkle over ice cream.

Money Plant *(Lunaria)*

This purple or white biennial is best as a filler plant until fall, when the silver pods begin to show at their best. Use dried in a winter bouquet or mixed with other dried material.

Monkey Flower *(Mimulus)*

These perennials with large, showy, snapdragon-like flowers like to grow beside streams and ponds, even on swampy land. The bush monkey flower *(Mimulus diplacus)* is a flowering shrub of the snapdragon family and grows to four or five feet. It blooms over a long period with flowers in shades of orange, yellow, and red. Grow in full sun in well-drained soil; the plants are drought tolerant.

Mother-of-Thousands, Strawberry Geranium, Aaron's Beard
(Saxifraga sarmentosa)

Many admirers have grown mother-of-thousands in hanging baskets or window boxes. Prettily colored, the leaves are light green, variegated, with silver above and reddish on the undersides. The flower stalk rises about a foot and produces white flowers in loose panicles.

From the rosette of leaves come runners that, as they touch moist soil, root and produce new plants. When a young plant acquires six leaves, it may be broken off from the parent and started on its own. This plant grows best in rich, sandy soil with a little filtered sunlight. Mother-of-thousands may be planted outdoors and will survive mild winters, even in the vicinity of New York.

Mullein, Flannel Leaf, Beggar's Blanket, Adam's Flannel, Velvet Plant, Feltwort, Bullock's Lungwort, Clown's Lungwort, Cuddy's Lungs, Tinder Plant, Rag Paper, Candlewick Plant, Witch's Candle, Hag's Taper, Torches, Aaron's Rod, Jacob's Staff, Shepherd's Club, Quaker Rouge *(Verbascum thapsus)*

For sheer diversity of names, this one wins the prize.

Mullein is valuable in alleviating human ills and has long been known to many people of varying cultures, all of whom agree on its value as a healing herb. The fresh and dried leaves and the fresh flowers are the parts used in home remedies. Officially, mullein has been recognized as a valuable demulcent, emollient, expectorant, and mild astringent.

Narcissus, Daffodil, Jonquil, Paper-white *(Narcissus spp.)*

This lovely perennial in solid borders and masses is one of the first flowers to welcome spring. The flowers may be yellow, yellow with white, orange, pink, apricot, white, or cream. But beware, the bulbs are poisonous and must never be eaten.

Sow African marigolds *(Tagetes erecta)* before planting narcissus bulbs to defeat certain nematodes that often attack the bulbs. Sulphur-containing substances called thiophenes are present in root exudates of African marigolds, as well as in many other plants from the Compositae and Umbelliferae families; these repel the nematodes.

Nasturtium *(Tropaeolum majus)*

Forms of this South American tendril climber brighten a fence or trellis with brilliant shades of yellow, orange, and red. It flowers best in full sun and clean soil. Potash added to the soil aids bloom development. Nasturtium, an old Latin word used by Pliny, was derived by him from *nasus,* the nose, and *tortus,* twisted, in reference to the supposed contortions of the nose caused by the hot, pungent odor and taste of these flowers. Nasturtium and rose geranium in a nosegay complement each other.

Nasturtium is an amiable flower that gets along in the worst sort of soil. It was an inhabitant of many an early American garden, being ideal for bouquets, and the flowers, leaves, and seeds were eaten. Flowers and leaves went into salads, and the seeds were pickled after being picked green; so treated, they were thought to be a nice substitute for capers.

Sow nasturtium seed around apple trees in spring to combat the woolly aphis. Sow a few in each hill to repel cucumber beetles. Sow with broccoli against aphids. Though nasturtium often have aphids of their own, they seem to keep them away from their companion plants.

Nettle, Stinging Nettle *(Urtica diocia)*

The name *diocia* indicates that the staminate and pistillate flowers, instead of being together on the same plant, are on separate plants. Therefore look for seed only on some, not all, nettle plants. Both flowers and seed are greenish and inconspicuous.

This weed causes much discomfort when touched. The stinging hairs cover practically the whole plant and prick the skin with their tiny silica tips, letting in enough formic acid to be felt. Relieve the itching with yellow dock leaves (usually found growing nearby). Crush and apply as a poultice.

Even so, the young leaves are very good to eat, though you must wear gloves when picking them. Wash and cook quickly. Boiling renders the stinging hairs harmless. Nettle, which is slightly laxative, is a healthy and easily digested vegetable, very high in iron. In England, a pleasant drink called nettle beer is relished by ailing aged folk.

This is a valuable plant for gardeners, especially good when used in the compost pile. Nettles help plants withstand lice, slugs, and snails in wet weather. They also strengthen the growth of mint and tomatoes and increase the aromatic qualities of many herbs such as sage, peppermint, marjoram, angelica, and valerian. Fruit packed in nettle hay will be free of mold and keep longer.

Night-Blooming Cereus *(Cereus grandiflorus)*

No mention of night-blooming flowers would be complete without this one, a strange cactus of the West Indies. Its bristling, tortured stems give birth in the darkness to the most spectacular of blossoms.

Truly a night bloomer, often at midnight, this lovely flower with the saxophone stem also emits a delightful fragrance. The waxy white blossoms with delicate pink sepals are breathtakingly beautiful. Once it has bloomed, however, the flower's sense of humor seems to assert itself; the spent blossoms hang limply, looking a bit like the legs of a freshly plucked chicken, and the rose sepals descend like bedraggled feathers from the yellow tubular stems.

Night-Blooming Jasmine *(Cestrum nocturnum)*

This member of the Nightshade family is cultivated for its fragrant, night-blooming, trumpet-shaped flowers. The leaves are somewhat oval; the fruit, following the flowers, is small and berrylike. All cestrums are extremely poisonous if eaten.

Orchid Cacti *(Epiphyllum)*

These incredibly beautiful plants are the so-called jungle cacti or leaf-flowering cacti. The name *Epiphyllum* is derived from *epi,* upon, and *phyllon,* a leaf, and refers to the location of the flowers. Epiphyllums may be grown in baskets suspended from the greenhouse roof. They require:

Light. Filtered light preferred, never direct noonday sun.

Humidity. Approximately 50 percent. Mist during summer months.

Temperature. 45 to 70°F preferred greenhouse temperature. Protect from frost.

Watering. Water when the soil surface has dried to a depth of 1½ inches. Water less frequently during winter.

Potting mix. Must be coarse and fast draining. Packaged indoor planter mix if coarse enough may be used, or a mix of the following proportions: four parts leaf mold, one part perlite, one part medium bark, one part horticultural charcoal.

Orchid cactus

Fertilizer. Mild fertilizer (with no higher than 10 percent nitrogen), once a month starting in April, ending in fall. Once in February and again in November, apply low-nitrogen fertilizer to promote blooms.

The orchid cactus comes in almost all of the colors of the rainbow. It should be kept potbound to induce flowering. Blooms normally occur on two- to three-year-old root-bound plants.

Orchids

All members of the family look a bit like the gorgeous flowers found in greenhouses and florists' shops. The family relations number more than 6,000 species and many are dainty wildflowers that grow in cool, damp American woods and swamps. These include the white, yellow, and purple lady's slippers; the calopogon; the violet-pink arethusa; the calypso; and the fragrant, pale pink moccasin flower.

In the tropical countries many orchids are air plants, attaching themselves to the bark of trees and sending roots into the air from which they take their food.

The orchid takes many unusual forms; the blossoms of one species look like butterflies. Another species furnishes vanilla. The tubers of still another are dried for their nourishing starch. They are sold on the market as "salep," which is used in medicine as a lubricant.

Orchids have the longest blooming period of any flowers. The blossoms of certain kinds may remain open for five weeks or even more.

The largest orchid is *Grammatophyllum speciosium,* native to Malaysia. A specimen recorded in Penang, West Malaysia, in the 19th century had 30 spikes. The plant was 8 feet tall with a diameter of more than 40 feet. The largest orchid flower is that of *Phragmipedium caudatum,* found in tropical areas of America. Its petals are up to 18 inches long with a maximum outstretched diameter of three feet.

This pink lady's slipper is a North American woodland orchid, and is as lovely as its many tropical relatives.

Oswego Tea, Monarda *(Monarda didyma)*

This perennial, which grows to four feet under ideal conditions, has very aromatic foliage. Large, brilliant scarlet flowers from summer to early fall entice hummingbirds.

Oswego tea (so named by the Shakers, who found the herb growing in profusion near Oswego, New York) was later known as bee balm. The healthful refreshment and delicious fragrance of this plant have made it a favorite among native American teas, and its down-to-earth beauty is valued in the flower garden. Sage or basil, freshly ground, or dried peel of orange or lemon, gives variety to the tisane.

Pansy *(Viola)*

The "flower with a face" is really a cultivated variety of violet. The lovely blossoms may be purple, violet, blue, yellow, white, brown, or a mixture of all these colors. In some climates pansies are best planted in the fall. The more you pick, the more pansies will bloom. If allowed to go to seed, they will stop blooming. You can increase pansies by taking cuttings from the center of the plant, but side shoots and branches will also grow. Place in a mixture of sand and loam, shade them from the sun, keep moist, and they will soon strike root.

Wild pansy *(Viola tricolor)* germinates well if grown near rye, and the growth of rye is improved by a few pansies. The same is not true if pansies are grown with wheat.

Pansy

Paper Flower *(Psilostrophe tagetina)*

This very showy perennial covers itself with bright yellow flowers, forming a cushionlike mound. It is excellent as a border plant. Flowers dry and stay on the plant, making them valuable for use in dried arrangements.

Pasque Flower, Wild Crocus *(Anemone patens)*

This wildflower, one of the first of spring, has lovely, large, pale blue or violet, bell-shaped flowers. They are two to three inches in size and appear before the foliage.

Sow outdoors in fall for germination the following spring, or cold stratify 30 days and sow in spring. The plants are nice in rock gardens and also for dried arrangements; the decorative seed heads look like fuzzy pom-poms. The name of the pasque flower means Easter flower, and the plant is sometimes used to dye Easter eggs green.

Pasque flower

Passionflower, Maypop (Passifloraceae)

According to legend, early Roman Catholic missionaries named these plants. They thought the 10 colored petals represented the 10 apostles present at the crucifixion. Inside the flower, colored filaments form a showy crown, which was thought to represent the crown of thorns. The five pollen-bearing anthers suggested Christ's wounds. The division of the pistil represented the nails of the cross. The bladelike leaf was symbolic of the spear that pierced his side. The coiling tendrils suggested whips and cords. Be this as it may, the flower is truly beautiful. The giant granadilla is red, violet, and white and is grown extensively in certain tropical countries for its fruits, which are believed to be aphrodisiac.

Patchouli *(Pogostemon patchouly)*
The fragrant oil of this shrubby East Indian mint is favored for perfumes.

Peppermint
See *Mint.*

Peruvian Ground Cherry *(Nicandra)*
This is a pretty little plant with small, pale blue flowers. It is also said to mean death to any bug partaking of its foliage. It grows in shade but produces more flowers in full sun. Set the seeds in fairly rich garden soil. Its blooming period (and its effectiveness) can be extended by keeping fading blossoms picked.

Petunia *(Petunia)*
This, one of the world's greatest summer plants, falls into four types: grandiflora doubles, grandiflora singles, multiflora doubles, multiflora singles. Petunias can "take it" but will bloom better and longer if fed liberally once a month — or if diluted fertilizer is added each time you water. Petunias live over the winter in mild climates. They attract beautiful moths at night, and the fragrance of some kinds is very pleasing.

Never underestimate petunia power; they perform well everywhere in the garden. They thrive in pots, flower beds, greenhouses, or wherever they have a sunny location, and they can be grown from cuttings or from seeds. Petunias help to protect beans from the Mexican bean beetle.

Phlox *(Phlox drummondii)*
The word phlox comes from the Greek word for flame. Its brilliant flower, however, never becomes flame-colored. Phlox are a true North American species and are favorite garden flowers because they are hardy and grow well in fertile soil. All annual phlox are derived from Drummond phlox, a species that grows wild in Texas. The familiar sweet William, whose bluish or pale lilac flowers are among the early summer blossoms, also belongs to the phlox group. Phlox are deliciously fragrant and for a long season in summer they dominate the garden.

Phlox are also attractive in hanging baskets with browallia or lobelia. They make a good ground cover with nicotiana or zinnia borders and are nice for beds and edgings. Sow where they are to grow; they dislike transplanting.

Piggyback Plant *(Tolmiea menziesii)*

The piggyback has the fascinating habit of growing baby plants on top of the mature leaves. The other surprising fact is that it grows wild along the Pacific coast from northern California to Alaska. If you live where winter temperatures seldom fall below 10°F, plant piggyback outdoors. In a shady, moist rock garden, a single plant will soon multiply into a colony. Scattered about the floor of a woodland, piggyback looks lovely in the company of hardy ferns.

Indoors it is definitely a winner. Give it good light and keep it a bit on the cool side, with a good soil mix consisting of equal parts all-purpose potting soil, sphagnum peat moss, and vermiculite. Don't let it stand in water but keep it evenly moist at all times.

Pine (various species)

Pine tar oil improves standard codling moth baits.

Plantain

This weed is often troublesome to gardeners, its seeds being spread by birds that eagerly eat them. Yet it has value as an emergency measure to stop bleeding. Crush or bite the leaves to let out the juice and apply directly to the wound. Bleeding will stop, even from a deep cut.

Plantain has been used for hundreds of years for healing broken bones. Keep a few plants in the garden in case of need.

Add the tender heart leaves to a green salad in early spring.

Pocketbook Plant *(Calceolaria)*

This multicolor perennial is spotted orange, yellow, or red with blossoms that mimic miniature pocketbooks. The plant is very effective in mass beds or along a shaded lawn area.

Poinsettia *(Euphorbia)*

This plant of the Spurge family has tiny flowers surrounded by large, colored bracts, or special leaves. The bracts are usually bright red but may be yellow or white. The brilliant red bracts contrast with the green leaves and make the poinsettia popular during the Christmas season. In tropical and subtropical regions, the poinsettia thrives outdoors. It may grow two to ten feet tall. It is a popular garden shrub in the southern states and

California. In cold climates it must be grown indoors. As a potted plant it grows from one to four feet tall.

The mealybug is sometimes a problem. Alcohol is lethal to the mealybug. Dip a small stick wrapped with cotton in alcohol and touch it to a pest for just an instant.

Root aphids may cause your plant to become weak and stunted, and plants may die in severe cases. To make it difficult for these pests to get to the roots, pack the soil firmly around the plant.

Poinsettia scab is sometimes prevalent in summer. Prune and burn scab-infected branches as soon as noticed.

Poor-man's-weatherglass, Pimpernel *(Anagallis arvensis)*

The small starlike, bright blue flowers of this low-spreading annual close with the coming of bad weather — believed by many to be a sure sign of rain. Plant seed in spring in full sun and poor, sandy soil. The plant will flower from May to August.

Poppy *(Papaver)*

The poppy has a bad name because opium is made from one species. Many varieties look good in groups in the perennial border or in rock gardens. Many different flowers are popularly called poppies, some native, some introduced. In this flower family are: the California poppy *(Eschscholzia californica),* corn or Flanders poppy *(Papaver rhoeas),* Iceland poppy *(Papaver nudicaule),* matilija poppy *(Romneya coulteri),* Mexican gold poppy *(Eschscholzia mexicana),* and the yellow poppy *(Papaver radicatum).*

Opium comes from the young seed capsule of *Papaver somniferum.* To obtain it, workers slit the capsules late in the day. The milky juice that seeps out solidifies overnight, and is collected by hand the next day. It takes about 120,000 seed capsules to yield 25 to 40 pounds of opium.

Poppies are actually robbers of the soil and inhibit the growth of winter wheat. They dislike barley but will lie dormant until winter wheat is sown in the field.

Portulaca, Moss Rose *(Portulaca grandiflora)*

This most gaudy of coverings for very dry spots is first cousin to the weed pussley (or purslane). It grows and

Portulaca

does well in hot, dry, shallow soil where no other flower will; for seaside gardens it is indispensable. Portulaca grows six to eight inches high and is of trailing habit. The blossoms are red, magenta, orange, and white, appearing from July to October. Culture is simple. Just scatter the seeds over the surface of raked ground when the weather is warm.

Pot Marigold *(Calendula)*

Pot marigold

This annual with yellow or orange blossoms is a nice background flower for pansies and candytuft. Plant it in fall for color through winter and spring. Pot marigold is good against asparagus beetles, tomato worms, and many other insects.

The pot marigold, or calendula, has been a popular annual for centuries. In the Tudor period it was known as the Sunne's hearbe or the Sunne's bride, and the name marigold is linked with the Virgin Mary.

Primrose *(Primula parryi)*

In summer this flower has intense cerise flowers with a yellow eye. The plant likes full sun or partial shade, and wet feet! It grows well with candytuft, pansies, calendulas, and violas.

Purslane *(Portulaca oleracea)*

Purslane is a persistent weed. Do not put it in your compost heap; it will survive and again be planted in your garden.

Pyrethrum *(Chrysanthemum coccineum)*

This interesting perennial grows to two feet with red, pink, or white daisies of three inches across. The crumbled flowers are made into a spray to control aphids and other soft-bodied insects. It is of low toxicity to man, animals, and plants and is also useful as a powder to control insect pests on pets or farm animals.

Queen Anne's Lace, Bird's Nest *(Daucus carota)*

The tiny white flowers are exquisite used in arrangements with larger, coarser flowers. Allowed to go to seed it will

Pyrethrum

become a pest, but the seeds serve as seasoners for
soups, stews, and baked fish; fresh or dried, they make
a fair substitute for anise or caraway seeds.

The herb is the wild prototype of our table carrot.
If it is found in rich soil, the root is sweet and palatable; located in sandy, hard soil, it is small and hard. It
is edible if steamed or cooked in a little water, or cut
into inch lengths and added to a soup or stew. Use a
reliable plant guide for positive identification if you try
this, however, because Queen Anne's lace closely
resembles other Umbelliferae that are deadly poisons.

Queen Anne's lace

A far better substitute for garden use is bishop's weed *(Ammi majus)*.
This lovely 2½-foot annual has lacy, white flowers like Queen Anne's lace
and is widely cultivated for cut flowers. It will grow just about anywhere.

Rafflesia

This small genus of plants has huge flowers but no leaves or stems. The
flowers grow as parasites on the stems and roots of several cissus shrubs in
Malaya. One species of rafflesia produces flowers more than three feet wide
and weighing up to 15 pounds. The stamens and pistils grow on separate
flowers, and need some agent to pollinate them. The flowers have five wide,
fleshy lobes and an unpleasant odor.

Ranunculus *(Ranunculus)*

This lovely perennial in yellow, orange, red, white, and pink is sensational
in masses, or use with snapdragons, pansies, and daffodils.

Rattlebox *(Crotalaria)*

See the chapter on Companion Planting with Flowers and Herbs.

Resurrection Plant, Rose of Jericho *(Cruciferae anastatica)*

This strange plant lives in the deserts of Mexico, Palestine, and Syria. It is
actually a seed, with small branches folded up into a ball. When ripened, it
drops off the mother plant and rolls about in the desert winds until the
rainy season. If placed in a saucer of water, the seemingly lifeless ball will
open into a beautiful rosette of fernlike leaves.

Another resurrection plant is bird's-nest moss. This plant reproduces by
means of spores.

Rose *(Rosa)*

See chapter 2, The Queen of Flowers; see also *Eglantine.*

Rubber Plant *(Ficus)*

This common houseplant is related to the fig. It does well in indoor heat and lack of humidity, growing tall rapidly and living a long time. It grows even better if the pot is rich in minerals and the plant is given enough sunlight, water, and room. Place it outdoors in summer so it will get enough sunlight to last during the winter months. Should it be attacked by scale insects, spray the plant with a control approved for indoor use.

Commercial rubber does not come from these rubber plants, but from a tropical tree that belongs to the Castor Bean family.

Sage *(Salvia)*

These aromatic plants of the Mint family have large, showy flowers, and require only the simplest of care. The salvias are a large group with both herbaceous and woody members. Among the shrub salvias is the "purple sage" so often referred to in songs and stories of the Old West.

Salvia officinalis is the source of the spice. Sage is a delicious flavoring for sausage, pork, duck, and poultry dressing. A favorite herb of Marcus Aurelius, it has figured frequently in love potions, recipes, brews, and stews throughout the ages.

Sea Onion, Squill *(Urginea maritima)*

Urginea belongs to the Lily family. Its name is derived from the name of an Arabic tribe in Algeria, who were probably the first to use the bulbs medicinally. These are tender bulb plants from the Mediterranean region, the tropics, and South Africa. Tiny new plants grow on the "mother" under a thin skin. From time to time they pop out and take root as they fall off. They are easily propagated by the gardener if the small bulbs are picked off or allowed to drop and set in moist soil.

Squills have a history of medicinal usage dating back about 4,000 years to the Egyptian Ebers Papyrus, which lists as a remedy for heart troubles a prescription including the bulbs of squills. Hippocrates, Theophrastus, and Dioscorides, as well as Pliny, all had much to say about squills, most of it wrong. From their day to the present the squill has been used in the preparation of medicines and also as an ornamental in our gardens.

A preparation made from squill is useful for colic in cattle, but should be used only under the direction of a veterinarian, for it can be poisonous. Indeed, red squill powder is manufactured as a poison for rodents.

Sedum *(Sedum)*

These succulent plants have attractive foliage and showy flower heads borne in late summer and fall. Plant in pottery containers, old shoes, boots, driftwood, or other unusual "pots" for a conversation piece, as well as in the rock garden. They are absolutely maintenance- and trouble-free.

Serpentaria, Virginia Snakeroot *(Aristolochia serpentaria)*

This small, aromatic perennial herb grows to a height of 8 to 15 inches. The flowers are usually hidden beneath the dry leaves and loose top-mold. Serpentaria is a traditional remedy for snakebite.

Sesame *(Sesamum indicum)*

The tiny but exquisite flower may be pink or white. This plant is grown mainly for its delicious seeds used to flavor bread, cakes, candy, and biscuits. The oil obtained from them is similar to olive oil. Sesame will grow in the southern states and should be planted at about the same time as cotton. It increases the effectiveness of pyrethrins.

Shamrock *(Oxalis* or *Trifolium)*

There has been much argument over which plant is the true shamrock. Some say it is a small clover plant with green leaves consisting of three leaflets, others insist it is the wood sorrel. The flowering shamrock sold by florists blooms best in warm weather and with generous sunlight. Water when necessary and do not repot often. Pot binding tends to encourage blooming.

The shamrock is the national flower of Ireland and appears with the thistle of Scotland and the rose of England on the British coat of arms.

Trefoil *(Oxalis acetosella),* sometimes called shamrock, is a delicate little wild plant that grows in shady places, often in backyards or along fences. Trefoil means "three leaves," each of which is heart-shaped.

Snapdragon *(Antirrhinum)*

The Greeks named this one *anti,* like, and *rhinos,* snout, to describe the curious shape of the flowers. However, nurseries are now producing penstemon- and azalea-flowered types of very different shapes. Two little-known trailing varieties, *A. asarina* (yellow) and *A. glutinosum* (cream and yellow), are delightful additions to the rock garden. Old-fashioned snapdragons are compatible with nicotiana, baby blue-eyes, and alyssum.

Snowdrops *(Galanthus)*

Winter jewels, undaunted by snow, snowdrops last a long time in bloom. They are lovely in patches of woodland under deciduous trees. Plant in fall so they have a long growing period. Increase your stock right after they bloom; replanting them pays off in a much bigger crop.

Soap Plant, Soap Root *(Chlorogalum pomeridianum)*

The powdered bulbs of this native from California and Oregon are toxic to armyworms and melonworms.

Sowbread

See *Cyclamen.*

Spider Plant *(Chlorophytum comosum variegatum)*

This interesting houseplant from South Africa develops young plants at the end of its flower stalks. The spider plant needs good light with or without direct sun, a cool room, and moderate humidity. It grows well in ordinary soil if kept moist. Propagate by removing young plantlets and potting them separately. The plants grow one foot tall with wider spread. The leaves are green with broad white center stripes.

Spurge *(Euphorbia)*

This plant has been rated by one of the world's outstanding nursery experts as among the 10 best perennials for its long-lived reliability, ease of cultivation, neat impressive form, and outstanding color. It looks a bit like cactus but is totally unrelated. Shapes run from clean geometrics through organ pipes, fat balls, and cylinders. Most strange of all are those with convoluted crests and snakelike, Medusa-head forms.

All euphorbias have small flowers without petals, enclosed in a cupshaped, leaflike structure with five lobes and a honey-secreting gland. The single female flower is normally surrounded by numerous male flowers.

Stapelia *(Stapelia)*

The enormous, hairy, star-shaped blossoms of this plant have a real stench.

Actually "stink bomb" seems more appropriate than "blossom," for when *Stapelia gigantea* opens one of its blooms, from 11 to 16 inches across, there is no doubt why it is called the carrion flower. But if you can overlook the odor, the bloom is remarkable — the sort of thing you'd expect to find in a science-fiction garden.

Giant stapelia isn't a good choice for a houseplant, but *Stapelia variegata* is fun to grow and the odor of the strange blossoms isn't nearly as potent. These plants are, however, very attractive to flies.

There are about 90 species of stapelia, mostly from South Africa. They belong to the Milkweed family. Other, more refined members include hoya and stephanotis, which have sweet-smelling flowers, and the ceropegia or rosary vine.

Star-of-Bethlehem *(Ornithogalum)*
This early-spring bloomer with white blossoms lightly striped with green, is excellent alone, in masses, or as an edging for a bed of daffodils.

Statice, Sea Lavender *(Limonium)*
The stiff flower stems bear literally hundreds of dainty flowers in many branched panicles. Statice is particularly good for drying as well as being graceful in the garden combined with larger flowers. The plants are superb for seaside gardens as they are unaffected by salt wind or salty soil. They grow well in garden soil; the richer the soil, the larger the flower heads.

Stinging Nettle
See *Nettle*.

Stinking Willie, Tansy Ragwort *(Senecio jacobaea)*
This weed, poisonous to cattle, causes a hardening of the liver.

Sunflower *(Helianthus annuus)*
This is one of our most valuable flowers. Its bright and cheerful blossoms dutifully follow the sun. Their blooms are visited by bees for pollen and nectar. The seeds, loved by birds, are rich in vitamins B_1, A, D, and F, and make a fine vegetable oil for cooking and salad dressings.

Also try sprouting the black sunflower seeds and using the sprouts with other greens as a salad. The black seeds are more delicious and nutritious than even the striped ones.

Sunflowers can provide not only a windbreak but also a quick-growing screen for any portion of the garden where visibility is undesirable — a compost heap, for instance. (See also Companion Planting with Flowers and Herbs for more information on garden use.)

Swan River Daisy *(Brachycome iberidifolia)*

This native of Australia is pretty in rock gardens with poppies and sedum, or used as an edging plant. Plant in masses. The name comes from the Greek, *brachys,* short, and *comus,* hair.

Sweet Flag, Calamus *(Acorus calamus)*

The alkaloid root works as a contact poison to insects, even though it is edible to humans. It commonly grows in swamps and along brooks.

Telegraph Plant *(Desmodium gyrans)*

This native of India belongs to the Pea family, Leguminosae. It has trifoliate leaves; the center leaf is elliptical and about two inches long, the two side leaves are about ½ inch in length. The leaves are usually in constant motion, rising and falling alternately, but not in regular time. The rise and fall of the leaves has been compared to railway telegraph signals. The plants are most active in early morning, especially the young ones. They make a wonderful conversation piece.

Use sandy soil when sowing the seeds of annuals in pots or when rooting cuttings.

Texas Bluebonnet *(Lupinus texensis)*

The state flower of Texas is beautiful grown in masses. It belongs to the Lupine family, and the spikes of sweet-pea-like flowers are a bright, rich blue. Nitrogen-fixing legumes, they thrive on well-drained, poor, sandy soils in full sun. These plants are easy to raise from seed but difficult to transplant.

Thistle *(Onopordum)*

Thistles, though beloved of butterflies, have never been popular with people. In spite of their beautiful flowers, the prickly leaves are unappealing. Thistles are rich in potassium (good in the compost heap), and would have high feeding value if it were not for their thorns. In grainfields they take away food and moisture, and in pastures they protect and thereby increase the spread of other weeds.

To get rid of thistles, timing is important. If cut before the blossoms are open, the thistles will spread from the rootstocks. If cut after the blossoms are pollinated, the situation is a little better. But if the blossom heads only are cut off shortly after pollination, the plant will bleed to death and wilt.

Thistle

Thyme *(Thymus serpyllum* and *T. vulgaris)*

This very valuable plant has been used in medicine since the very earliest days of herbal treatment. It is a powerful antiseptic and general tonic. As an aphrodisiac, thyme crops up with almost monotonous regularity in literature throughout the ages.

Thyme yields an essential oil that accounts for its antiseptic properties and is a good vermifuge. The oil, called thymol, is found in many orthodox preparations such as disinfectants, dentifrices, and hair lotions.

Tillandsia *(Tillandsia)*

These tender, evergreen plants have attractive flowers and large, beautifully colored bracts. They belong to the Bromelia or Pineapple family. *T. usneoides,* the Spanish moss, is another family member.

Toadflax *(Linaria vulgaris)*

Toadflax, found in waste places and often growing among corn, has powerful dissolvent properties and has traditionally been used to treat obstructions in all parts of the body, particularly the intestines, kidneys, and bladder. The leaves are small and flat; the flowers are in racemes of yellow and orange, marked white, and of the familiar snapdragon form. The plant is also considered one of the best jaundice remedies known to the herbalist.

Tulip *(Tulipa)*

The name comes from a Turkish word for "turban." Between 1634 and 1637, tulips became so fashionable in Holland that the craze was called tulipomania, and the bulbs brought fantastic prices. The Tulip Festival, which takes place in May when the flowers bloom, is a renowned event in the Netherlands.

Though they are sun lovers, tulips grow better in the North than in the South, for the bulbs need a period of cold. Since mice like to eat the bulbs, it sometimes is advisable to plant them in a small wire cage sunk in the earth and covered with soil. Scilla bulbs may also be planted with them as a protection against mice. Do not plant tulips near wheat, as they discourage its growth.

Turkey Mullein, Doveweed *(Eremocarpus setigerus)*

Greenish flowers; dark gray, shining seeds; and stinging hairs characterize the turkey mullein. The leaves contain a narcotic poison and were used by Native Americans to stupefy fish and poison their arrow points.

Other plants used to stun fish were blue curls (*Trichostema* spp.), vinegarweed or camphor weed, wild cucumber (*Marah* spp.), and members of the Gourd family. Turkey mullein is also toxic to cross-striped cabbageworms.

Unicorn Plant, Devil's-Claw, Elephant-Tusk *(Proboscidea)*

The showy, reddish purple to coppery yellow flowers are large and attractive but few in number. More spectacular are the large, black, woody pods ending in two curved, pronglike appendages that hook about the fetlocks of burros and the fleece of sheep. In this way, the pod is carried away from the mother plant and the seed is scattered. The attractive pods are used for many decorative purposes; some even are painted to resemble birds. Young pods are eaten by desert Indians as a vegetable. The mature fruits are gathered by the Pima and Papago Indians, who strip off the black outer covering and use it for weaving designs into basketry.

Vanilla *(Vanilla)*

The extract from this group of climbing orchids is used to flavor chocolate, ice cream, pastry, and candy. The vanilla vine, cultivated in Mexico for hundreds of years, has been introduced into other tropical areas, mainly Madagascar and the Comoro and Reunion Islands. However, it is said to set seed naturally only in Mexico. Elsewhere it must be hand-pollinated, adding greatly to the cost of its production. The cultivated plant lives for about ten years, producing its first crop at the end of three years.

The flowers, though dull in color, are very fragrant. Vanilla is obtained from the prepared seed capsules of *V. fragrans (planifolia),* which are six inches long and beanlike in shape. To grow vanilla in a greenhouse, a tropical atmosphere is required; in winter a temperature of 60°F is suitable.

Verbena *(Verbena)*

Vervain or verbena was the holy herb used in ancient secret rites; it was also supposed to cure scrofula and the bite of rabid animals, to arrest the diffusion of poison, to avert antipathies, and to be a pledge of mutual good faith — hence it was worn as a badge by heralds and ambassadors in ancient times.

Most of our perennials come from South American and are hardy only in favorable climates. They come in many colors and types, and are nice for edging or hanging baskets. Verbena is attractive grown with yarrow and dusty miller.

Victoria Water Lily, Royal Water Lily *(Victoria regia)*

The plant, a member of the Water Lily family, was named *Victoria regia* in honor of Queen Victoria. The round leaves with upturned edges measure up to seven feet across and are strengthened by a marvelous network of veins capable of sustaining weight up to 150 pounds. A child can easily sit on the floating leaves.

The huge flowers are nocturnal; it is a breathtaking sight to watch them open in early evening, rapidly moving from a bud to a creamy white, wide-open, deliciously scented flower. Closing the next day at about noon, they open again three or four hours before dusk, with the color turning to a definite pink. They fade the next morning and sink below the surface of the water.

Violet *(Viola)*

Violets are among the "artillery flowers" — the seedpods, when ripe, split apart and the seeds are flung hither and yon to begin new plants.

Violets have a delightful, fresh, springlike fragrance, and the edible leaves and blossoms are so rich in vitamins C and A that Euell Gibbons

Violets are a favorite flower of almost everyone. They're beautiful, no matter which species is grown.

(Stalking the Healthful Herbs) calls them "nature's vitamin pill." The violet blossoms are three times as rich in vitamin C, weight for weight, as oranges.

Violets are used in many delicious recipes, which include violet syrup, candied violets, and even a violet bombe made with candied violets, ice cream, and whipped cream.

Viper's Bugloss *(Echium)*

These plants are biennials, usually blue with gray-green foliage. They are fine for rock gardens and especially so for seacoast gardens. For a pretty combination, plant with columbine or armeria.

Wallflower *(Cheiranthus)*

This perennial is usually orange or golden. Before sowing seed, water the drills with a spray of rhubarb leaves boiled in water to protect against clubroot.

Combine wallflowers with daffodils and tulips; in cool climates combine with snapdragons and dusty miller. New strains exist in lovely pastel shades of cream, lemon, apricot, gold, salmon, light pink, rose, ruby, purple, copper, and rust. Wallflowers are good grown with apple trees.

Wandering Jew *(Tradescantia)*

The endearing habit of all the wandering Jews is that they are luxuriant in their growth habits. They are many-branched with a compact leafing pattern that is enhanced by a variety of color forms — from shades of green, to variegated white and green, to green and red.

Wandering Jews do best under filtered light because they originate in the rain forests of the tropics and semitropics. Use potting mediums of equal parts of loam, peat moss, and perlite. Pinch them back occasionally to keep them looking tidy.

Wandflower *(Dierama)*

From the Greek *dierama,* a funnel, the name describes the shape of the individual flowers hanging from long, slender stems. These perennials from South Africa cannot withstand wet, cold winters; use as houseplants in northern areas.

Water Lily *(Nymphaea)*

Water lilies, as with many other plants, have been hybridized and now come in an almost endless variety of magnificent creations, beautiful in form and color. The lilies mentioned here are less showy but interesting nonetheless in their own way.

White pond lily *(Nymphaea alba)* grows wild on ponds, lakes, and other still waters. The name is from the Greek for water nymph. The flowers are large, solitary, rounded of form, and sweetly scented with prominent yellow stamens. The root is soothing and astringent with antiseptic properties. The leaves are sometimes used for binding over wounds or inflamed areas of the skin.

The yellow pond lily *(Nuphar lutea)* is also medicinal. Its common name is brandy bottle, from the brandylike scent of its flowers and the shape of its seed vessels, which are like the traditional brandy flagons. These lilies grow wild in the shallows of lakes.

White Hellebore, False Hellebore *(Veratrum)*
This was a safe, popular insecticide against slugs, caterpillars, and other leaf-eating pests in early American gardens. It was used as a dust, or dissolved for a spray: one ounce to three gallons of water.

Wild Cucumber, Manroot *(Echinocystis fabacea)*
The powdered root is toxic to European corn borer larvae.

Wild Mustard *(Brassica arvensis)*
Wild mustard is fairly common in cultivated areas and waste places. Gather the young leaves in spring and they may be steamed, or use them in a cold salad or soup. Wild mustard growing among fruit trees or grapevines is beneficial, according to Beatrice Trum Hunter in her book *Gardening Without Poisons*.

Windflower *(Anemone)*
The name is from the Greek *anemos,* wind, and *mone,* habitation. The plant is so called because some species are found in windy places. The windflowers are suitable for the border, for the rock garden, and for cutting. Their blue, pink, and white coloring combines well with narcissus.

Wormseed, Jerusalem Tea *(Chenopodium ambrosioides)*
Some parts are toxic as extracts or dusts on several species of leaf-eating larvae.

Wormwood *(Artemisia absinthum)*
This name is loosely applied to many artemisias, but it properly belongs only to *Artemisia absinthum,* a hardy perennial with woolly gray leaves and a strongly bitter odor. As a tea, spray it on the ground in fall and spring to discourage slugs and on fruit trees and other plants to repel aphids.

Southernwood is a close cousin, growing about three feet tall with gray-green divided foliage. Silky wormwood *(A. frigida)* is excellent against snails. Plant it among your flowers in full sun and a dry location. Other family members include tarragon, mugwort, silver mound, fringed wormwood, and dusty miller. These are somewhat more moderate in odor than wormwood and southernwood.

Yucca, Amoles *(Yucca)*

Yucca has many names, the loveliest being the Spanish *candelabra de Dios* (candles of the Lord). Yucca's great clusters of creamy, bell-shaped florets appear on the stiff, woody stalks ranging from three to nine feet tall. In some species the immense symmetrical flower heads form the distinct shape of a cross. The blooms, which last from four to six weeks, are very fragrant, particularly in the evening hours.

Yucca makes an excellent specimen plant as an accent for rock gardens, having the same cultural requirements as many others used for this purpose. It grows well with pine tree moss, an upright ground cover that grows six to fifteen inches high with little tufts of needlelike foliage. Tall tulip varieties and daffodils interplanted around yucca in clumps add color while the moss is greening up.

In the Southwest many varieties of succulents and cactus grow well with yucca plants, which are valued for their ability to bind a sandy soil, particularly in areas of high winds.

Yuccas are both beautiful and edible; Native Americans even eat the flowers. The stalks are rich in sugar. The leaves produce a fiber used in making baskets and mats.

There are many species of yucca. Soap tree yucca *(Y. elata)* is treelike, often branched, and has the tallest flower stalk of any of the yuccas. It is very ornamental with creamy white, lilylike flowers. Native Americans beat its roots in water, using the milky liquid produced for washing their hair. This shampoo is thought to help the hair retain its natural color well into old age.

The large, pulpy fruits of *Y. baccata* can be eaten raw or roasted, or cooked and dried for future use. Cattle eat the flowers.

The powdered leaves of Spanish dagger *(Y. shidigera)* are toxic to melonworms, bean leaf rollers, and celery leaf tiers.

The hardiest type, Adam's needle *(Y. filamentosa),* will grow in the North if given some winter protection.

The yucca plant and the yucca

The fibers of yucca leaves have long been used by Native Americans for making rope, matting, sandals, basketry, and coarse cloth.

moth are symbiotic. The word "symbiosis" means "living together," and any organisms that do so are referred to as symbiotic, whether they benefit one another, harm one another, or have no effect at all. In the instance of the yucca, the moth feeds but also pollinates, leaving enough seeds to start new plants.

Zantedeschia

See *Calla Lily*.

Zinnia *(Zinnia)*

This is the easiest and most satisfactory annual to grow, and the hybridizers have made them so elegant that they can surely find a place in every garden.

Zinnias are bright and cheerful. The older varieties were beautiful in their day, but zinnias are now available in a rainbow of colors from white to purple. They even come in many striking bicolors.

The prairie zinnia *(Zinnia grandiflora)* is a spectacular bedding and border perennial shrublet. It forms ground-hugging cushions less than six inches tall and is completely covered with deep yellow flowers from mid-summer through fall. Plant this close relative of the annual garden zinnias in full sun. Prairie zinnia is slightly toxic to celery leaf tiers.

Lamb's-quarters gives added vigor to zinnias, as well as marigolds, peonies, and pansies.

The Queen of Flowers

The Rose family, one of the most important in the plant kingdom, includes about 2,000 species of trees, shrubs, and herbs. Some of the loveliest flowers and most valuable fruits belong to it. A few members of the family are: apple, apricot, blackberry, cherry, cinquefoil, eglantine, peach, pear, plum, quince, raspberry, spiraea, and strawberry. Its many ornamental plants include the meadowsweet, mountain ash, and hawthorn. Plants of this family give us many useful products such as attar, an oil from rose petals, used to make toilet water and perfume. Several fine woods are used in cabinetmaking.

Plants of the Rose family have regular flowers. Each has five petals, a calyx with five lobes, many stamens, and one or more carpels. They bear seeds, so they are classed as angiosperms. The sprouts have two seed leaves, therefore they belong to the dicotyledonous plants.

Different species of wild rose are native to every state of the union except Hawaii. Often they represent the so-called transition shrubs between forest and meadow or prairie. Many sucker freely and can be invasive, but they are much hardier and more disease resistant than their hybrid relatives.

Old Roses of Romance and Legend

Once upon a time, roses were different from what they are today — less dramatically beautiful in form and color but far, far more fragrant. Most of our modern roses are descended from these older types.

Fragrance is the rightful heritage of the rose. In the minds of most of us, the ideas are inseparable. Even long ago when the rose was a simple flower, it was known as the Queen of Flowers. Surely it must have been the unsurpassed quality of its fragrance that gave it this prestige.

Recently flower lovers have been uneasy because of the scentless, or nearly so, roses appearing on the market. This trend toward mere beauty in roses is greatly deplored.

What is meant by the pure odor of roses, sometimes referred to as the "true old rose scent"? This is the property of that famous trinity: *Rosa centifolia,* the cabbage rose; *Rosa damascena,* the damask rose; and *Rosa gallica,* the French rose. This lovely scent has been inherited by many modern Hybrid Perpetuals and also by some Hybrid Teas, though in a lesser degree. The old H.P. 'General Jacquemont', which first saw the light in 1852, is the parent of a long line of deliciously scented roses, and it is still popular today.

The fragrance of a rose flower is in its petals. Red roses, perhaps because they are closer to the grand varieties of early times, are generally the most richly endowed with fragrance. Next come the pink varieties. Yellow roses are the least scented, and white almost scentless.

Old-Fashioned Roses

Rose

Old-fashioned roses have been hard to find, but are enjoying a revival and are now offered by many nurseries. Aside from the fragrance, they have another advantage: Many are hardy not only where winters are severe but also where summers are hot. They are excellent for different landscaping effects.

Roses will grow, and grow well, practically anywhere if you are careful about a few things. Buy only first-quality bushes, plant them with care in a sunny, well-prepared bed, maintain a regular dust or spray schedule, water and feed at correct intervals, and remove spent blossoms.

The American Rose Society suggests these planting pointers for roses: Plant them where they'll get sun at least half the day. Plant during winter where ground isn't frozen. A raised bed works well for roses in many areas.

Pruning

It is not easy to give definite rules for the pruning and care of old-fashioned roses. Each old, rare, or unusual rose is an individual, with its own type and habit of growth.

Old, shrub, and species roses should not be pruned in the spring as with the Hybrid Teas, for if you do, you will remove the canes that would have produced their great spring flowering.

However, roses that bloom repeatedly should have weak growth removed and be trimmed to shape the plant. Pruning them is more a matter of shaping and thinning than of cutting back. Removing spent flowers encourages the growth of new flowering stems.

Treat varieties with but one annual flowering like flowering shrubs. Leave them alone, and put away your pruning shears until after they bloom.

Some of the loveliest and most intriguing of the old-fashioned beauties have long canes that arch over naturally from their own weight. Others have canes that grow straight up, which will bloom only at the top unless pegged or pruned.

To achieve a bushy, many-branched plant, shorten the long canes by one-third after the plant blooms and shorten lateral canes by a few inches. If you desire, keep this up until late summer, then leave the plant alone until after it blooms in the spring.

Climbers

The various types of climbers behave quite differently, but all must have a support to look their dramatic best. Support for climbers can be of conventional patterns, or design and build a support that is suited to your own needs.

Species Roses

Botanists have discovered species of rose in various parts of the world and brought them into cultivation. These roses are fascinating individualists, for all developed distinct characteristics enabling them to survive in their native habitats. Some are extremely hardy and have one annual flowering; others, native to the subtropics, are tender and bloom repeatedly.

Miniature roses may be used as edgings or in beds, or when potted as points of emphasis on patios. Give them a rich loam, and mulch plants in the winter with soil or straw.

Rosa rubrifolia is a beautiful shrub, so named because everything about it is red, from the soft pink 1½-inch single flowers with their reddish brown calyxes, to reddish brown canes, dark greenish red foliage, and bright hips the color of Queen Anne cherries. Blooming off and on through the season, it grows to six feet, is quite hardy, and is native to the mountains of China and southern Europe.

Rosa roxburghii is more commonly known as chestnut rose, for the unopened buds look like little chestnut burrs. It is one of the most beautiful and unusual roses in existence. Its light green foliage has new tips shaded with copper and gold. The silvery gray branches shed their bark as many trees do, and the very double 2½- to 3-inch flowers of many small petals glow pink at the center with silvery pink on the outside. It blooms repeatedly and makes an excellent bank cover. It grows quite large in mild climates.

Rosa soulieana was discovered in western China. Its relaxed canes lie on the ground and grow from 12 to 20 feet long. In June and July they are covered with corymbs of 1½-inch, single white flowers with a distinct fragrance that perfumes the air. It makes an excellent bank cover, for over the years its canes will take root and hold the soil. Grown on a retaining wall, it will cascade to the ground like a waterfall. Growing up a tree such as weeping willow, the canes will fountain down very dramatically. When the petals fall, small orange hips form. Occasional flowers appear after its mass summer blooming.

Japanese Roses

These are the pure rugosa roses that have been developed from species originally found in Japan; sometimes they are known as Japanese roses. They are hardy anywhere and very disease resistant. They should not be confused with hybrid rugosas, which have been developed by cross-pollination with other types of roses.

Grow Your Own Vitamin C

Vitamin C, found in greater concentration in rose hips than in oranges, is essential to good health and may have benefits that are not yet fully understood. Most animals have the enzymes to synthesize their own vitamin C, but man and apes do not. Since the body does not store vitamin C, our supply must be constantly replenished; there is little danger of an overdose, as the body eliminates what it does not use.

Some rose hips, those of the *Rosa rugosa,* contain 20 times as much vitamin C as citrus fruit, and the wild Scandinavian types are even richer. The hips are rich in vitamin E as well. The rugosa blossoms with a single-petaled rose. Rugosas make a dense hedge, molding a desired contour in the garden. Planted 18 inches apart, they make a bright living fence. Bees hover around the flowers because of their intense perfume.

Some kinds include: 'Will Alderman', clear lilac pink; 'Blanc Double de Coubert', pure white; *Rugosa magnifica,* carmine; and 'Fru Dagmar Hastrup', with five petals of clear pink and lower growing than most of this type.

For either a hedge or a specimen planting, the method is much the same. If possible, set your roses out immediately after arrival. For individual plants, dig holes; for a fence, it's better to dig a trench about a foot across and one foot deep.

Put some well-rotted manure or compost several inches below where the roots will rest; this promotes a stronger start and quicker results, helping the roses produce usable hips much sooner.

Rugosas need little care but will establish more rapidly after transplanting if cut back. Leave three or four buds or leaf nodes on each stem. Rugosas, like other roses, respond well to mulching to retain moisture, especially during the summer. As it decomposes, the mulch also feeds the plants.

Using Rose Hips

To receive the most benefit from this fantastic source of vitamin C, remember that the more roses you pick, the fewer the hips (these are the fruits that mature after the flower petals fall). Gather the hips when they are fully ripe, but not over-ripe. If they are orange, it is too early. If dark red, it is too late. In the North, the hips usually ripen after they've been touched by the first frost.

After picking, cook your rose hips immediately and quickly to retain the greatest amount of vitamin C. If this is not convenient, pack them in tight containers and keep refrigerated.

The hips, taken when fully ripe, can be split longitudinally and the inner seedlike structures removed. This gets rid of the hairs that are attached to them. The blossom end is usually removed and the pulp can be eaten raw or stewed, or can be used to make jam or jelly. Rose juice blended with apple juice makes a different but very tasty jelly. Be sure to cook your rose hips (and jelly) in glass or enamel saucepans.

Harvest your own supplies of vitamin C by collecting rose hips, and use them in jam, soup, syrup, marmalade, and rose-hip tea.

To make rose-hip marmalade, soak the cleaned rose hips for two hours in plain cold water then let simmer for two hours; and strain. Measure the puree and add one cup of brown sugar to each cup of rose-hip puree. Boil down to thick consistency. Pour into sterilized glasses and seal.

Enjoying Trees and Shrubs

Acacia, Wattle, Mimosa *(Acacia)*

These tender trees and shrubs with ornamental foliage have attractive flowers in spring. They may be grown outdoors in mild climates. Some species seem to know which ants will steal their nectar; they close when ants are about, opening only when there is sufficient dew on their stems to keep the ants from climbing. The sophisticated acacia actually enlists the services of certain protective ants, rewarding them with nectar in return for protection against other insects and herbivorous mammals.

White-thorn acacia *(A. constricta)* has fragrant masses of yellow flowers, amply protected by long, straight, white thorns. It grows in Texas, Arizona, and Mexico, and makes a good barrier plant for traffic control.

Azalea *(Rhododendron)*

Azalea

Botanically, all azaleas are rhododendrons, but most gardeners call the smaller-leaved and deciduous types azaleas. Azaleas are one of springtime's delights, blooming early in May and June in a wide range of colors. About 40 species grow in North America. Azaleas are truly gorgeous, and blossoms range in color through pink, red, white, yellow, and purple. Their long pollen stalks extend beyond the petals. Some of the leaves are narrow, others egg-shaped. In some azaleas, the flower has a covering of sticky hairs that keep ants away from the sweet nectar. A long, slender pod with hairs holds the seeds. The plants live best in acid soil and partial shade.

The Arnold Arboretum in Boston, Massachusetts, established in 1872, was the first extensively organized effort to collect and introduce ornamental plant varieties from foreign countries. Of the several collectors sent out by the Arnold Arboretum, Ernest H. Wilson was the most famous. During his travels throughout the Orient, Wilson gathered one of the finest collections of the azalea varieties of Japan. Since then azaleas have been hybridized into the glorious flowers we have today.

Blood-twig, Siberian Dogwood *(Cornus alba)*
This shrub is unbelievable for winter color. Its bright red stems provide intense contrast against evergreens or winter snow. See also *Dogwood.*

Bonsai
Bonsai are miniature trees grown in pots. The aim of bonsai culture is to develop a tiny tree that has all the elements of a large tree growing in a natural setting. Over the years, the Japanese have devised standards of shape and form that gradually became the classic bonsai style. Many ordinary shrubs and trees take to bonsai — quince, forsythia, even a scrubby little American elm shoot.

Begin by cutting back the roots; if your plant has a taproot, cut it off to the end. Trim other roots if numerous, but not too much. Shape the top and put the plant in a clay pot with a hole in the bottom for drainage. Rocks at the bottom are helpful, and maybe a screen to keep out the bugs.

The soil mix is a third each of sand, compost, and soil. Screen out the mix in three sizes, through quarter- eighth-, and sixteenth-inch screens, with the larger lumps at the bottom.

Set the plant in the soil, water well, and in the beginning limit sunshine to mornings. Branches may be shaped by clipping, or trained on an attached wire covered with twig tape (a greenish brown color) to hide the wire. Twist-ties may also be used to hold branches in the unnatural position.

Plants should not become root-bound. Nor should the pot be too big. The pots may be sunk in the ground to winter the plants from November 1 to March 1. If the plant is in a container that might crack, move it to a clay pot.

Bonsai were developed in the Orient, but now their popularity has spread around the world. Some bonsai are hundreds of years old — and still tiny — but don't let this deter you from trying to grow your own shrub or tree.

Broom *(Cytisus, Genista)*

Plant these lovely spring-flowering shrubs in a hot corner on poor sandy or gravelly soil if you wish them to flower lavishly. If fertilized heavily, they will be barren of bloom. Brooms come in many brilliant colors and are breathtakingly fragrant. They grow very quickly, filling in that dull patch just after the azaleas finish. The branchlets do not lose color in winter and, of course, you can make your own brooms from them!

Box, Boxwood *(Buxus)*

Because of their handsome appearance and beautiful foliage, the common box and the edging box are greatly valued as garden ornamentals. Most will thrive in any good garden soil, but are particularly useful for planting on limestone ground. Many are grown for topiary work, either to stand out individually or for hedges and dwarf borders for garden beds and paths.

Cacao *(Theobroma)*

The source of chocolate is the seeds or "bean" of the cacao tree. Native to tropical America, the trees have been cultivated for more than 4,000 years. After the canes are dried they are shipped to chocolate factories, cleaned, roasted, and ground into a pastelike substance called chocolate liquor. Pressing out the fat from this produces dry cocoa.

Researchers have discovered that cocoa contains sizable amounts of phenylethylanine, a substance produced by human brain cells during emotional episodes.

California Buckeye *(Aesculus californica)*

Flours that are made with meat and hulls of the nuts are toxic to larvae and adults of Mexican bean beetles; also, certain parts of this plant are toxic to humans.

Cercis

See *Redbud.*

Cherimoya *(Annona cherimoya)*

This small, unusual, tropical American tree grows wild in Peru and is now cultivated in California and Florida. The tree bears fragrant yellow flowers followed by egg-shaped or heart-shaped fruit weighing a pound or more. Its white smooth pulp tastes like a mixture of pineapple, peach, and banana.

The tree grows quickly and has very ornamental foliage; the fruit is about four inches across. However, it normally takes two years to fruit and the flowers must be hand-pollinated with an artist's paintbrush for the flowers to set.

Chinese Wingnut (*Pierocarya stenoptera*)
The powdered leaves of this ornamental tree are slightly toxic to Mexican bean beetle larvae.

Coffee Bush (*Coffea*)
Coffea has shiny dark green foliage and white, starlike, fragrant flowers, followed by berries, which are harvested when they are scarlet. Then the fleshy outer pulp can be removed and the "beans" dried. Freshly roasted and ground, they make real coffee.

Cold-Climate Trees
Southern gardeners delight in magnolias, but farther north the autumnal foliage of such trees as silver, red, and sugar maples; red and white oaks; and white birch brings a similar pleasure.

For flowering trees there are black and honey locusts as well as bristly locust, which has large, deep rose-colored flowers from late May to mid-June. Other "blossomers" include eastern redbud, tulip poplar, wild black cherry, catalpa, white-flowering dogwood, and little-leaf linden with its inconspicuous but very fragrant flowers.

Cornelian Cherry (*Cornus mas*)
This shrub will cheer you up when the delightful fluffs of yellow bloom dot every leafless branch in February. They are followed by green foliage and, in turn, by scarlet fruits attractive to birds and great in jellies and preserves. The purple-red fall foliage makes this shrub of year-round interest. Specimens can be pruned to produce alluring stem and bark patterns. Cornelian cherry is also excellent for spring forcing.

Corylus, Harry Lauder's Walking Stick (*Corylus avellana* 'Contorta')
Here's something very unusual for your flower arrangements. Like the crooked cane of the old-time Scottish comedian Harry Lauder, its branches are so fantastically twisted and contorted that it is almost corkscrewlike in appearance. Plant it where you can enjoy its strange silhouette against the winter snow.

Cotinus *(Cotinus)*

Unequaled for its lovely display in early spring is the cotinus, the so-called smoke tree. *C. coggygria* 'Royal Purple' is regal indeed with its coppery purple-black foliage and plumed inflorescence of the same color.

Crape Myrtle *(Lagerstroemia)*

Masses of spectacular flowers make this shrub a southern favorite; it is dramatically beautiful when in bloom in the summer. And it comes in lovely colors of white, pink, watermelon red, and royal purple.

Crape myrtle stands heat and drought well, and is not only easy to grow but also easy to root. Cut off a branch, strip the lower half of leaves, and insert the cutting (or clone) in moist soil.

Daphne *(Daphne indica)*

This small evergreen shrublet has white or purplish flowers in January. It is said that the daphne "can boast of being the most powerfully fragrant plant in the world." It grows as far north as Washington, D.C., and persists over winter if given a warm wall to sun its back against.

D. laureola (spurge laurel) grows luxuriantly in shrubberies where it is hardy and often produces its small green flowers as early as January. The plants have a delicious scent like primroses that can be detected at a distance of 30 yards.

D. mezereum is often grown as an ornamental. However, it produces poisonous berries, and eating even a few can be fatal to a child. Its fragrant, lilac-purple flowers in stalkless clusters of three bloom before the leaves come out.

Dogwood *(Cornus)*

The western dogwood, *C. nuttallii,* a very handsome tree, has beautiful blossoms and an agreeable, honeylike fragrance. *C. amomum,* the red-stemmed dogwood, has fragrant inner bark that Native Americans use for smoking.

Eucalyptus, Gum Tree *(Eucalyptus)*

This tree has a remarkable capacity for storing solar energy. Experiments in South Africa have shown that a forest of such trees produces yearly approximately twenty tons of fuel per acre. The dry timber is heavier than coal and gives out as much heat when burned.

These trees thrive best in hot, moist regions, but some varieties are extremely drought-resistant. Foliage of most eucalypti is fragrant. The lance-shaped leaves are long, narrow, and leathery. The feathery flowers look like bells and are filled with nectar. In California, eucalypti are planted around orange and lemon groves as windbreaks.

The resin, called Botany Bay kino, protects wood against shipworms and other borers. The bark of some species furnishes tannin, which is used medicinally. The leaves contain a valuable oil that smells somewhat like camphor and is used as an antiseptic, deodorant, and stimulant.

Gather bark, stems, leaves, and seeds of long-leaf eucalyptus and make a decoction by boiling. Use to spray plants affected with aphids.

Young blue gum *(E. globulus)* is handsome for a houseplant or for planting in the garden for summer foliage effects.

Euonymus *(Euonymus)*
Euonymus alata (winged or cork bark euonymus) is a prize for flower arrangements. The twigs develop pronounced corky wings that are very well defined. Plant this shrub in sun for spectacular fall foliage as well as for the color effect of the orange fruits.

Evergreens
Needles are useful for soil building and make good humus for azaleas. Evergreen plantings make good windbreaks.

Forsythia, Golden Bells *(Forsythia)*
The yellow blossoms of this lavishly beautiful shrub are one of the joys of February. Forsythias are outstanding as specimens and excellent for forcing. Branches cut in January and February will force in just a few days. Prune older wood immediately after blossoming to keep the shrub in good health and heavy flowering.

When food is scarce, birds may pick and tear at the unopened buds, but happily the plant has a reserve set that are rapidly brought into action if the season's normal quota is pillaged. Almond trees make good neighbors.

Fothergilla *(Fothergilla gardenii)*
This early-blooming deciduous shrub is noted for its one-inch spike of honey-scented, cream-white flowers appearing in early spring. An out-standing characteristic of this shrub is the change of its leathery, dark green

summer foliage to a spectacular display of brilliant yellow and orange red in the fall. To achieve this, plant the shrub in full sun and in an acid soil with good drainage.

Frangipani, Perfume Tree *(Plumeria)*

There are more than 40 species of these warm-weather ornamentals. With their exceedingly sweet-smelling flowers, they are considered the most fragrant of ornamental plants. Their waxy blooms of deep rose and white consist of five petals overlapping in star fashion to a narrow throat supported by a thick short stem. Blooms form bouquets in clusters often 8 to 11 inches across and continue opening in the same cluster for many weeks. In some parts of the country they bloom year-round.

Frangipani cuttings root easily, and if desired, the tree can also be propagated by seeds from the occasional paired, tightly filled seedpods. Sizable trees are sold by nurseries to furnish immediate beauty for outdoor gardens and, where they are not hardy, they make lovely pot plants.

Fruit Trees, Flowering

Few things are lovelier than the blossoming of fruit trees in the spring. Not to be overlooked are the marvelous, easily grown flowering crabs. Some bear fruit that makes a delicious jelly, but they are grown mostly for their beauty. Fiery crimson crab is grown for its gorgeous blossoms but is laden in the fall with small scarlet crab apples that cling for a long time after the leaves have fallen.

Another valued ornamental is the Bradford pear, which is one of the earliest trees to bloom in the spring. The abundant blossoms appear in clusters of 10 or 12. They are off-white, nonfragrant, and borne on short spurs. Collectively, they appear as a solid mass of white in vivid contrast to other spring foliage and flowers. The glossy green, thick, and broadly oval leaves appear just as the flowers start falling. Their wavy margins cause them to flutter in the wind and, like the flowers, they are abundant. The Bradford pear is gorgeous again in the fall. Early frosts bring about changes in the color of the leaves to deep hues of purplish red, then crimson. The tree rarely fruits, and when it does so, the fruit is inedible.

Other fruit trees often grown as ornamentals include almond, cherry, peach, plum, and quince.

Dwarf fruit trees, grown espaliered against a wall, provide an interesting and attractive way to use a narrow space.

Fuchsia *(Fuchsia exoniensis, F. corallina)*

This vigorous, nearly prostrate shrub spreads to three feet or more. Its branches, covered with large, dark green leaves, arch gracefully. All summer long there is a sparkling display of long flowers with brilliant red calyxes and a rich purple skirt. The shrub is beautiful for banks or to overhang a wall, and grows in sun or shade.

Gardenia, Cape Jasmine *(Gardenia jasminoides)*

This is a beautiful broad-leaved evergreen shrub, two to six feet tall, with dark lustrous leaves and exquisite large, white, waxen flowers of enchanting fragrance. The double-flowered form is famous as a buttonhole flower. The shrub blooms from May to September in the South, where it is often used for hedges. Use as a background for lower-growing flowers as the white blossoms blend well with all colors.

Guelder Rose, Highbush Cranberry *(Viburnum opulus)*

The highbush cranberry is a valuable wild plant, yielding food, drink, medicine, and beauty, but it is not a cranberry, nor is the almost identical guelder rose of England a rose.

These tall shrubs, reaching from 6 to 10 feet, are related to the honeysuckle, the elderberry, and the blackhaw. The attractive white flowers appear in showy cluster three to four inches across, with large sterile blossoms about the edge of the cluster and much smaller fertile ones near its center. The flowers are followed by bountiful clusters of bright red berries that become better-tasting and soft when touched by frost. The berries hang on the bushes all winter. Birds eat them, but not until early spring, when other food is scarce. This is an excellent plant for bird lovers to place in a wild garden.

Hawthorn *(Crataegus oxyacantha)*

The hawthorn is a beautiful May-blooming shrub with sweet-scented blossoms and lovely pink, rose, or white double flowers. Not all varieties are fragrant, however, and the blossoms of some of the American hawthorns have a disagreeable odor. Be sure of the kind you plant.

Hawthorns make excellent hedges around the flower garden and for windbreaks, shade in hot weather, and protection against intruders.

Heathers and Heaths *(Calluna and Erica)*

These dwarf evergreen shrubs are excellent for edging or in front of taller evergreens in a foundation planting. Their foliage, which persists in winter, takes on attractive shades of green, bronze, and gold.

Heathers and heaths resemble each other closely in their growth characteristics; however, the heathers (*Calluna*s) are hardier than the heaths (*Erica*s). Heathers flower for the most part in summer and fall, some continuing into winter, while the heaths bloom in late winter and spring. They come in shades of deep rosy red, brilliant pink, and white. Heather may be lilac mauve, silvery pink, red-purple, and pure white. The heath *Erica carnea* 'Springwood White' is one of the first shrubs to bloom in winter.

Honeysuckle *(Lonicera)*

There are numerous kinds of honeysuckles, characterized by the sweet honeysuckle scent and full of nectar for the bees.

In fairly recent times a decoction of the stems was used for the gout, while an infusion of the flowers was believed helpful for asthma sufferers.

The winter honeysuckle *(L. fragrantissima)* suggests the scent of roses. Blooms usually occur before leaves open, and the fragrance of the profuse, tiny blossoms carries for yards from late February to April. The plant grows well in sun or shade even in a northern location, and sometimes is evergreen in a sheltered spot.

Hydrangea *(Hydrangea macrophylla)*

As many as 35 species of these deciduous shrubs or vines with large bold flower clusters and leaves are found growing in the United States. *H. macrophylla,* widely called hortensia, is the pot or tub hydrangea that florists force for spring bloom.

Potted hydrangeas are often made to produce blue flowers by adding aluminum sulphate to the soil weekly at the rate of ½ pound to five gallons of water. After two or three applications, apply four ounces of ferrous sulphate per five gallons of water for a few weeks. This treatment is continued as long as it is necessary to keep the soil acid.

Blue-flowered hydrangeas produce flowers of various pinks if grown in nonacid soil; a neutral or slightly alkaline soil will give the results you desire. Add sufficient lime to raise the pH of the soil to a figure between 6.7 and 7.2. The addition of lime works best in the fall. Lift out the hydrangea. Shake the roots free of as much soil as is safely possible. Then mix the lime thoroughly with the soil before replanting. Have your soil tested if you want to be certain.

H. macrophylla is one of several that are extremely poisonous. Cyanide compounds are present mostly in the leaves and branches.

Idesia *(Idesia polycarpa)*

This attractive deciduous tree is found wild in southern Japan and in central and western China. The Chinese type is hardy as far north as Boston, Massachusetts. The yellowish green flowers are followed by bunches of small fruits resembling bunches of grapes. Fruits are red when ripe. Some trees produce all female flowers, others all male, and yet others, both. The all-male-flowered trees do not fruit and the all-female-flowered ones only do so when a male tree is nearby.

Indigobush *(Amorpha canescens)*

Indigobush is a deciduous shrub with narrow spikes of lovely, tiny purple flowers in late summer. Because of a deep taproot, it is drought tolerant. Plant in full sun or partial shade. *Amorpha fruticosa* is similar but much bigger, with attractive flowers in large clusters. Butterflies adore it.

Jasmine *(Jasminum nudiflorum)*

The so-called winter jasmine is one of our most brilliant winter-flowering shrubs. The cheerful butter yellow flowers and red-tinged buds appear in profusion in midwinter. Before October is over, if you grow it on a south or west wall, the earliest flowers will brighten a garden already entering its first bare stages of winter. Then, until February or March, your winter jasmine should be a never-failing source of blossom for your house. Most generous flowers appear when this hardy plant is grown in a lime-free soil in a position fully exposed to the sun.

Jojoba *(Simmondsia chinensis)*

Jojoba is a dense, mounding, evergreen desert shrub that may grow as high as eight feet and equally wide. It is an excellent landscape plant even for a formal garden, for hedges, background, foundations, and screens. Mature plants are hardy to 15°F, but seedlings are sensitive to frost.

Jujube, Christ's-thorn *(Ziziphus spina-christi)*

This may be either a shrub or a small tree. They bloom late, small greenish white flowers giving way to elongated fruits sometimes called Chinese dates. These can be used in the kitchen or as a tonic food for people and animals.

It is an attractive plant with shiny, bright green leaves, and the small, woolly flowers in clusters are richly honey-scented. The fruit is a prized delicacy of the Bedouins. However, the thorns of this shrub dig cruelly into human flesh. Legend says that Christ's crown of thorns was made of its branches. Legend also says that the *christi* name was given to the shrub because Christ loved its fruits. They are refreshing and alleviate fatigue in the heat of summer.

Kavakava *(Piper)*

Kava and ava are the names of two shrubs related to the pepper plant. People have cultivated them for centuries in the Pacific Islands and Australia. The kavas are erect shrubs and may grow as tall as five feet. They have small yellowish cream flowers and round leaves. They may be easily raised in greenhouses and can be grown from stem cuttings.

The roots yield a juice called kavaic acid. Peoples of the South Pacific use the roots to make a fermented drink called kava, ava, or kavakava.

The kavas are in the family Piperaceae. The two kinds are *Piper methysticum* and *P. excelsum.*

Kerria *(Kerria)*

A valuable plant that flowers well even in dense shade, this small, tough shrub grows upright with thin branches that remain bright green all winter in all but the coldest regions, and even there it grows when given protection. It blooms in mid-May with a wealth of 1½- to 1¾-inch bright yellow flowers. And it doesn't stop there — the spring-blooming period is followed by light, sporadic flowering through the summer and an impressive show again in early fall.

Kochia, Burning Bush, Summer Cypress *(Kochia)*

For a quick-growing ornamental, try kochia. It grows 30 inches tall and makes a nice annual hedge. The feathery foliage turns red in the fall.

Kolkwitzia, Beauty Bush *(Kolkwitzia amabilis)*

This is a handsome flowering shrub from China. Its clean foliage is untroubled by insects or diseases. In June the whole plant becomes a fountain of bell-shaped, light pink flowers. It reaches a height of seven to eight feet and will grow anywhere, thriving even in dry, sandy, poor soil.

Magnolia *(Magnolia stellata, M. soulangeana)*

Magnolias are of special interest because they have the largest flower of any tree in our gardens. The lustrous evergreen leaves, the big deliciously fragrant white blossoms, the conelike fruits that flush from pale green to rose, all have helped to give the magnolias a preeminent place in every country where ornamental planting is valued.

Magnolias are reasonably hardy and in sheltered locations may be planted as far north as Massachusetts. They prefer a rich, moist soil. Transplanting is, however, a difficult operation and is best done when new growth starts. The flowers show up marvelously against a dark background of evergreens.

Mahonia *(Mahonia)*

These evergreen shrubs have compound, hollylike leaves, fragrant yellow flowers, and berries that are both edible and delicious. Plant mahonia for foundations, background, screens, and ground cover.

Mesquite, Honey Pod *(Prosopis)*

These interesting and beautiful multiple-trunked deciduous trees or large shrubs are found growing in desert areas. The clusters of creamy white flowers attract bees, which make an excellent honey from their nectar. The fine-textured, fernlike foliage gives light shade. These plants grow slowly in nature but faster in cultivation. They do well in lawns and are nitrogen-fixing members of the Bean family.

The mesquite is almost an object of worship to desert dwellers. The long, fat pods supply a nutritious food. Cattle thrive on the young shoots when other forage is lacking. The deep-reaching roots, 60 feet or more in length, are hauled out of the ground for fuel, posts, railroad ties, furniture, and paving blocks. The wood is also cut into building and fencing materials, two great needs of the desert.

Oleander *(Nerium oleander)*

Beautiful but poisonous, this houseplant may be grown outdoors in the South. It makes a shrub about 15 feet tall, with leathery lance-shaped leaves and showy, roselike flowers in red or white. Oleander is easily grown from cuttings. All parts of the plant are poisonous but effective against codling moths.

Japaca or yellow oleander *(Theretia peruviana)* also has insecticidal properties. All parts except leaves and fruit pulp are used to make a cold-water extraction effective against a number of insect pests, especially aphids.

Osage Orange, Bodark, Bois d'Arc, Boxwood *(Maclura pomifera)*

The name refers to the Osage Indians, who used the wood for bowmaking. The plant grows wild in Oklahoma, Texas, and Arkansas. The yellow fruit looks much like an orange but is inedible. Cut and oven-dried, the fruit is sliced and used to make lovely flowers (which may be painted) for decorations.

The pioneers planted Osage orange for a living fence around their farms before barbed wire came into general use. Posts sprout easily and soon became trees. The wood is also used for making wagon wheels. A yellow dye is made by boiling chips in water.

Roots, wood, and bark repel insects, particularly crickets and roaches.

Otaheite Orange *(Citrus limonia)*

This plant is sometimes classed with limes, but the purple flower buds and outer petal surfaces indicate a lemon relationship. However, because of the fruit's shape and color, it is commonly known as the Otaheite orange.

This naturally small shrub, usually raised from cuttings and grown in pots, is very ornamental. It is fragrant when in flower and attractive in fruit. The fruit is small to medium in size, round, orange-colored, with orange, juicy, blandly sweet pulp.

Philadelphus, Mock Orange *(Philadelphus)*

Mostly hardy, these deciduous shrubs vary in size from small dense bushes two to three feet high to large ones fifteen to twenty feet high and equally wide in diameter.

Breeders have produced many beautiful hybrids of mock orange. One of these, *Philadelphus virginalis,* is among the best and most fragrant. The sweet-scented mock orange, *P. coronarius,* is the most common. Its flowers are strongly scented, and although they are delightful in the garden, their scent is too strong indoors for many people. The double-flowered varieties are less strongly scented than the common kind and last longer as cut flowers.

Mock oranges are among the oldest shrubs in cultivation, dating as far back as the sixteenth century. Like the lilac, they were brought to America and planted in the dooryards of the early settlers. The small, inedible fruits are often used as pomanders.

Phellodendron, Cork Tree *(Phellodendron)*

These are handsome, deciduous trees with short trunks and widely spreading branches. Male and female flowers are borne by different trees in summer.

Phellodendron belongs to the Rue family, Rutaceae, and several kinds have the aromatic odor peculiar to other family members. They also share in the repellent properties of rue and a decoction made from the bark is repellent to insects.

The name is taken from the Greek *phellos,* cork, and *dendron,* tree, and refers to the corky bark of several kinds. The Amur cork tree *(Phellodendron amurense)* is one of these and is prevalent in Manchuria, northern China, Korea, and Japan.

Pruning Principles

Early-flowering ornamental trees and shrubs form their buds in summer and fall. Therefore, do any necessary pruning only during the month after they have flowered; if you prune them in late winter or early spring, you will be cutting off the buds. Some early-flowering trees and shrubs are dogwood, crab apple, forsythia, rhododendron, rose, and viburnum.

Pussy Willow *(Salix mutabilis discolor)*

This one has dainty, pearly catkins. Cut twigs for indoor decoration in January and February, place them in water, and watch them unfold. Children find these delightful. The French pussy willow *(S. caprea)* produces silver-pink catkins that are deliciously honey-scented.

Pyrostegia *(Pyrostegia ignea)*

This showy, tender climbing shrub from Brazil produces rich, crimson-orange, tubular flowers in large drooping panicles. The name pyrostegia is derived from *pyr,* fire, and *stega,* roof, and refers to the upper lip of the flower. This high climber is an absolutely marvelous choice for covering the rafters of a large greenhouse or for growing outdoors on arbors in the South.

Quince

Quince *(Cydonia)*

The quince, a shrub or small tree, is one of the loveliest members of the Rose family. Though it is grown mainly for the fruit, the rosy flowers that bloom early in the spring are very attractive. They are long-lasting when cut and give a delightful Japanese-style effect placed in a low bowl.

The pear-shaped fruit has a golden yellow color and a fragrant smell. Quince is never eaten fresh, as it is quite hard and has an acid taste, but it is very pleasing when cooked or used in marmalades, preserves, and jelly. Plant quince shrubs with garlic; it improves the flavor of the fruit. The tree has long been cultivated, but has never been popular in this country.

Redbud, Judas Tree *(Cercis)*

Redbud grows wild in Oklahoma and Texas. It is unbelievably beautiful in early spring when every branch and twig is covered with bright violet-red flowers. Transplant small specimens in early spring. Shrubby in growth, it seldom attains a height of more than 12 to 15 feet, and may be grown as a large shrub or small tree. Members of the Bean family, redbuds are also nitrogen-fixing trees.

The redbud and the dogwood come into blossom at approximately the same time and complement each other, one rose pink and the other sparkling white.

Rose

See the chapter on The Queen of Flowers; see also *Eglantine.*

Rosemary *(Rosmarinus officinalis)*

This evergreen shrub of the Mint family is noted for its fragrant leaves. It has tiny, pale blue flowers and dark green leaves. In masses, blossoming rosemary looks like blue-gray mist blown over the meadows from the sea. Its name comes from the Latin *rosmarinus,* meaning sea dew. A thick growth of prostrate rosemary planted around the flower bed will act as a border for snails and slugs; the sharp foliage apparently hurts their soft, slimy skin.

Cooks use the plant in seasoning and its oil is used in perfume. The oil is secured by distilling the leafy tips and leaves. It gives the characteristic note to Hungary water; eau de cologne cannot be made without it. (See the chapter on Cosmetics and Fragrances.)

Rosemary oil is in all pharmacopoeias; it should not, however, be taken internally. The flowers are a stimulant, antispasmodic, emmenagogue (promoting menstruation), and rubefacient (causing redness of the skin). The leaves are rubefacient and carminative (cleansing).

Rose of Sharon, Shrubby Althea *(Hibiscus)*

The hibiscus shrub is distinguished by rose, purple, white, or blue flowers about three inches wide. The flowers appear in late summer when few other shrubs are in bloom. It does well even under unfavorable conditions, in either the city or the country, and is a good shrub for the gardener who has little time.

Sarsaparilla *(Smilax)*

This group of woody or herbaceous vines has hardy, tuberous roots and veined evergreen leaves. The vines grow in temperate and tropical climates and bear small clusters of red, blue, or black berries. Some species yield the drug sarsaparilla, which was once widely used as a spring tonic. It is also used as a flavoring for soft drinks and medicines.

True sarsaparilla *(S. officinalis)* is related to asparagus. Native Mexicans have long used the roots of the vine in a concoction they believe cures impotence.

Sourwood, Lily of the Valley Tree *(Oxydendrum arboreum)*

Closely rivaling the dogwood in interest and the beauty of its flowers and foliage, this plant is to summer what dogwood is to spring. The small, fragrant, bell-shaped flowers resemble lily of the valley and are borne during July and August in showy clusters 8 to 10 inches long. The attractive leaves assume deep red and scarlet tints during the autumn and form a contrast with the interesting seedpods. The plant is slow growing, which is considered an asset under certain conditions.

Spindle Leaf Tree, Spindle Tree *(Euonymus europaeus)*

This deciduous shrub or small tree is wild in parts of Europe. The leaves color well in the fall and its red fruits with orange seeds are very attractive in autumn. The fruit has a paralyzing action on aphids. The wood of the tree was once popular for butchers' skewers.

Sumac, Lemonade Tree *(Rhus glabra, Rhus typhina)*

The parts used are the flower heads, picked early to midsummer, and the fruits as they begin to turn a bright red. Dry for future use. To prepare a tasty summer drink, steep a heaping teaspoonful of the ground flowers and/or fruits, fresh or dried, in a cup of hot water. Cover five or six minutes with a saucer. Stir and strain. The native peoples of upper North America sweetened this drink with maple syrup, the tart fruits being soaked in water until needed for use. The fruits of the staghorn sumac are distinguished from those of the smooth variety by being far more hairy; use less of the staghorn because they are more acid.

Bury bags of sumac leaves around the base of apple trees infested with woolly aphids. Tannin has been discovered as an active principle in sumac leaves.

Summer-Flowering Shrubs
If you want spectacular bloom in July and August, here are some suggestions: hydrangeas (many varieties), *Abelia grandiflora, Buddleia davidii, Ceanothus americanus, Clethra alnifolia, Hibiscus syriacus, Holodiscus discolor, Hypericum densiflorum, Indigofera amblyantha, Itea virginica, Lespedeza bicolor, Perovskia atriplicifolia, Sorbaria arborea, Stewartia pentagyna, Tamaris pentandra,* and *Vitex negundo incisa.* These do well in the hot and dry areas of the southwestern states.

Tulip Tree *(Liriodendron tulipifera)*
This near relative of the magnolia has showy yellow blossoms that resemble garden tulips in size and form. A good shade tree with fast growth, it is ideal for young folks who have just purchased their first home or for older people when they move to treeless suburbia. In the lumber trade, tulip tree is called yellow poplar.

Uva Ursi, Bearberry, Manzanita, Wild Cranberry, Bear's Grape, Sagckhomi *(Arctostaphylos uva-ursi)*
This low-growing evergreen has pretty pink flowers from April to June. Plant in early fall or spring in land that is loamy and free of lime. Herbalists use a tea made from the leaves in treating diabetes, Bright's disease, and all kidney troubles.

Weigela *(Weigela)*
This lovely shrub flowers from May through July. The rosy blossoms resemble foxglove in shape, are borne in immense quantities, and are attractive to hummingbirds. Give them a moist soil and full sun, away from competition of tree roots. As they bloom on twigs of the preceding year, prune after flowering.

Wild Cherry *(Prunus)*
The avid tent caterpillar likes to eat wild cherry trees, and landowners

sometimes try to get rid of the trees for that reason. However, entomologists have discovered that if an insect is deprived of its native feeding plant and learns to eat another plant, it will never return to its original feeding plant. What this means is that if all the wild cherry trees were destroyed, the tent caterpillar would go to other trees, principally apples and pecan. Worse than that — it would never go back to the wild cherry.

Keep this in mind and don't destroy the wild cherry trees; they are valuable as trap plants for concentrating the tent caterpillars where they can do little harm. Even when completely defoliated, the wild cherry instinctively protects itself against permanent damage. In about three weeks it may be again in full leaf.

The enemies of the tent caterpillar, the calosoma beetles and braconid wasps, as well as other insect friends, help keep tent caterpillars under natural control.

Winterfat *(Cerotoides [Eurotia] lanata)*

A bit of an oddity, this shrub grows three feet tall and is covered with woolly hairs, white but becoming rust-colored with age. In fall the twigs are covered with woolly white fruits, resembling lamb's tails, and are wonderful for dried arrangements.

Witch Hazel *(Hamamelis)*

This very fragrant hardy ornamental blooms at a time when few other shrubs are blossoming outdoors. Its bright yellow flowers are not injured even in zero temperatures. On a cold, frosty morning witch hazels "shoot" their seeds as the seedpods crack open with a snap.

The well-known medicinal lotion is derived from an extract of the plant dissolved in alcohol.

Ylang-Ylang, Flower of Flowers *(Cananga odorata)*

The name comes from the pennant-shaped, long-petaled flowers, and means "flower that flutters."

The ylang-ylang is not a graceful tree, but its peculiarly shaped blossoms make up for any shortcoming in its stature. The flowers are noted for their heady fragrance that permeates the air for a considerable distance around them. Just one of the fleshy, three-inch-long flowers will perfume an entire room.

As the flowers, almost hidden at first, reach maturity, the petals turn yellow. Then they gradually darken with age and their fragrance becomes proportionately stronger. The tree is generous with its flowers, which, strangely, never fall; they just dry up and gradually blow away. The birds consider these delicate tidbits.

Plant this brittle, upright tree where it will be protected from strong winds. It is fast-growing and will easily reach 25 feet within five years. Though listed as a rarity, it isn't difficult to find in nurseries that specialize in unusual trees.

Vines

There is always a place in every flower garden for a truly outstanding vine. In addition, vines are often used to screen out an unsightly area, to create shade, or as protection for other plants. Many vines add grace to hanging baskets.

Some suggestions for annuals are: cathedral bells *(Cobaea scandens)*, 30 feet; cypress vine *(Quamoclit pennata)*, various colors, 25 feet; cardinal climber *(Ipomoea quamoclit sloteri)*, scarlet, white-throated tubular flowers, 30 feet; marble vine *(Diplocyclos palmatus)*, attractive leaves; and black-eyed Susan vine *(Thunbergia)*.

Perennial vines of interest include: coral vine *(Antigonon leptopus)*, 30 feet; Chilean jasmine *(Mandevilla suaveolens)*, fragrant white flowers; butterfly pea *(Clitoria ternatea)*, double light blue flowers; flag of Spain *(Quamoclit lobata)*, crimson flowers, heart-shaped leaves; perennial sweet pea *(Lathyrus latifolius)*, many colors; Madeira vine *(Anredera pseudobaselloides)*, vigorous climber, fragrant white flowers; wisteria, blue or purple clusters in spring; queen of vines; and yellow jasmine *(Jasminum humile)*, a delightful evergreen bearing many clusters of bright yellow bells in summer.

Here are some further notes on vines for the yard and garden (plus an aid to recognizing one that you certainly will not want to plant but may encounter accidentally).

Bean, Scarlet Runner *(Phaseolus coccineus)*

This is the king of the ornamental beans, growing over 10 feet tall with large clusters of bright scarlet flowers that blossom all summer. It is very prolific; the more pods you pick, the more the plant produces. The pods are 12 to 16 inches long with large black and scarlet beans that are absolutely delicious freshly cooked. If left on the vine to mature, the beans can be made into attractive necklaces. Pierce while still green and let dry for few days on a long hat pin. String on heavy thread with small gold beads in between.

This flowering bean is ideal for growing up the side of a porch, garage, or house as a vine for shade. The scarlet runner has unusually large leaves that maintain a lush green color all summer, and the flowers attract hummingbirds — which add to the beauty of the scene.

Scarlet runner beans are both delightfully pretty and excellent to eat. They're a fine choice if you need a vine that will grow quickly to hide an unattractive fence. Keep them away from onions and garlic.

Summer savory, strawberries, potatoes, beets, celeriac, and summer radishes are good companions, but do not plant members of the Onion family nearby.

Chinese Fly Catching Vine *(Aristolochia delibis)*

The long peculiar flowers are insectivorous; their odor serves the purpose of attracting the insects required to ensure pollination and fertilization. The small leaves are attractive, and the plant has hanging-basket-shaped fruits. Use for hanging baskets. This vine is an important medical plant in China and Japan.

Cinnamon Vine, Chinese Yam, Chinese Potato *(Dioscorea batatas)*

This quick-growing vine will hide an unsightly area as it ranges up to 30 feet in a single season. In July and August it puts out profuse white, cinnamon-scented flowers borne in loose clusters. The roots are large tubers, potato-like in flavor, and considered edible in the tropics. The leaves are shiny and quite attractive. Its flowers are borne on the axils, where little tubers about the size of a pea also appear. These tubers, sown like seeds, will produce a full-sized vine the second year. Cinnamon vine likes the sun but is not at all capricious as to soil. For quick growth, start the small tubers indoors in pots.

Clematis *(Clematis)*

Large-flowered hybrid clematis is one of the loveliest vines known and blossoms abundantly in many colors. A wide range of cultivars is available and more are continually developed.

Also of interest is the smaller-flowered clematis called virgin's bower. There are a number of colors and varieties of these rather small, deciduous vines, highly prized for their often showy flowers. Give virgin's bower a place on fences, trellises, or posts. It likes a cool, shaded spot in rich soil and full sun to partial shade.

This is a marvelous companion plant for enlivening the rather somber branches of pine trees; Japanese gardeners often train it to grow on them. It is not a parasite and does not harm the tree.

Clinging Vines

Vines growing on masonry walls or on trellises on wooden walls add insulation. In summer they lower indoor temperature by protecting the outside walls from the sun's direct rays. Choose deciduous leafy vines (they will drop their foliage in winter to let the sun warm the dwelling), and plant them on southern and western walls.

In cold weather, evergreen vines on the north surface will head off the wind and keep the inside warmer. Try Boston ivy or Virginia creeper for summer insulation and an evergreen species such as English ivy for cold-weather protection. Clinging vines are not recommended for wooden walls because their stems and tendrils hold moisture, causing the wood to deteriorate. Achieve the same insulating effect with trained twining vines such as wisteria or climbing roses on trellises.

Dutchman's-Pipe *(Aristolochia durior)*

This foliage vine with its handsome, heart-shaped leaves creates dense, cooling shade. It grows rapidly, reaching up to 30 feet in height.

Grape *(Vitis)*

Grapes

The sunlight on the leaves and not on the grapes determines whether or not grapes can be grown. Grapes will color normally if they have adequate leaf surface in proportion to the amount of fruit being produced. To obtain perfect bunches of grapes, they are sometimes placed in bags. If you want to do this, use brown paper bags. Grapevines need a sunny, well-ventilated location. A grape arbor is so decorative that you may wish to place one in your flower garden. Hyssop planted near grapevines will increase yield. Though grapes are usually propagated by cuttings, they do have flowers, beloved of bees, and fertile seeds. Wild mustard is beneficial to grapevines.

Kiwi *(Actinidia chinensis)*

The so-called Chinese gooseberry is a native of China and is commercially grown in New Zealand. The plant is a rampant grower, shooting up possibly five inches in one day and up to eight feet the first year. The fruit tastes like a blend of strawberry, pineapple, and guava, and keeps well in the refrigerator.

Hardy varieties of kiwi have been developed and can be grown even in the North. Train grapelike vines on arbors, trellises, or fences for November harvesting. Grow in pairs of one male and one female vine; additional female vines may be planted with one male.

Moonflower, Man-of-the-Earth, Wild Potato *(Ipomoea pandurata)*

This is a very hardy tuberous vine with flowers similar to those of morning glory but larger. They have a delicious fragrance, slightly reminiscent of lemon, fresh and clean.

Morning Glory *(Ipomoea purpurea)*

This popular favorite possesses a simple beauty, especially in the modern versions of standard varieties. Rapid in growth, it must be provided with something to twine about; if not, it will twine on whatever is nearest, no matter what it is. Morning glory is a great success in a window box. With light support it should reach the ceiling by midsummer, blooming every foot of the way. It is great for covering trellises and arbors and for hiding unsightly areas.

Morning glory seeds will germinate sooner if boiling water is poured over them before covering with soil. This does not harm the seeds and will soften the shell, causing the seeds to sprout more quickly. Other extra-hard-coated seeds may be treated the same way.

This vine takes plant parenthood quite seriously, and will vigorously reseed itself.

Morning glory has uses as a companion plant. (See the chapter on Companion Planting with Flowers and Herbs.)

Poison Ivy Look-Alikes

Virginia creeper is frequently mistaken for poison ivy, which it does some-

Virginia
creeper

what resemble. Yet its five leaflets, compared to only three for all forms of poison ivy and poison oak, make it easily recognizable. Other innocent plants that sometimes suffer from an identity crisis are the harmless Boston ivy *(Parthenocissus tricuspidata)* and marine ivy *(Cissus incisa)*.

The real culprits to watch for are, first, poison ivy *(Rhus radicans)*. Usually this is a vine, but may sometimes, especially in open sun, be a shrub from a few inches to several feet high.

Poison oak *(Rhus toxicodendron)*, found in the South and West, is sometimes called oak-leaf poison ivy. It is shrubby, with leaflets covered by downy hairs and lobes resembling small oak leaves.

Be careful around these two, for even particles of the irritant oil wafted through the air on smoke or pollen can affect the eyes or lungs of allergic people. Jewelweed, which often grows nearby, is very good to use as a remedy against poison ivy. It relieves the itching almost at once. Boil a pot of the jewelweed and strain the juice. Keep juice refrigerated or freeze cubes of it and bag them for future use.

Trumpet creeper

Trumpet Creeper *(Campsis radicans)*

This woody, high-climbing vine is very hardy. Although a native of the woods, it is often planted in gardens. The flowers are three-inch-long, orange tubes with flaring scarlet lobes and grow in clusters. They yield copious nectar and attract many insects. The shade of red-orange is somewhat harsh, so use this vine with discretion. The fruit is a long pod with a many-winged seed. Some people are allergic to the leaves and may get dermatitis from touching them. Although this is a beautiful vine, it can be a nuisance along roadsides in the South.

Wisteria *(Wisteria)*

This truly magnificent vine increases in beauty with every passing year. Drought-tolerant, it does well planted in a sunny location. *W. floribunda* has long racemes of pure white flowers; when in bloom it resembles a waterfall.

Acetone extract from seeds of wisteria is somewhat toxic to codling moth larvae.

The Life of Plants

All-America

To qualify for this label, a new seed variety must be started at 30 sites across the country, each site representing a different climate and soil. Only those seeds that grow well at a wide range of sites and are a distinct improvement over the nearest existing variety win this citation.

Allelopathy

Some plants release chemicals into the soil that are toxic to other plants. This phenomenon is now receiving attention as a way to control weeds. Researchers hope to breed weed resistance into commercial crops in much the same way that disease resistance is instilled.

An example of allelopathy is the so-called "soft chaparral," a unique association of evergreen shrubs and trees in the semiarid land of western North America. No more than eight feet in height, these thickets of broadleaf evergreens and stunted shrubs and trees have the amazing ability to invade grasslands and encircle themselves with dry moats of bare soil three to six feet wide.

Scientists have determined that these xerophytic (arid-climate-loving) plants release fragrant chemical compounds called terpenes from their leaves into the surrounding air. The soil around the shrubs absorbs the terpenes, which accumulate more rapidly during the dry season, in an amount sufficient to inhibit the germination and growth of other plants in the surrounding area. Commonly known terpenes include camphor, rosin, natural rubber, and turpentine.

Bracts

What we sometimes think of as blossoms are often petal-like bracts such as the highly colored bracts of the poinsettia. The dogwood and the bunch-berry have tiny purple flowers surrounded by white, petal-like bracts. Bracts are leaflike structures that may form a circle beneath an inflorescence.

Carnivorous (Insectivorous) Plants

Venus flytrap

These plants trap insects for food. They usu-ally live in moist places where they get little or no nitrogen from the soil. They must obtain it from the decaying bodies of the insects they trap. For this they have special organs and glands that give off a digestive fluid to help them make use of their food.

Some of these plants have flowers that are colored or scented like decaying meat to help them attract insects. Pitcher plants have tube-shaped leaves that hold rainwater in which the insects drown; other carnivorous plants have rosettes of leaves with sticky hairs, such as those borne by the sundews. Some plants such as the bladderworts grow in water.

The Venus flytraps make interesting houseplants; in the absence of insect prey they are usually fed tiny pieces of meat, generally hamburger. Their leaves consist of two hinged lobes. When an insect is attracted to a leaf, the lobes snap shut, and the insect is digested by the plant. If you grow carnivorous plants indoors, water them with distilled or soft water to avoid toxic salt buildup.

Composite or Compositae

This family is the largest and most highly developed of flowering plants. It consists of more than 20,000 species of herbs, trees, vines, and shrubs.

Composite plants have efficient methods of reproduction. They pro-duce many seeds and have good methods of scattering them.

Some family members, such as calendula, chamomile, wormwood, tansy, and arnica, are used to make drugs. Chrysanthemums, asters, and dahlias are grown for their beauty; others are weeds and wildflowers, such as ragweed, goldenrod, sagebrush, thistle, and burdock.

Cross-Pollination

Seeds may be produced by either self- or cross-pollination (see *Pollen,* below). In the former case only one plant is involved; in the latter, two. Pay attention to your nursery catalog to know whether you will need two plants for fertilization to occur.

Bayberry *(Myrica pensylvania),* beloved of early Americans for candle making, will not bear its berries unless male and female forms keep company together.

If you have a single holly, don't discard it; buy the missing member of the pair and your holly will bear berries.

The willowy leaves of the spiny sea buckthorn *(Hippophae rhamnoides)* are a lovely silvery gray, and pollinated female bushes bear an abundance of orange berries. No need to arrange individual marriages; plant one male buckthorn amid a small harem of ladies.

Fragrance

Flowers exude a powerful, seductive odor when ready for mating. This causes a multitude of bees, birds, and butterflies to join in a saturnalian rite of fecundation. Unfertilized flowers emit a strong fragrance for as many as eight days or until the flower withers and falls; yet once impregnated, the flower ceases to exude its fragrance in less than half an hour. One tropical plant *(Colcasia odorata)* increases in temperature at time of flowering, repeating this phenomenon for six days from three to six each afternoon.

Fragrant flowers are usually light in color or white, with the purples and mauves coming next. Thick-textured flowers such as magnolias and gardenias are often heavily scented. The perfume of a plant is not always found in its flowers. It may be in the root, seeds, bark, the gum or oils, even in the leaves or stalk. Certain families, such as the Labiatae (lavender, rosemary, mints), are especially gifted with perfume.

This invisible quality of flowers is one of their most important assets; however, many of our modern hybrids have lost their fragrance. The so-called "unimproved" kinds often retain this. The modest little sweet-scented candytuft, *Iberis odorata,* is an example. The wild carnation seems to spray its admirers with its spicy incense. The scent of old-time roses, lilac, and violets is enchanting. Most of the older varieties of iris are also sweet with perfume. If you would have fragrance in your flower garden, seek out the older, less showy varieties. Note also that flowers are less scented in periods of extreme heat and drought.

Gibberellic Acid

In the mid-1920s, a Japanese scientist working on rice diseases discovered a remarkable colorless substance named gibberellic acid. Less than one drop of it on a camellia bud causes the flower not only to be much larger but also to bloom much earlier than usual. This has greatly extended the season of blossoming for camellias.

Another experiment has shown that a lawn can be made to start growing in early spring at below normal temperature after being treated with gibberellic acid at a concentration of one ounce per acre. Scientists believe the gibberellins are natural plant products.

Greensand

Greensand is found along the New Jersey and Virginia coasts, among other places. This granular, half-soft marine deposit contains about 6 percent potash, and is an olive green, iron-potassium silicate, also called glauconite. Greensand is available from several natural-fertilizer companies and is recommended as a major natural source of potash as well as nitrogen and phosphorus. (See Sources.)

Hybrids

The production of new flowering plants occurred only after the sexual basis of plant reproduction was understood and the principles of heredity and genetics were laid down. It was then possible to take a plant with one desirable characteristic (for example, flower size) and cross it with a plant having another desirable characteristic (such as a specific color).

Hybrid plants are formed by taking the pollen from one plant and transferring it to the ovary of another. The resultant seeds are first-generation hybrids and can be planted to produce the superior flowers, fruits, and vegetables found in seed catalogs.

The mule, a sterile cross between a horse and a donkey, is a first-generation or F_1 hybrid. If mules could reproduce, their offspring would be F_2 hybrids. The "F" stands for filial or offspring, the digit for the generation.

Just as mules have greater vigor than either parent, so have hybrid plants. In general they grow faster, bigger, and more uniform, and bear more flowers and fruit. That's especially true for the F_1 generation. Offspring of F_1

plants — the F_2 generation — have more vigor and uniformity than regular plants, but less than the F_1. F_1 hybrid seed is expensive because seedsmen can't let bees do the pollinating, but must brush the proper pollen on by hand. F_2 seed doesn't need hand-pollination, so is less costly.

Inflorescence

The word inflorescence means "a flowering" or a "flower cluster." The largest known inflorescence is that of *Puya raimondii*. The jolly green giant is a rare Bolivian plant with an erect panicle (diameter 8 feet) that emerges to a height of 35 feet. Each of these bears up to 8,000 white blossoms. This is also said to be the slowest-flowering plant, the panicle emerging only after 150 years of the plant's life. After blooming, it dies.

LUTHER BURBANK (1849–1926)

Burbank was an American plant breeder and horticulturist who developed many new trees, fruits, flowers, vegetables, grains, and grasses. Among the plants he developed are the Burbank potato, the giant Shasta daisy, the spineless cactus, and the white blackberry. He also improved many plants and trees already known.

One of the methods he employed was the selection process, continued through many generations until a plant that was superior with respect to a single characteristic or group of characteristics became isolated. He employed this method in the development of the "stoneless" plum.

First, Burbank selected from a large collection of plums one that had a thin "pit" or stone. He permitted this tree to carry on pollination and set fruit. Then he chose from this tree a few plums that had the thinnest stones. He planted the seeds from these, and when the resulting trees fruited, he again selected the fruits with the thinnest stones. These were planted and when the resulting trees matured, Burbank again selected the fruit with the thinnest "pits." After several selections of this type, he produced a plum with an extremely thin stone; this was marketed as a "stoneless" plum. In using this method, only the desirable variations are retained. Burbank also used this method in developing the Shasta daisy. There is really no magic about the selection process; anyone with time and patience can use it.

Burbank's first discovery was the potato that bears his name. As a young gardener in Massachusetts, he planted the contents of a seedpod from the rarely blooming 'Early Rose' potato. The pod produced 23 widely varying seedlings. Burbank sold the best plants to a dealer, who named the variety 'Burbank'.

Light Pollution

As if noise, air, and water pollution weren't enough, we now have light pollution! Safety lights, installed by many people in their backyards, upset the timetables of plants and cause them to confuse night with day.

The amount of sunlight that a plant needs each day is called its photoperiod. Plants that flower when days are short are called short-day plants, and include chrysanthemum, Christmas cactus, gardenia, kalanchoe, aster, and poinsettia. Plants that flower when days are longer are called long-day plants and include marigold, petunia, black-eyed Susan, China aster, coneflower, feverfew, calceolaria, and weigela. And then there are the "day-neutral plants," which have hormones to induce flowering whether days are long or short. In this category are African violets, roses, snapdragons, and tomatoes.

The growth pattern is altered when plants are near the night lights because the plants grow when they should be "sleeping." This is detrimental to trees, particularly in northern regions, because they continue to grow in the fall when daylight is shorter and they should be ceasing growth to prepare for winter. New growth is moist and tender. When a tree continues to grow well into the frost season, it becomes more sensitive and is more easily injured. Lighting also makes the leaves more sensitive to air pollution.

High-pressure sodium lamps are twice as efficient (for lighting purposes) as the mercury-vapor lamps, and emit more red and yellow light. Mercury-vapor lamps, generally used on highways and city streets, give off a bluish green light that contains a few red rays and many ultraviolet rays. Natural sunlight gives off light in the visible region from blue to green to yellow to red. The red region of the spectrum regulates the photoperiod.

Chlorophyll for photosynthesis — the food-making process that occurs only in nature and which is the chief function of the green leaves of plants — is activated by red and blue. The blue region also attracts night-flying insects.

Research by the U. S. Department of Agriculture indicates the red part of the spectrum is the growth-triggering light. During the 24-hour period of a day, the light-dark cycles trigger the flowering, branching, dormancy, bulging (as with onions), and other plant-growth responses.

DO PLANTS SLEEP?

Plants sleep during a period called dormancy. They are affected by the cycles of winter, spring, summer, and autumn, as well as wet, dry, cold, and hot seasons. Many plants also close up and sleep at night.

In the Beltsville, Maryland, nursery where tests were conducted, it was found that plants near the sodium lamps grew more rapidly into the fall season and also grew much later than plants of a like age that had been screened from night lighting. Trees that had been exposed to the light suffered severe winter dieback the following spring.

The sensitivity of 17 species of trees to security lights (night lights) was rated by USDA horticulturists. Trees tested having the highest sensitivity were Norway maple, paper birch, eastern catalpa, sycamore, American elm, and zelkova. The intermediate sensitivity group included red maple, gingko, honey locust, golden rain tree, Japanese pagoda tree, and littleleaf linden. Trees exhibiting low sensitivity were American holly, sweet gum, Austrian pine, Bradford pear, and willow oak.

These lights also have an adverse effect on gardens, because plants need to sleep as well. Generally speaking, plants are affected within a radius of about 25 feet of the lights.

Laws affecting night lighting of commercial property vary from state to state, but as our need for protection grows, lights are becoming more widely used. It is good to be aware of the effect they have on growing plants, so that you can place your garden in a more favorable location or plant varieties with lower sensitivity to light.

Officinalis

Any plant with *officinalis* as part of its name is or has been listed in the official pharmacopoeia, a book containing standard formulas and methods for the preparation of medicine, drugs, and other remedial substances. The plants listed may vary from country to country. For instance, the British pharmacopoeia lists some plants not found in the American. Also, some plants formerly listed in the American have been deleted down through the years.

Organic Matter

An important ingredient often lacking in garden soil is organic matter: fully or partially decayed remains of plants, animals, or animal by-products such as manure. Besides its gradual release of nutrients needed for plant growth, organic matter is valuable for several other reasons:

1. It improves soil aeration.
2. It improves the water-holding capacity of the soil.
3. It reduces soil crusting.

4. It stimulates the growth of beneficial microorganisms, some of which may destroy harmful microorganisms or prevent their growth.
5. It assists nematode control by supporting parasites, predators, and diseases of nematodes.

Osmosis

This is the passage of one fluid into another through a membrane between them. It occurs with both liquids and gases. This passage, or transfusion, results in a mixture of the two fluids. Osmosis takes place through a semipermeable membrane that allows certain substances to pass through and keeps others out.

Plants depend on osmosis. Minerals dissolved in water pass from the soil to the plant through root membranes. Osmotic pressure probably helps raise the sap to the high branches of trees.

Plant Mimicry

The orchid *Trichoceros parviflorus* grows petals to imitate the female of a fly species so exactly that the male attempts to mate with it and in so doing pollinates the orchid.

The carrion lily develops the odor of rotting meat in areas where only flies abound. Other flowers that rely on the wind for pollination do not waste their time making themselves fragrant or beautiful to appeal to insects or birds but remain relatively unattractive.

Plant Quarantine

Plant quarantine is a law that regulates the movement of plants and other materials that may carry a plant disease or insect pest. The quarantine keeps the disease or insect from spreading from infested areas to those free from these hazards. Some laws list plants that may not be shipped in or out of a locality. They may also give directions for moving, packing, and labeling.

In a quarantine, officials examine all plants at the border of the quarantined area and keep out the dangerous types. Foreign plant quarantines control the shipping of plants from other countries.

Pollen

The tiny yellow grains seen in most flowers are pollen. They are used to form seeds. Plants make the pollen in the saclike anthers of their flowers.

The anthers are the male organs of reproduction. The female organs include the pollen-receiving stigma leading to the ovary, which is the egg-bearing part of the plant. Pollination is simply the transfer of pollen from the anther to the stigma. When this occurs, fertilization has taken place.

Self-pollination occurs in flowers that can transfer pollen from their own anthers to their own stigmas. Cross-pollination means that the flower must depend on wind, insects, birds, flies, or some other means to carry its pollen from one flower to another.

Pollen has been considered a great energy producer for centuries and it is reportedly consumed by many athletes. It is also believed to be an aphrodisiac.

The pollen of most plants is highly inflammable. When thrown on a red-hot surface, it will ignite as quickly as gunpowder.

The wind scatters the pollen of many plants, including all the grasses and cereal grains such as corn, wheat, rice, and oats.

Proliferation

In the plant kingdom, proliferation means new growth by cell division or buds. An example of this is the daylily, which not only makes seed and may

---

THE WILL TO LIVE

Why do some plants live and others do not? Like people, plants do not always respond in an exact relationship to their environment and care. Some have a will to survive, others don't.

An occasional tulip bulb planted upside down will circle laboriously around and reach up triumphantly for the light. A cactus growing in the desert will top itself with a brilliant blossom. Tiny seedlings seem to have a built-in will to live. And, of course, some varieties of plants have it more than others; for example, it's very hard to kill sansevieria (mother-in-law tongue) or a rubber plant. And some flowers and herbs grow and spread on their own without help from gardeners.

Plants have also developed various means of self-protection. Mechanical weapons include thorns on roses, prickles on thistles, and spines on cacti. Sumac (some types) uses poisonous chemical weapons, and nettles have irritating acids.

be divided by its tubers but also makes new plants at joints of the flower stalk, sometimes growing aerial roots. (See *Daylily* in the Flower Lore chapter.)

The so-called airplane plants also propagate themselves in a similar manner by sending out runners.

Roots

Roots are one of the three organs that most plants must have in order to grow. The other two organs are the stems and leaves. The roots of most plants grow in the ground and draw their food material from the soil, but some plants have their roots in water or even in air.

Roots hold the plant in place and supply it with water and nourishing salts from the soil. Roots that form first and grow directly from the stem are called *primary roots.* Branches of the primary roots are called *secondary roots,* and branches of these are *tertiary roots.*

Roots with different forms have special names. A primary root that grows much larger than any of its branches is called a *taproot.* When taproots grow very thick and store up food for the rest of the plant, they are called fleshy roots. A cluster of thick primary roots is called *fascicled roots.* Threadlike roots are *fibrous.* Roots may also grow on the stem or in other unusual places. These are called *adventitious roots.*

Roots are also called soil roots, aerial or air roots, and water roots, depending on where they grow. Roots that get their food from other plants are called parasitic roots.

Scientific Names

These are the names botanists give to all plants. They are in Latin and are the same in all countries. Scientific names have two parts, the genus and the species. For example, the prairie rose is *Rosa setigera.* This means that it belongs to the genus *Rosa* and the species *setigera.* The relationship of plants is determined mostly by their reproductive parts.

Seeds, Survival of

Seeds possess an enormous potential for survival. It is not unusual for large seeds, 100 years old and more, to grow when planted. During World War II, in England, the bomb craters blossomed with flowers and other plants that had not been seen within the memory of man. Evidently the seeds were sleeping deep in the earth until brought again to the surface, where light and moisture caused them to germinate.

In 1982 scientists tested lotus seeds found in an Asian lake-bed deposit. They were found to be viable, and radiocarbon dating showed that they formed on lotus plants between 1410 and 1640.

Other claims are doubted by scientists. These include stories of viable wheat found in the tombs of Egyptian pharaohs, and Arctic lupine seeds found in the Yukon and believed to be at least 10,000 years old.

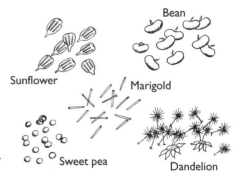

A seed is a little bundle of determination-to-grow, and it is the most important part of the plant. The roots, the leaves, the flowers all exist so there can be seeds. As shown above, there's a great variety among seeds, from the airborne dandelion seeds to the relatively large beans.

Sex

The first botanist to demonstrate that flowering plants have sex and that pollen is necessary for fertilization and seed formation was a German, Rudolf Jakob Camerarius, who published his *De Sexu Plantorium Epistula* in 1694. The heated controversy engendered by this book lasted a generation before it was finally established that plants had sexual organs and could in fact be elevated to a higher sphere of creation than previously thought.

Bisexual plants have flowers that bear both male and female parts.

Dioecious plants. Male and female parts are found on separate plants.

Monoecious plants. Male and female parts are borne in different flowers but on the same plant. A good example of this is the squash plant. Gardeners frequently tell me that their squash plants are blooming but not bearing. The answer is that the male flowers appear first. As the plant grows, the female flowers (which will bear the fruits) appear and are fertilized, often by bumblebees. The female flower is borne at the end of a small bulb that gradually enlarges to form the fruit.

Synergists

Usually derived from plant products, synergists are nontoxic substances that are added for a strengthening effect. Pyrethrum, for instance, is greatly strengthened by the addition of asarinin from the bark of southern prickly ash, sesamin from sesame oil, and peperine from black pepper.

Terminal Shoot

This term indicates the shoot that forms the end of the main stem or of a main branch of a tree or plant. All other shoots are called side shoots or laterals.

Tetraploids

Seeds or plants exposed to radiation are often grossly changed. A drug, colchicine, extracted from the fall-blooming crocus, profoundly changes plants too, sometimes doubling the number of chromosomes in every cell so that a normal diploid becomes a tetraploid. Such plants have enormous vigor, larger blossoms, or bigger fruit.

The brown-eyed Susan, a meadow plant, was treated with colchicine and changed into the vigorous and beautiful gloriosa daisy, a tetraploid. The same has been done with ageratum, phlox, snapdragons, and zinnias.

The small French marigold has double the chromosomes of the large American type. The result of crossing is an intermediate type, a triploid that is sterile; because it fails to produce seed, it continues blooming with tremendous vigor all season.

Which Plants Go Where?

Accent Plants

These plants are planted singly or in small groups to provide emphasis in the yard or garden. Usually they are of distinct color or form; an accent tree, for example, might be the Italian cypress, the Atlantic cedar, or the handsome sugar or rock maple.

To avoid monotony in a perennial border, interplant with a tall, stiff species. These exclamation marks of the garden include good tall plants such as Siberian iris, lythrum, and some daylilies. Or use plants with light gray foliage to break up the monochrome of green. Silver mound artemisia, santolina, and *Dianthus plumarius* give the desired effect.

Boulder

Tuck succulents and tiny rock plants into crevices and crannies of an ancient boulder. Rub with moss and lichen and let sun and rain be its benison. I have a planted boulder and love it.

Cold-Resistant Annuals

This term describes the first annuals to plant in the spring and those that will survive nippy autumn days. These annuals are also used for winter planting along the Pacific coast and in the Gulf States.

Pansies head the list. They are hardy and available in early spring throughout much of the country; some are even ready for late-fall planting in the milder climates.

If you need fragrant annuals for your garden, try stocks. These delicious annuals are fine for cutting and last well indoors. Snapdragons resist the cold and begin to provide their colorful spikes early in the gardening season. For strong yellows or oranges, plant calendulas. The newest hybrids are compact, floriferous, and very hardy.

Larkspur or delphinium, annual poppies, centaurea, dusty miller, annual phlox or aster, primulas, cineraria, dianthus, and carnations all will perform enthusiastically for you in the early spring and will continue through several fall frosts.

Desert Gardening

Wise desert gardeners keep lawn areas small and use rocks, gravel, and patio paving generously, along with raised beds, pools, and water plants. Choose trees that can "take it," such as cottonwoods, poplars, Siberian elms, black locusts, chinaberry trees, as well as evergreens such as athel tamarisk, Arizona cypress, and Aleppo pine, for shade and wind control. In low deserts include more evergreens, such as beefwood, black acacia, and eucalyptus. Survival and fast growth are important criteria for desert plants.

Night-flowering cactus, Mexican fan palm, yucca, and low-growing lavender lantana make good companion plants.

For easy upkeep, grow annuals and perennials like creeping rosemary, feathery wormwood, senna, African daisy, salvia, and fairy primrose. For seasonal color, plant pyracanthas, oleanders, yuccas, and showy crape myrtles. Remember: If plants can't take heat, drying winds, and alkaline soil and water, their beauty counts for little.

Drought-Resistant Flowers

Cornflower, calliopsis, sunflower, morning glory, ice plant, four-o'clock, rose moss, and zinnia will grow in regions with deficient rainfall.

Fences

Robert Frost said, "Good fences make good neighbors." They also keep out unwanted animals. A living fence such as multiflora roses may also act as a deterrent and give lovely bloom as well. And think of the vitamin C in all those rose hips.

Fire-Retardant Plants

While no plant will completely keep a fire from advancing, some plants resist burning better than others and thus may slow a fire's progress. However, if winds carry sparks, even protective fire-retardant plants can be breached.

Useful trees and shrubs are: callistemon, *Ceratonia slilqua, Heteromeles arbutifolia,* Myopurum, *Nerium oleander* (dwarf varieties), *Prunus lyonii, Rhamnus alaternus,* Rhus (evergreen kinds), *Rosmarinus officianalis prostratus, Schinus molle, Schinus terebinthifolius,* and *Teucrium chamaedrys.*

Perennials and vines: achillea, agave, aloe, artemisia (low-growing varieties), atriplex, campsis, *Convolvulus cneorum,* gazania, ice plants, *Limonium perezii, Portulacaria afra, Santolina vivens, Satureja montana, Senecio cineraria, Solanum jasminoides,* and yucca (trunkless varieties).

FLOATING GARDENS OF XOCHIMILCO

The Floating Gardens, about three miles beyond the village of Xochimilco, are the brightest and prettiest sight in Mexico City. (In fact, Xochimilco means "place where the flowers grow.")

The flowers have been growing there since the height of the Aztec Empire, when many nobles lived near Lake Xochimilco. In those times workers built big rafts, covered them with earth, and planted vegetables and flowers. The rafts floated and the roots worked down through the earth into the water. These "floating gardens" gradually increased in size and became anchored by the interlacing roots of the plants. Now, the island rafts no longer float but are solid islands surrounded by canals. Flower vendors move about in the canals selling their colorful wares from canoes.

This type of garden was one of the earliest uses of what is now called hydroponics.

Hang It All!

Hanging baskets never fail to attract attention, be it cascading petunias gracing an old-time porch, a gay ivy geranium attached to a lamp post, or a dainty fuchsia suspended from a tree branch. Hanging baskets have a magic all their own.

A hanging basket is really a pot plant gone glamorous and needs to be fed to keep going. Slow-release houseplant fertilizers are a handy way to do this.

Here are some suggestions of suitable candidates for various positions.

Plants to grow in sun:

FLOWERING: lantana, ivy geranium, phlox (annual), lobelia, dwarf French marigold, nasturtium, oxalis, petunia, bougainvillea, sweet alyssum, verbena, monkey flower (mimulus), shrimp plant, dimorphotheca, pinks (dianthus), cascade chrysanthemums, pansy (early spring), Tiny Tim tomato.

FOLIAGE: English ivy, Sprenger asparagus, donkey-tail *(Sedum morganianum)*, variegated vinca, peppermint geranium, purple passion *(Gynura sarmentosa)*, flowering inch plant *(Tradescantia blossfeldiana)*, setcreasea, siebold sedum.

Plants to grow in shade:

FLOWERING: fuchsia, achimenes, browallia, coleus (trailing) , black-eyed Susan vine *(Thunbergia)*, tuberous begonia, columnea, episcia, flowering maple, star-of-Bethlehem *(Campanula isophylla)*, torenia.

FOLIAGE: English ivy, German ivy, Swedish ivy, grape ivy, kangaroo ivy, pick-a-back plant, variegated archangel, spider plant *(Chlorophytum)*, inch plant, zebrina (tradescantia), philodendron, rosary vine, Christmas cactus, strawberry "begonia" (saxifrage), epiphyllums, patience plant, pothos, Boston fern, rabbit's foot fern (and other ferns).

Lawn

Lawns are the greenest show on earth. Where the flower beds are the picture, lawns are often the frame. A lawn is a great asset to cooler living, for an acre of grass in front of your home gives off 2,400 gallons of water every hot summer day. This has a cooling effect equal to a 140,000-pound air conditioner (which amounts to a 70-ton machine). Along with trees, shrubs, and flowers, a lawn helps purify the air, putting oxygen back into it so we can breathe much easier.

If you live in a dry location and have difficulty getting grasses to flourish, consider establishing a lawn of fragrant camomile (Anthemis nobilis). Drought has little effect on this green plant. Sow it just like grass. When cut it will give out a fragrant odor. To get it started in spring, sow a mixture of camomile and lawn grasses together; as the season advances, the strong-growing camomile will take over the lawn as the grasses begin to lose ground.

Low-Light Areas

A dim location is the perfect spot for a dieffenbachia, a tropical plant from South and Central America. It can survive on only two hours of sunlight a day but must have humidity. The plant grows well grouped with palms, aglaonemas, ferns, and dracaenas.

Patio Pyramid Planter

A pyramid planter can be a most interesting focal point for your garden, balcony, or patio. A lot of different fruits and flowers can be shown off to advantage. Or use it for a miniature herb garden. Even midget vegetables will grow in one of these. For indoors, the planter is mounted on casters for easy movement; watering is provided for by way of a top reservoir.

Planter

Want something different in a container? Often free for the gathering, sculptured by wind and wave, driftwood makes a beautiful "pot" for cactus, sedums, and other small plants. Or fill it with lacy green ferns set with their own peaty earthballs in plastic bags, punctured at the base for drainage.

For indoors, look for a fine piece of handcrafted pottery, a dainty basket, or a filigree of old iron; Western boots, well worn, also make unusual planters. An old coal scuttle is dandy for summer flowers. It does not tip over, can be punched with drainage holes, and there is lots of room for deep root growth.

Something extra special for an apartment balcony is a birdcage on its stand. Paint it black and fill it with a tumble of white marguerites or red or yellow cascade petunias. Or paint it turquoise blue and use pink geraniums, white petunias, and green ivy.

Seashells make attractive planters. If you prefer not to deface a shell by cutting or drilling to provide drainage, water the plants sparingly. Plants such as velvet plant *(Bynura),* aloe vera, succulents, sedums, and miniature English ivy will grow well in these containers. (See also *Patio Pyramid Planter.*)

Pond-Edge Planting

Suitable plants for the edge of a pond are: *Iris pseudacorus, Iris versicolor,* arrowhead, sweet flag, cardinal flower, flowering rush, marsh marigold, and astilbe. Tiger lilies do not like wet soil, but *Lilium canadense* and *Lilium superbum* do.

Purple loosestrife is beautiful, but should generally be avoided because its invasiveness has made it a serious problem for wetlands in many areas.

The water lily is seen in a variety of colors. Small air sacs in the leaves keep this plant afloat.

Rock Garden

There are hillside rock gardens and valley rock gardens, as well as those on level sites; there are rock gardens in sun and rock gardens in shade, as well as those that include water.

All rock gardens should include dwarf material in trees and shrubs. Nurseries that specialize in choice rock-garden plants usually have a good selection. The extremely dwarf evergreen trees, for example, grow slowly and never develop out of proportion to a miniature landscape.

Make the rock garden attractive in winter by using a number of evergreen rock plants (many of which are technically shrubby or subshrubby). Examples are perennial candytuft and *Iberis sempervirens.* The rock roses *(Helianthemum)* are brilliant in early summer with a myriad of satin-textured blooms resembling little wild roses in pink, crimson, orange, gold, white, and scarlet. The silver saxifrages are very useful for creating the all-the-year-round picture of true Alpine rock gardens. For cooler, shadier rock gardens try the mossy saxifrages. The genus *Dianthus* includes many splendid plants well adapted for sunny locations and well-drained sites. There are also bellflowers or campanulas, thymes, stonecrops or sedums, primroses or primulas, houseleeks or sempervivums, gentians, bulbs, and ground covers.

Roof Terrace, Plants for

Consider sun and shade just as for ground-level gardens, and study the prevailing wind direction before you make plant selections and decide on locations. Use good soil mix, and you can successfully grow begonias, lobelias, nicotianas, and impatiens. Japanese yews make nice accents.

Sandy Soil

Sandy soil, sometimes found near the seashore, need not be a problem if the right flowers are planted. Among annuals adaptable for sandy soils are calendulas, California poppies, sweet alyssum, marigolds, nasturtiums, portulaca, cleomes, and petunias. Shrubs may be Russian olive, *Rosa rugosa,* hydrangeas, rose acacia, tamarisk, and Siberian pea tree.

Scatter Plants

Instead of using herbs alone in a stiffly formal herb garden, try scattering them throughout your flower garden. For their protective qualities include: marjoram, oregano, lavender, santolina, blessed thistle, camomile, lovage, chervil, lemon balm, and bergamot.

Shade

Two delightful plants for shade that team well with each other are native bleeding heart *(Dicentra eximia)*, with lacy foliage and pink, nodding, heart-shaped flowers; and lily of the valley *(Convallaria majalis)*, a dainty, fragrant perennial with tiny white flowers. A third plant for shady spots is hosta (funkia), a plant much valued for its large, decorative leaves.

Achimenes, which comes in various colors, is an excellent pot plant for shady locations on the north. It blossoms almost continuously from late spring until fall frost.

Stepping Stones

For a flagstone walk, plant creeping thyme *(Thymus serpyllum)* between the stones in a sunny position. The plant seems to thrive from being walked upon and gives off a pleasing fragrance with each step you take.

Street Noises

Trees and hedges muffle street noises. The best trees and shrubs for this purpose are dense evergreens, which also give year-round privacy. Hemlock, yew, and arborvitae are good if they will grow in your area. Keep the lower branches from dying off by pruning carefully; most noise comes from near the ground. If you have a choice of sites when you build, choose one above street level to keep noise at a minimum.

Stumped by a Stump?

You can make it into a thing of beauty if not a joy forever. Sometimes an old tree must be cut down because it is rotten, yet the stump may not be dug up and removed. Scoop out the middle of the stump and fill it with good soil. In the fall, plant tulip bulbs. After they have bloomed in the spring, succeed with petunias, snapdragons, or some other colorful flower.

Swimming Pools

You can have a carnival of color without the pain of constantly cleaning up if you choose wisely for your poolside planting. And don't plant anything bristly, sharp, or thorny. Plants should also be as litter-free as possible.

Shrubs. Here are some beautiful but practical suggestions: camellia,

Crassula argentea, Fatsia japonica, Griselinia, Juniperus, Raphiolepis, Viburnum davidii.

Trees. Cordyline, dracaena, *Ficus auriculata, Ficus lyrata, Firmiana simplex,* Musa, palms, *Schefflera, Strelitzia,* tree ferns.

Vines. *Beaumontia grandiflora, Cissus, Fatshedera lizei, Solandra maxima, Tetrastigma.*

Perennials. Agapanthus, *Agave attenuata, Aloe saponaria, Alpina zerumbet,* artichoke, *Aspisdistra elatior,* canna, *Clivia miniata,* cyperus, gazania, hemerocallis, *Kniphofia uvaria, Liriope, Ophiopogon,* philodendron (treelike types), *Phormium,* sedum, succulents, yucca, *Zoysia tenuifolia.*

Remember that the litter produced by plants (and this should be reduced as much as possible) should be large enough to be removed by hand rather than by passing into the pool's filter.

Window boxes

Some popular plants suitable for many types of window boxes include geranium, lantana, dwarf marigold, nasturtium, petunia, salvia, sweet alyssum, ageratum, verbena, and trailing vines (for sun). For shade use achimenes, tuberous and wax begonias, impatiens, fuchsia, and torenia. For colored foliage use coleus and caladium; for a trailer, German ivy.

Winter Flowers

Winter gardens call for tough plants, so don't think in terms of man-made hybrids. Alpines are the obvious choice. In their natural habitat there are two seasons, winter and August. This means they must bloom, ripen seed, and store food between the melting of snowbanks in late July and the new snows of September. In our less orderly climate, Alpine bulbs still obey their mountain timetable. If you choose a naturally warm site, you may have "spring in January" with pastel-shaded snow crocuses in bloom.

Brilliant orange *Crocus korolkowii* is one of the earliest blooming of all temperate-climate flowers, often blooming before winter's snow has melted, during a prolonged January thaw. It may even disappear beneath a late winter snow and suddenly reappear after the first sunny day.

WANT INSTANT GARDEN COLOR?

Try annual bedding plants such as petunias, geraniums, salvia, ageratum, zinnias, and marigolds. For best effects, mass flowering annuals in large clumps of color rather than a staccato line of single plants.

Companion Planting with Flowers and Herbs

Allium *(Allium)*

Onions belong to the Lily family, Liliaceae. Actually, *allium* is a Latin word for garlic. Vegetable alliums are chives, garlic, leek, onion, and shallot, all of which are excellent protective companions for roses.

The ornamental alliums are more decorative to plant with roses and will also provide excellent protection from mildew and black spot as well as aphids and many other pests. They thrive on the same care and culture as onions and are very easy to grow.

Flowering onions come in many colors beside blue and purple — in greenish white, yellow, rose, and dark red. They like plenty of compost but will do well even on dry soil. Some of the larger varieties such as 'Jewel of Tibet' grow to a height of five feet and have a blossom head up to eight inches in diameter. These should be staked in windy climates. Alliums are winter hardy and may be left in place year after year.

An interesting ornamental allium is *A. senescens glaucum,* a low-growing plant with silvery blue leaves that curl and twist in a style suggestive of Japanese art. The two-inch umbels of soft rose pink are profuse in August and September. This plant not only makes a fine protective ground cover for roses but is also appropriate for edging rock walls or for the front of the border. Add to its useful qualities its hardiness and drought tolerance. Plant seeds ten to twelve inches apart.

Alliums also repel moles. Here are some other beneficial services of the Onion family:

Onion. Repels cabbage butterflies and helps all members of the cabbage family.

Chives. Good companion for fruit trees and tomatoes.

Garlic. Good against fruit tree borers.

Members of the Onion family were so valued in ancient times that it is said the builders of the pyramids were paid in leeks, onions, and garlic. Onions are not only healthful; certain members of the family such as garlic are said to be an excellent aid in preserving a youthful complexion.

Borers

Garlic planted around fruit trees will repel borers, but this is best done when trees are young and newly planted. Nasturtiums are also good. To foil borers in squash plants, soak the seeds overnight in kerosene.

Buckeye *(Aesculus pavia)*

The flowers of the dwarf or red buckeye attract and kill Japanese beetles.

Bulbs

Flowering bulbs such as crocus and colchicum (which are poisonous if eaten) are very attractive but often are simply allowed to come up without an accompanying ground cover. They are much prettier if low-growing companion plants such as white alyssum, *Phlox subulata, P. divaricata,* armeria, saponaria, common thyme, and vinca minor are used as a framing ground cover.

Buttercup Family

Root secretions from these plants poison soil for clover by retiring growth of nitrogen bacteria. Clover will disappear in a meadow where buttercups are increasing. Delphinium, peony, monkshood, columbine, and double buttercup belong to the same family. Unless the soil is very rich, other plants will not grow well in their vicinity. This is a strong, vital family, but they grow only for themselves.

Calendula *(Calendula officinalis)*

See *Marigold.*

Camomile *(Anthemis nobilis)*

This plant of the Aster family has strong-scented foliage and flower heads that contain a bitter medicine principle. It is used as an antispasmodic, stomachic, and perspiration ingredient for breaking fevers.

Camomile in small quantities increases the essential oil in the peppermint plant, but as the proportion of the camomile plants increases, the amount of peppermint oil diminishes — too much of a good thing!

Camomile tea is effective against a number of plant diseases, especially in young plants. It can be used to control damping-off in greenhouses and cold frames. Make tea by soaking dried blossoms for a day or two in cold water.

The powdered heads of rayless camomile *(Matricaria matricarioides)* are fairly toxic to diamondback moths.

The flower heads of scentless false camomile *(M. nidora* or *M. camomile)* are said to be as effective as commercial pyrethrum in controlling face flies.

Chinaberry *(Melia azedarach)*

This shade tree repels grasshoppers and locusts. Make a repellent tea with either live or dried leaves. The powdered fruit is somewhat toxic to European corn borer larvae.

Chrysanthemum *(Chrysanthemum)*

The name is derived from the Greek *chrysos,* gold, and *anthemon,* flower. There are 100 species of both annuals and perennials, some of which are known as pyrethrum. Chrysanthemums are protective to strawberries.

Chrysanthemums themselves may be protected by an all-purpose spray made from three hot peppers, four large onions, and one whole bulb (large) of garlic, ground together. Cover with water and allow to stand overnight. The following day, strain the mixture through a fine sieve. Add enough water to make a gallon of spray. This spray may also be used on roses and azaleas. Bury the mash around roots of plants.

Columbine *(Aquilegia vulgaris)*

These beautiful plants are very attractive to red spiders in some areas, so keep them in the flower bed and out of the vegetable garden. Those columbines grown in humus-rich soil are less susceptible to damage by leaf miners.

Columbines are strong growers themselves but do not assist other plants and often are detrimental. They are heavy feeders, so if you want to grow them as ornamentals, give them plenty of compost and feed other plants grown in their vicinity equally well. They will grow well in combination with rhubarb if both are given plenty of well-rotted cow manure.

Native Americans considered flowers of wild columbine *(A. canadensis)* a highly effective tranquilizer.

Coreopsis *(Calliopsis)*

Coreopsis in the flower bed is useful as an insect control for nearby plants. It also is an attractive annual (of the Compositae family) whose yellow, red, or maroon flowers grow on tall, slender stems. It looks like a daisy and may have one or two layers of petals.

Cornflower *(Centaurea cyanus)*

Cornflower, in the proportion of 1 to 100 seeds, is noted for its salubrious effect when grown with rye. Also called bachelor's-button or bluebottle, it also is beneficial to other small grains if grown in about the same proportion. The flowers supply bees with abundant nectar even in the driest weather.

It was a custom among Russian peasants to decorate the first sheaf of the rye harvest with a cornflower wreath, after which it was placed in front of an icon.

Cornflower

Dandelion *(Taraxacum officinalis)*

Dandelions, even if they grow in thick patches on your lawn, are not competing with grasses because of their long, very deep taproots. These transport minerals, especially calcium, upward from deeper soil layers (even from beneath hardpan, which they can penetrate), and deposit them nearer the surface. They are therefore returning to the soil minerals that have been lost through seeping downward.

Dandelions are closely associated with clover and alfalfa, which also prefer good, deep soils.

Juliette de Bairacli Levy states in her *Herbal Handbook for Everyone*: "This is one of the most esteemed plants of the herbalist. . . . It is blood-cleansing, blood-tonic, lymph-cleansing. Also has external uses for treatment of warts and hard pimples. A diet of greens improves the enamel of the teeth."

Dandelion helps other flowers grow. It stimulates fruits to ripen faster. The roots, dried and ground, are sometimes used as a coffee substitute. In

early spring the unopened buds are delicious cooked with leeks, lightly seasoned with butter, salt, and pepper. The hearts may even be eaten raw if the
leaves are tied together and the heart blanched. They are very rich in
vitamin A.

A pale yellow dye can be made from dandelion blossoms; a deeper
yellow-brown color is obtained when the dye is made from the plant's roots.

Dusty Miller *(Centaurea cineraria)*

Plant this around prized flowers to repel rabbits and other animals. William
J. Park, former president of Park Seeds, who gave me this suggestion, considered the variety 'Diamond' to be the most effective and the prettiest.

Elder *(Sambucus)*

Elder is noted for repelling certain insects. An old method of trapping cutworms consisted of placing compact handfuls of elder sprouts in every fifth
row or hill of cultivation and tamping them down. Cutworms gathered in
this trap material, where they could be regularly collected.

Elder is a powerful patriarch of the plant world; wherever it grows, it
discourages other herbs. Animals usually dislike the rank elder taste.

Elder leaves are effective against moles if placed in their runs; they find
the odor offensive. Branches of elder have been used against maggots.
Bruise them first to increase the odor, then rake the leaves across the
seedbed after sowing.

Feverfew *(Chrysanthemum parthenium)*

Sometimes this plant is called pyrethrum. It is not the same plant, but it has
insect-repellent properties of its own, perhaps because of the spicy scent of
its foliage.

Four-o'Clock *(Mirabilis)*

Japanese beetles, a pest on peach trees and many other plants, like the
foliage of the four-o'clocks and are apparently unaware that in eating it they
are committing suicide. Dig up the four-o'clocks in the fall and if carefully
overwintered, they can be used again the following year. The foliage of this
plant is also poisonous to humans; don't let children take a bite of it.

Foxglove *(Digitalis)*

The tubular purple or white flowers grow about 2 inches long in a 12- to

24-inch, one-sided cluster. The summer-blooming flowers are often spotted within.

Foxglove has a growth-stimulating effect on nearby plants and is a good companion for pines. It does well in a forest border and in open woodland for naturalizing. Foxglove tea in the vase is said to prolong the life of other cut flowers.

The flower is the most valuable source of the powerful heart stimulant digitalis. Natives of North America knew and used

Some people plant soybeans and corn as a lure or trap crop for deer; others plant castor beans and foxglove to repel them. An effective fence has to be at least seven feet high.

foxglove for heart problems before it was known to Europeans. In England the extract was recommended by so-called witches (or herb women) for this purpose before it was recognized by physicians. The drug is cumulative in its action and should never be used as a medication except under the direction of a physician.

Severe poisoning comes from eating the fresh or dried leaves, which do not lose their toxicity by cooking. Children have been poisoned by sucking the flowers and swallowing their seeds.

Geranium *(Pelargonium)*

Geraniums will repel cabbageworms and are good to plant among roses, grapes, and corn against Japanese beetles. Use the white variety near corn.

Among the diverse scented geraniums are the peppermint geranium *(P. tomentosum),* which has velvety, grapelike leaves and small white blossoms; the lemon-scented *(P. crispum),* with long-stemmed, conspicuous flowers of a deep rose color and crispy, fruit-fragrant leaves; and nutmeg and apple geraniums, which have small, almost rounded, soft gray leaves distinguished by the scent of spice or apple. Try making apple jelly flavored with rose geranium leaves.

Gladiolus *(Gladiolus)*

Peas or beans and gladiolus have inhibiting effects on each other.

Herb of Grace, Rue *(Ruta graveolens)*

This is a very bitter-tasting herb, strongly aromatic, and once important for medicinal purposes but no longer taken internally. Contact can cause a rash if you are allergic to it.

Plant rue with roses to foil the Japanese beetle. It is also helpful grown with fig trees. Cats detest rue, so rub it on your upholstered furniture to keep them from clawing. Use against fleas in the dog's bed, and a few sprigs hung in a room will drive out flies. Rue and basil are incompatible.

Insecticidal Flowers

Asters, chrysanthemums, cosmos, coreopsis, nasturtiums, and French and African marigolds are good to plant throughout the flower garden.

Japanese Beetle *(Popillia japonica)*

This bronze-blue, iridescent beetle feeds on all kinds of ornamentals. To control, a rotenone preparation is recommended. In lawns, treat the turf with a bacterial spore dust, which will infect the grubs with milky spore disease.

Beetles are sometimes caught in traps filled with geranium oil. They may also be lured to feed on trap crops of African marigold, evening primrose, four-o'clock, or woodbine. They are poisoned by leaves of castor bean and blossoms of white geranium.

Jimsonweed *(Datura stramonium)*

This weed spreads usually by having its seed carried by birds. It is very poisonous, causing a kind of intoxicated state, but has a certain medicinal value. It is helpful when grown with pumpkins.

Larkspur *(Delphinium consolida)*

Common larkspur's alkaloids — delcosine and delsoline — have been found effective against aphids and thrips.

Lily of the Valley *(Convallaria majalis)*

This delightfully fragrant garden flower, in Germany called the Mayflower, grows wild in the southern Allegheny regions. It likes a rich, humusy soil and partial shade. Do not put narcissus with it in a vase as it will cause the narcissus to wither, perhaps because the leaves and flowers of lily of the valley are poisonous.

Marigold *(Tagetes)*

Nematodes, wormlike inhabiters of the soil, are microscopic in size, and the root-knot types injure many garden plants. These tiny worms like sandy, warm soils and have been known to devastate entire gardens. Chemical soil disinfectants kill them but kill the plants as well, so the discovery of a protective flower is very valuable.

Marigolds are very beneficial in discouraging nematodes that attack potatoes, strawberries, roses, and various bulbs, especially if these strong-scented beauties are grown for several seasons in ground where nematodes are suspected. Experiments have shown that marigolds suppress meadow nematodes for up to three years and control other nematodes for one or more years without injuring the plants.

An easy way to use marigolds for nematode control is to rotate plantings of marigolds with crops that are susceptible to nematode injury. To lessen competition it is also wise to interplant marigolds two or more weeks after the plants that they are grown to protect.

Marigolds control nematodes with sulphur-containing substances called thiophenes that are produced in the roots and kill the pests when released in soil. Both French and African marigolds have similar root excretions. The chemicals are produced slowly, so the marigolds must be grown all season to give lasting control. Interplanting them may not greatly help garden plants during the first season, but the benefits become apparent in the following years as the nematode population is reduced.

Tomatoes interplanted with marigolds will grow and produce better. Plantings with beans help protect against the Mexican bean beetle. They also help deter weeds and may be planted as a crop against invasions of ground elder, bindweed, and ground ivy. The older types with strong odor in both foliage and blossom are considered the most useful.

Pot marigold *(Calendula officinalis),* or calendula, planted in the vicinity of choice evergreens, will repel dogs. This is an old-fashioned herb whose dried flowers were used by our grandmothers to flavor soups.

Morning Glory *(Ipomoea)*

The Indians liked to grow wild morning glory with corn — probably one of the earliest examples of companion planting — since they believed that it gave the corn added vigor. It is believed that morning glory seeds also will stimulate the germination of many types of melon seed.

Kentucky Wonder beans and morning glory planted on the same trellis grow and blend together. Both will last all summer if kept well watered.

Narcissus *(Narcissus)*

A planting of African marigolds *(Tagetes erecta)* a year before planting narcissus bulbs will defeat certain nematodes that often attack the bulbs. (See *Marigolds* above.)

Nasturtium *(Tropaeolum)*

Nasturtiums planted with squash will keep away squash bugs, but be sure to give the flowers a head start since the squash grow more quickly. If aphids appear in the nasturtiums — a sign that there is a lime deficiency in your soil — dust the plants with lime and they will disappear.

Nasturtiums sown in a greenhouse will help to repel whiteflies. When planted near broccoli in the garden they will keep down aphids and benefit potatoes, radishes, cucurbits, and any member of the Cabbage family. Under apple trees they will protect against woolly aphids.

Nasturtiums, planted nearby or made into a spray, repel a range of harmful insects from vegetables and fruits. They also improve growth in the neighboring crops.

Use sprays made from nasturtium leaves on the same crops that benefit from the nasturtium plants. Add a small amount of soap powder; the sprays will adhere better.

Pepper *(Capsicum)*

A California study found that natural juices squeezed from succulent plants such as green peppers were effective in protecting other plants from viruses. They work against diseases transmitted by insects or wind. The sprays were found effective against tobacco mosaic virus, potato virus, and several other viruses carried by aphids. Strangely, the compounds do not kill the viruses but change the plant so it is not susceptible.

Old-time gardeners planted hot peppers among their flowers to discourage insect pests. Some of the lovely and unusual ornamental peppers would be excellent choices.

PESTS AND THEIR CONTROLS

These herbs and flowers act as troubleshooters for various pests:

PEST	PLANTS
Ant (and the aphid that ants carry)	Pennyroyal, spearmint, southernwood, tansy
Borer	Garlic, tansy, onion
Cutworm	Tansy
Eelworm, see Nematode	
Flea beetle	Wormwood, mint, catnip
Fruit tree moth	Southernwood
Gopher	Castor bean
Japanese beetle	Garlic, larkspur (poisonous to humans), tansy, rue, geranium (use white geranium)
Leafhopper	Petunia, geranium
Mexican bean beetle	Marigold, rosemary, summer savory, petunia
Mouse	Mint
Mole	Spurge, castor bean, mole plant, squill
Nematode	Marigold (African and French), salvia (scarlet sage), dahlia, calendula (pot marigold), crotalaria
Plum curculio	Garlic
Rabbit	Allium family
Rose chafer	Onion family, geranium, petunia
Slug, snail	Prostrate rosemary, wormwood
Squash bug	Tansy, nasturtium
Striped pumpkin beetle	Nasturtium
Tomato hornworm	Borage, marigold, opal basil
Whitefly	Nasturtium, marigold, nicandra (Peruvian ground cherry)
Wireworm	White mustard, buckwheat, woad

Petunia *(Petunia)*

This is a member of the Nightshade family, Solanaceae. The word "petunia" is derived from *petun,* a South American name for tobacco, since the tobacco plant belongs to the same family. Petunia protects beans against beetles.

Rattlebox *(Crotalaria)*

From its seedpods, which rattle when shaken, crotalaria derives its common name. Prized not only for its racemes of yellow sweet-pea-like flowers, it also is toxic to nematodes.

C. retusa is three feet high with maroon reverse petals. *C. spectabilis,* the species tested for nematode control, is four to five feet tall with smaller flowers.

Rose *(Rosa)*

Roses do not like boxwood because its outspreading, woody roots interfere with the roots of rosebushes. But garlic, onions, and other members of the Onion family, including ornamental alliums, are beneficial. (See *Allium, above.*)

Sunflower *(Helianthus annuus)*

Sometimes called *maiz de Texas* (Texas corn) or *tourne-soleil,* the common sunflower is an American plant that has been widely cultivated and much improved. It is a soil-improver when grown in moderation through certain farm crops. However, sunflower seed will not germinate well where grass is growing in close proximity.

Sunflowers

Sunflowers are now believed to produce leaf substances that inhibit other species. This may be due to a defense mechanism of the plant. Needing little nitrogen itself, the sunflower produces a substance that inhibits nitrogen-fixing bacteria in the soil, thus delaying the day when grasses and other succeeding plants may take over.

Sunflowers and potatoes have an inhibiting effect on each other that results in both being stunted. Potatoes also are more likely to be infected by phytophthora blight. Sunflowers and pole beans should not be planted together since both compete for space and light with resulting poor growth.

Sunflowers also have their good points as companion plants. It has been found that corn and sunflowers are protective to each other and insects are reduced on each. Cucumbers benefit when sunflowers are grown near them to provide a windbreak. In my hot climate I grow sunflowers on the west side of the cucumber patch to provide shade in the afternoon. Both cucumbers and sunflowers like a rich soil, so I dig in plenty of compost to prevent one from starving out the other.

Tansy, Parsley Fern *(Tanacetum vulgare)*

Tansy has a very strong, bitter aroma. The Latin *tanacetum* derives from a Greek word indicating immortality because the dry blossoms do not wilt. The distilled oil repels flies and mosquitoes. The plant has been used against intestinal worms *(Oxyuris)* and in wine against stomach and

Tansy

intestinal spasms. The Russians used it as a substitute for hops in beer and rubbed it on the surface of raw meat to protect it from flies. Tansy planted near the entrance to the house deters ants. Tansy is a friend of both vegetable and flower gardeners, since it will repel ants, borers, cucumber beetles, Japanese beetles, and squash bugs.

Trap Cropping

Some plants earn their living by repelling potential trouble, others by luring insect pests away from more valuable plants. Japanese beetles are attracted to white and pastel zinnias, white roses, and odorless marigolds; and nasturtiums attract aphids.

Wallflower *(Cheiranthus cheiri)*

A spray of rhubarb leaves will protect wallflowers against clubroot. Boil the leaves in water and sprinkle it where the wallflower seeds are to be sown. Wallflowers are believed to be beneficial to apple trees.

Weeds

Some weeds have been found helpful in flower beds. Lamb's-quarters gives added vigor to zinnias, marigolds, peonies, and pansies. Growing among rosebushes, a carpet of low-growing weeds from the despised Purslane family improves the spongy soil around their roots. Lupine, a legume, helps corn and other cultivated crops. Morning glory planted near corn enhances root vigor.

Gardening Tips and Techniques

For the Soil's Sake

Composting for Soil Enrichment

The importance of abundant soil humus is to create a favorable environment for root growth. A soil in good tilth has a granular structure that readily permits rain and air to penetrate and also retains moisture for long periods to permit maximum growth. It's good garden practice to use compost in combination with mulching.

You can start a compost pile at any time of the year. Build your pile in a pit, trench, freestanding stake-and-chicken-wire form, or any large container such as a plastic trash barrel. Build the pile with layers of organic matter in such a way that they will decompose easily.

Use grass, weeds, leaves, stalks, branches, and wood chips. Use any organic matter, but kitchen scraps should be vegetable materials such as carrot tops, lettuce, and coffee grounds; don't include meat or dairy products. A shredder to grind up the material will appreciably shorten the length of time for the compost to ripen. Put down a six-inch layer of organic matter, and sprinkle it with finely ground agricultural lime. Add a one-inch layer of soil to introduce the microorganisms needed for speedy decomposition.

Layer these materials up to about four feet high and keep the entire pile moist. Make the top of the pile slightly concave so that moisture will seep into the pile. Turn the pile to reintroduce air into the compost and speed decomposition of organic material.

Is all this worth it? Yes. A four-inch layer of compost worked into the soil to a depth of six inches will almost guarantee gardening success with both flowers and vegetables. If you don't have enough for that, you can concentrate your compost where it's most needed (around the roots of transplants, for instance).

Earthworm Castings

The castings (droppings) of the earthworm are rich in nitrates, phosphates, potash, and calcium — all elements necessary to plants. They also contain trace elements of sulphur, boron, zinc, copper, manganese, chlorine, iron, molybdenum, aluminum, and selenium — all needed to keep a plant healthy.

Gardeners everywhere are beginning to realize the value of earthworm castings. They report that their use results in vegetables of better taste and larger size with yields often doubling. Tomatoes especially benefit from castings.

Castings will not burn even the most delicate plant. There is no danger of adding too much to your soil. Worm castings can be found packaged, ready to use, in some garden centers, and worms are easy and fun to raise at home.

Here are some suggestions for using castings:

Indoor plants. For established pots, add one cup of castings to a six- or eight-inch pot and water thoroughly. Increase proportionately for larger pots. Castings will be absorbed into the soil during normal waterings.

Sick or dying houseplants. Remove one to two inches of the old planting mix (being careful not disturb the plant any more than necessary). Replace with castings.

Potting or repotting. Mix one-third castings with two-thirds peat moss, or any good soil. Add enough of this mixture to set the plant at its original depth. Pot the plant, fill around it with the castings, and press gently to firm the soil. Water thoroughly.

Root stimulator. Use castings to make up the planting root ball for newly planted fruit trees, rosebushes, and berry vines. This application of castings (where other fertilizers are too strong) provides a head start for the plant and will produce remarkable results even for years to come. Seeds also germinate much faster in castings.

Nitrogen-Fixing Plants

Colonies of nitrogen-fixing bacteria form on the roots of members of the Bean family (Leguminosae). These organisms take nitrogen gas from the air and convert it into nitrates that can be used by plants.

It is far better to encourage these minute creatures to manufacture nitrates than to apply nitrogen-containing chemical manures. They charge nothing for their work, and their own death makes the earth more productive. To increase nitrates in the soil, grow peas and beans in different parts of the garden each year.

Since the entire family of Leguminosae has the same properties, grow sweet peas and lupines in the flower garden for the same reason. When clearing ground in autumn, never burn the roots of leguminous plants. Break them up instead and add them to the compost heap. The tiny nodules on the roots contain the nitrogen.

pH

The pH scale measures the acidity or alkalinity of a substance. It's an important measurement for gardeners, because soil pH within the proper range is needed for good results in the flower or vegetable garden.

Soil tests for pH may be made at home using one of the test kits sold by garden centers and catalogs; or a soil sample may be sent to a professional laboratory. Ask your county extension agent for information on local soil-testing facilities.

To get a reliable soil sample, use a clean spade to cut a one-inch-thick, seven-inch deep slice of undisturbed soil. Take similar samples from several points in the garden and mix all in a clean bucket. Then dip out a pint jar of the mix to take to the laboratory, being sure to label it with your name and address. The lab will charge a small fee to cover costs of chemicals and a technician. The report will include not only the pH level, but also recommendations on how to correct an overly acid or alkaline condition. Other tests for nutrient levels can also be done on request; ask for information.

Here are the pH preferences of some commonly grown flowers: chrysanthemum 5.7 to 7.0, daylily 6.0 to 7.0, iris 5.0 to 6.5, ageratum 6.0 to 7.5, begonia 5.5 to 7.0, marigold 5.0 to 7.5. They will attain their best growth in this pH range and are less likely to do well above or below.

Off to a Good Start

Astrological Aspects

For centuries farmers have plowed and planted according to the signs of the zodiac. The same method can also be used for flowers. Use them in conjunction with a good gardening almanac that gives the correction for time changes in each part of the country.

PLANTING FLOWERS BY THE MOON

PLANT	MOON PHASE (BY QUARTER)	SIGN
Annuals	1st or 2nd	Libra
Asters	1st or 2nd	Virgo
Bulbs	3rd	Cancer, Scorpio, Pisces
Bulbs for seed	2nd or 3rd	Cancer
Chrysanthemums	1st or 2nd	Virgo
Clover	1st or 2nd	Cancer, Scorpio, Pisces
Coreopsis	2nd or 3rd	Libra
Cosmos	2nd or 3rd	Libra
Crocus	1st or 2nd	Virgo
Daffodils	1st or 2nd	Libra, Virgo
Dahlias	1st or 2nd	Libra, Virgo
Deciduous trees	2nd or 3rd	Cancer, Scorpio, Pisces
Flowers for beauty	1st	Libra
for abundance	1st	Cancer, Pisces, Virgo
for sturdiness	1st	Scorpio
for hardiness	1st	Taurus
Gladiolas	1st or 2nd	Libra, Virgo
Golden glow	2nd or 3rd	Libra
Honeysuckle	1st or 2nd	Scorpio, Virgo
Iris	1st or 2nd	Cancer, Virgo
Lilies	1st or 2nd	Cancer, Scorpio, Pisces
Moon vine	1st or 2nd	Virgo
Morning glory	1st or 2nd	Cancer, Scorpio, Pisces, Virgo
Pansies	1st or 2nd	Cancer, Scorpio, Pisces
Peas, Sweet	2nd	Cancer, Scorpio, Pisces, Libra
Peonies	1st or 2nd	Virgo
Peppers, Ornamental	2nd	Scorpio, Sagittarius
Perennials	3rd	Cancer, Pisces, Libra
Petunias	1st or 2nd	Libra, Virgo
Poppies	1st or 2nd	Virgo
Portulaca	1st or 2nd	Virgo
Roses	1st or 2nd	Cancer
Sunflowers	2nd, 3rd, 4th	Libra
Trumpet vine	1st or 2nd	Cancer, Scorpio, Pisces
Tulips	1st or 2nd	Libra, Virgo

During the increasing light (from new moon to full moon), plant annuals that produce their yield above ground. (An annual is a plant that completes its entire life cycle within one growing season, and has to be seeded anew each year.)

During the decreasing light (from full moon to new moon), plant biennials, perennials, bulbs, and root plants. If you wish to save flower seed, let flower heads mature for as long as possible before gathering but not so dry that the seedpod shatters. Gather seed in a dry sign such as Aries, Leo, Sagittarius, Gemini, or Aquarius.

Clone

Recently the word "clone" has been appearing often in the news. Actually, plants have been cloned for thousands of years. The word itself comes from the Greek and means a twig or slip. Cloning plants is very easy because many plant cells have the power of regeneration.

With onions, for instance, I put cloning to work. When my onions sprouted, softening gradually in the process, I used to throw them out. No more. I plant these onions in the fall, sometimes in the garden, sometimes in my rose bed. From one onion a cluster of five or six will grow, delicate in flavor, and giving me early table onions the following spring.

The first year I pulled them all, but in succeeding years I left several clumps as an experiment. In time they grew large. I harvested them at maturity with the rest of my crop. They kept very well but in time sprouted again and were replanted. A good onion — like an old soldier — never really dies! It doesn't even fade away.

Cold Frame

A cold frame on wheels allows the gardener to place it in sun or shade as the season requires. Make the sides of the frame out of ¼-inch plexiglass. Attach with screws to 2 X 4s supporting a plywood bottom. The top is a plexiglass sheet with a 2 X 2 attached underneath to hold it up and allow air to pass through. When turned over it is sealed shut, keeping out animals and insects. Use old tricycle or bicycle wheels for the frame. If there's a late freeze coming, you can wheel this cold frame into the garage at night to keep it warm.

Cuttings

These are vegetative portions of plants used for reproduction. A cutting may consist of the whole or part of a stem (leafy or nonleafy), leaf, bulb, or root. A root cutting consists of the root only; other cuttings have no roots at the time they are made and inserted.

To ensure success, you must make cuttings when the tissues are in the right condition, prepare them properly, insert them in the right rooting medium, and keep them in a favorable environment until they are able to regenerate themselves as new plants. Detailed directions are given in many gardening guides; see your local library or garden center for help in getting started.

Take a cutting of the plant part to be used of the correct size so the regeneration of new parts is encouraged; this may mean the removal of leaves, or parts of leaves.

Many different rooting media are used for cuttings. One of the most popular is sharp sand; or use sand and peat moss, or vermiculite and sandy soil. Cuttings of some plants such as the African violet may be rooted in water.

For plants in all rooting media, prevent the tissues from drying before the new plant is established. This avoids loss by disease and encourages rapid reestablishment. The introduction of special root-inducing hormones and the use of bottom heat may speed this process. In the greenhouse, heat is usually provided by hot-water pipes, electric heating cables, or fermenting manure.

Divisions

In midsummer, many perennial garden flowers begin a rest period. Divide at this time to form new plants. Suitable candidates include peony, German iris, Oriental poppy, madonna lily, painted daisy, phlox, and columbine. Usually plants that flower in spring and early summer may safely be divided in late summer and fall. Those flowering in summer and fall should be divided in early spring before new growth appears.

Crown division is one of the easiest methods. To make a crown division, lift the plant carefully and remove some soil from the roots. Cut the crown into several pieces with a knife. Use the individual sections of vigorous plants to make new plants.

How often to divide? Peonies may remain in the same spot for many years. Divide Shasta daisies and phlox every three years. Replant daylilies and iris every five years. Divide chrysanthemums and hardy asters every two to three years in the spring. Some plants, such as Oriental poppies, do not adjust well to moving; transplant these only when they lose vigor from overcrowding.

Flower Pots

Let your dishwasher sterilize your flower pots. First scrub your pots clean to remove soil and accumulated salt. Put clay pots on the bottom rack, and plastic ones on top with pan lids on top to weight them. Nest several sizes to maximize space. The pots will come out clean, sterilized, and ready to use.

Forcing

Forcing ensures a supply of fruits, flowers, or vegetables earlier than they would be available if cultivated in the usual way. Forcing necessitates the use of warmth, supplied for large operations by hot-water or steam pipes, electric heating, or by a hotbed made of fresh manure and leaves. For home use, though, the warmth of a heated room is all that's needed.

Pussy willow *(Salix)* is a favorite for spring forcing. Cut the ends of the branches in January or February, place in water, and watch them unfold their large, closely packed catkins. Black pussy willow *(S. melanostachys)* is unusual and truly different; its catkins are so dark that they appear almost black against the red twigs.

Mini-Greenhouse

To root African violets, rex begonias, roses, and small evergreen cuttings, use a greenhouse made from a clean, label-free, three-pound peanut butter jar turned upside down on its lid. Fill the lid with moist gravel. Then place a pot containing the moist, sterile rooting medium, and cuttings on the gravel. Tip out any excess water. Twist the jar down over the lid to seal.

Pasteurizing Soil

To pasteurize potting soil for seed starting and houseplants, follow these directions: Thirty minutes in a 140°F oven is optimum for killing undesirable pests and will not destroy all beneficial plant organisms; 30 minutes at 180°F kills most weed seeds and all plant pathogenic bacteria and fungi; temperature above 185°F may damage the soil's chemical structure. Use a reliable oven thermometer.

Soil should be moist, not wet. Spread it evenly on an old cookie sheet or tray. Soil mixes should not be high in manure or compost because the heat will release too much fertilizer at one time and be toxic to plants.

Pots and occasionally tools also need decontamination. A solution of one part bleach to ten parts water will sterilize them.

Pelleted Seeds

Tiny seeds such as those of petunia are available from some garden catalogs in a pelleted form. Pellets — in the case of petunia seed, about the size of shot — contain a little plant food as well as seed disinfectant. Easy to sow in flats, they often germinate and grow much better than common seeds. Seedlings suffer less from damping-off. Pellets also allow you to space the seeds, thus eliminating the disagreeable job of thinning.

Planting Errors

Most plant failures are caused by improper planting.

Far too many of us place a $10 plant in a $1 hole. Prepare the best possible foundation for your plant. If the plant is bare root, make the hole large enough for the roots to spread out naturally.

Plant purchases are often made on impulse with no thought to where the plant will be placed, nor what its ultimate size will be, nor how it will adjust to other plants in the immediate vicinity. The urge to use plants that will give a quick effect often results in overcrowding.

Flower seeds often are sown too thickly. Pull out or transplant the surplus plants as soon as they begin to crowd each other.

Seed Catalogs

Everything in a seed catalog is "superb," "magnificent," and usually resistant to something. But just as in an insurance policy, you've got to watch the wording. For instance, there's that phrase "reseeds itself." That one you can believe, especially if it refers to something like bluebells-of-Scotland.

"Likes full sun" is also to be believed.

"Grows in shade" needs a little interpretation. What it actually means is "filtered sunlight," a spot dappled with a few shadows now and then, as under a tree. Few plants grow well in full shade.

"Naturalizes well" means that if you give the plant half a chance, it will take over. So beware.

"Grow in clumps of three or more" means just that. Grown alone, it will barely make an imprint on your consciousness, yet grown in a small group the plant can be very lovely.

"May be divided" means you must — if you don't want the plants to choke themselves to death.

"Once established" means that getting this plant to do what you want may take a long, long time.

Seeds

Almost all the plants mentioned in this book appear in the catalogs listed under Sources (see pp. 237–238). You can buy seeds and nursery stock with confidence from these dealers.

Seeds, Sowing

To evenly distribute tiny seeds, such as portulaca, place them in a clean squeeze bottle, the kind used for mustard. Turn the bottle upside down, press the tip gently against the soil where you want to seed, and squeeze lightly. A few seeds will come out, and when the bottle is lifted, soil covers them.

To make it easier to see small seeds shaken into a seedbed or furrow, place them in a clean salt shaker with enough talcum powder to coat them. This method also saves seed as you get more even distribution and less need for thinning.

Here's a method to plant petunia seed directly into peat pellets without failure. Take a wet pencil tip, pick up one tiny seed at a time, and apply it to the moistened peat of the pellet. For insurance, use two seeds per pellet and remove one if both sprout.

Seeds, Sprouting

When starting seeds in pots, use a plastic coffee can lid to cover the pot until the seeds sprout. It works better than fragile plastic wrap to hold in moisture, and also prevents quick cooling or heating when the weather is changeable.

Some kinds of flower seeds sprout faster if they are tortured. One tough nut is the flower named canna. It is also called Indian shot because the seeds of canna are round, heavy, and oily like buckshot. Nature made canna seed coats resistant so that not all of them would sprout the first year. You can fool Mother Nature by cutting through the coats to admit water. Use a triangular file or nail clippers. Soak the nicked seeds in warm water overnight, blot dry, and plant in warm soil; the seeds should sprout in two to three weeks.

Scald the seeds of the hibiscus called mallow. Bring water to a boil, turn off the heat, drop in the hibiscus seeds, and leave them in the water overnight. The hot water won't kill the seeds, but it will cut through the natural oils.

Seeds, Storing

Until recently, home gardeners would do little to prolong the life of leftover garden seeds, especially those naturally short-lived such as onion, parsnip, delphinium, and larkspur.

The following is an inexpensive method of storing leftover garden seed from open-pollinated plants. (Saving hybrid seed is not recommended, as they seldom come true.)

1. Unfold and lay out a stack of four facial tissues.
2. Place two heaping tablespoons of powdered milk on one corner. The milk must be from a freshly opened pouch or box to guarantee dryness.
3. Fold and roll the facial tissue to make a small pouch. Secure with tape or rubber band. The tissue will prevent the milk from sifting out and will prevent seed packets from touching the moist desiccant.
4. Place the pouch in a widemouthed jar and immediately drop in packets of leftover seeds.
5. Seal the jar tightly using a rubber ring to exclude moist air.
6. Store the jar in the refrigerator, not the freezer.
7. Use seeds as soon as possible. Discard and replace the desiccant once or twice yearly. Dried milk is hygroscopic and will quickly soak up moisture from the air when you open the jar. Therefore, work quickly when you remove seed packets; and recap the jar without delay.

This method is of special value to gardeners who make repeated plantings of short rows to keep a constant supply of flowers or vegetables.

Transplanting Tips

Flower and vegetable plants can crowd each other when seeds are planted too closely together. Crowding delays maturity, stunts growth, and distorts the roots of carrots and other root crops. At the same time, there may also be skips; transplant enough seedlings to fill the skips, then discard the surplus.

Here's how to transplant so there is as little shock as possible.

1. Start when the plants are small; if they have four to six leaves, they're big enough.

2. Transplant at sundown on a cloudy day. Wind can injure as much as sunlight.

3. Wet soil thoroughly around the roots of seedlings that are to be moved. Do this a few hours beforehand so that the plants will be plump with water.

4. Dig transplanting holes before you uproot any seedlings. Fill the holes with water and let it soak in.

5. Shove a trowel in deeply to pry up plants. Move seedlings with as much soil around the roots as possible.

6. Move one plant at a time. Transplant quickly; don't delay.

7. Immediately soak the soil around each transplant. Don't wait until you have completed the row. For a week thereafter, sprinkle the transplants at least daily.

8. Never apply garden or houseplant fertilizer — liquid or dry — around newly transplanted seedlings. Their roots are too damaged to take it up.

9. If you must move large seedlings with many leaves, trim back half the foliage to reduce the leaf area through which water is lost. Use a shovel to move a big root ball and try to keep it from breaking up when you set it in place.

Growing Concerns

Crop Rotation

Crop rotation in the flower garden cuts down on certain insect pests. Spatial relationships are also important among flowering plants because crowding will reduce vigor.

Cultivation

In preparation for planting, the soil of the flower bed should be in a good state of tilth, with plenty of organic matter added, preferably in the form of compost, for those flowers that require it. This is particularly important in the South and Southwest, where the hot sun tends to burn the humus out of the soil. Replenish the bed with compost each season.

A small area may be spaded; for larger flower beds a rotary tiller is invaluable. The type with the tines to the rear is easy for elderly persons to handle, permits deep or shallow cultivation, and adds greatly to the pleasure of gardening.

Disease Problems

Plants are attacked by fungi, rusts, and other diseases for a variety of reasons. Extreme weather conditions, either drought or excessive rains, weaken plants. Peony leaves turn brown around the edges in wet weather. Or insect pests may injure them so that fungus diseases and rots find an opening. Other insects infest plants with certain virus diseases.

Raw organic materials used as fertilizer can cause a plant to succumb to whatever comes along because it cannot digest the crude material provided. The plant's chemistry is altered in such a way that it actually may attract insect pests. Well-decomposed compost is as good for your flowers as it is for your vegetables.

Intensive Care

An intensive-care spot for plants can be a sheltered area under shrubs where houseplants can safely spend the summer. This is a good treatment for plants that have been on display in dark or smoke-filled rooms, in drafts, or exposed to too much sunshine. Plants can often be brought back to health and become attractive again if given a period of rest under more ideal conditions.

An intensive-care area can also be a place near the porch or patio to start seedlings or root cuttings, or a cold frame for starting young seedling plants.

Keep extra plants growing in a secluded area for replacement purposes as the life spans of earlier plants are reached and they must be pulled. Young zinnias make a fine summer replacement for more delicate spring plants that must eventually be removed. Keep some young shrubs or evergreens growing in case you lose one by death or disfiguration. Prepare for such misfortunes by starting extra specimens in your intensive-care "unit" in case of need.

Mulch

A good mulch can often double the time a flower bed can go between waterings, and it also has other advantages.

Organic mulches act as insulators because of their low heat-conducting properties. On the other hand, a mulch such as pea gravel is a good heat conductor. Dark gravel mulches tend to warm light-colored soils and organic mulch tends to keep soil cool. Use this principle to slow down or speed up plant growth in the spring.

Organic mulches decrease weed seed germination. Mulch limits the splashing of mud onto flowers and foliage, in turn reducing possible disease development. And well-chosen mulches are more than useful; they can also be attractive.

Pinch a Plant, Pinch Back, Pinch Out

These terms have the same meaning and are used by gardeners to describe the removal of the growing tip of a shoot to ensure the development of side shoots. The term pinching out is also used to describe the complete removal of small side shoots, as is done when tomatoes are trained to a single stem and when the stems of chrysanthemums, fuchsias, and other plants are trained to form "trunks" of standard (tree-form) specimens.

Tip pinching makes a plant grow bushier; just pinch out the growing tip of the tallest stem close to a leaf joint.

The following annuals are improved by proper pinching: ageratum, carnation, cosmos, marigold, phlox, petunia, salvia, snapdragon, verbena, and dwarf-type dahlias (grown as annuals).

Season Stretchers

Extend the growing season a couple of weeks or more by using hot caps or plastic row covers for flowers or vegetables that do not grow above eighteen inches high. Also, study your seed catalogs, and choose some of the many quick-maturing varieties.

Spray Damage

When spraying plants with fungicides to control disease, insecticides to control pests, and fertilizers for foliar (leaf) feeding, there is always a danger of damaging the leaves with the spray fluid. This may occur if the spray is not sufficiently diluted, if the plants are in a soft condition, or if the weather and atmosphere are unfavorable. Also, plants growing in a smoky atmosphere may be damaged owing to the liberation of copper by the acids in the atmosphere.

Whenever possible, choose a still day for spraying, so that the spray material may be directed where it is needed. This prevents the spray from drifting in the wind and endangering other plants. Do not use oil sprays or other types of spray on fruit trees at blossoming time. The spray might injure bees, bumblebees, or other insects pollinating the fruit.

Water

We know that seeds and the roots of growing things need water, but the water also carries nourishment. Sometimes elements for plant nourishment are in the rain itself, sometimes plant food previously put in the garden is dissolved by the rain. The most fertile soil and the best climate conditions cannot produce a single green leaf if there is no moisture.

It is important to use water wisely, especially in areas with little rain. To conserve moisture, soak furrows before planting seeds, and then cover with dry soil. Though invisible to the eye, the moisture is there where the seeds need it to germinate.

When setting out new nursery stock, especially in dry weather, dig the hole and water deeply several times before planting the shrub or tree. Then the water will be available to the roots. Splashing a little water on top after setting won't do the job. When the hole is half-filled with soil, pack firmly and fill with water. As water soaks down, fill in with soil and leave a saucerlike depression, putting a layer of loose mulch in the depression.

Mulch is important over all the garden: It prevents a crust from forming and lets water soak down easily and more slowly, preventing runoff. Check soil under mulch to see if watering is needed.

For vine crops such as tomatoes or even decorative vines, it's good to sink a perforated tin can on one side of each plant. Whenever the plants need water, fill the cans. Once you start watering, continue until there is a good rain, or you may lose your plants.

Hints for the Yard and Garden

Banana Peels

Plant, don't pitch! Tear the peels or cut them with scissors into small pieces and bury them around your roses. Peels provide 3.25 percent phosphorus and 41.76 percent potash. But don't overfeed; three peels per bush at a time is about right. Stockpile extras by freezing them in half-gallon ice cream containers.

Clothespins

Use snap or spring clothespins to train fuchsia and small vines in pots and baskets. Catch the stem through the indentations and clip the jaws to other stems, pot rims, or stakes. Also use to hang along stems as weights if you are working toward a trailing plant. Remove after a few weeks and the stem will stay in place.

In the garden, use snap clothespins — the type with a spring and two grooves — to train grapevines on the trellis. The innermost groove should fit over the wire and the outer one around the stem. As the vine grows, adjust the pins. Remove at pruning time when they are no longer needed. This idea works well with espaliers or with anything you need to train to wires.

Espalier

For small plants to train as miniature espaliers, try the annual balsam. Pinch off the side shoots so the plant will grow tall and slender; you will be rewarded with a mass of blossoms. The espalier form is still used for training fruit trees on frameworks or against a wall, although it is not as popular as it once was.

Flagstone Flattery

A flagstone walk gives interest and drama to the flower garden. To lay the stones in concrete, first wax the upper surface of each flagstone with liquid or paste wax. Cement will not adhere to a waxed surface, so it will be easy to clean off any spills or smears when the job is finished.

Foam, Packing

Save that packing foam next time you receive a package. Because it is light-weight, noncompacting, and water-repelling, package foam is good material for hanging baskets and planters.

Frost Protection

Evergreen branches, which are springy, are excellent frost protection for perennials and herbs.

Grass

To keep neat edges on grass along flower beds, paint grass edges with tractor fuel. Use an old four- or five-inch paintbrush. This application will check Bermuda, carpet, and St. Augustine grasses.

Knee Pads

These can be as simple as iron-on pads, inside or out, for your blue jeans, or a pair of rubber pads with adjustable straps. They make small garden chores like weeding much easier.

Labels

Many flowers look so much alike when they are not in bloom that it is easy to make a mistake when they are dug for replanting or sale. Iris, for instance, are almost impossible to tell apart. Write on the leaves with a magic marker pencil, or for a more permanent label, cut old venetian blinds in one-foot lengths and write the name of the plant with a wax pencil.

When potted, the plant may be inexpensively labeled with a plastic knife. Print out the name of the plant with a name-tape printer, press it onto the knife handle, and push the blade into the soil. This is neat, inexpensive, and long-lasting, especially with potted plants.

Plant labels can also be made from one- by three-inch strips cut from used bleach jugs. Scratch or write on these with a large needle inserted in a two-inch section of wooden broom handle. Next, rub dark shoe polish over the label, and wipe off the excess. This makes the writing both visible and permanent.

Somewhat unusual but neat and practical are the gutter spikes available in seven- or nine-inch lengths from hardware stores. To prevent them from rusting, dip them in rust-resisting enamel and let dry. Then attach the labels with copper wire or plastic twist-ties and drive the spikes into the ground beside the plants.

Milk

It is sometimes helpful to spray milk over plants suffering from mildew, mold, or tobacco mosaic.

Potato Chip Can

Tall potato chip canisters can be used as dusters for flowers and vegetables. Punch holes in the bottom and drop in a few marbles or pebbles for agitators; fill the canister two-thirds full of rotenone, Dipel, or other garden insect dust; put on the lid; and you are ready to do battle.

Shock Absorbers

Many garages will give away discarded shock absorbers for the asking. Place them at the end of garden rows. When watering, slip the hose around them to prevent it from whipping over plants.

Shoe Bag

Get a see-through plastic shoe bag and store the small separate items such as gloves, plant tags, and twist-ties in the pockets. This is a time- and temper-saver, and ideal for the greenhouse.

Smoking

Smoking is not only dangerous to your health, but it's dangerous to your plants' health as well. The tobacco mosaic virus also affects members of the Tomato family and can be communicated by the hands of a smoker working in the garden.

Sugar

Sugar kills nematodes by drying them up. Five pounds of sugar per 100 pounds of soil will kill nematodes within 24 hours. Helpful fungi are the enemies of nematodes, and plenty of humus in the soil will promote their growth.

Sunscreens

The sun's harsh rays dehydrate and dry out your skin, reinforce the lines that come from squinting, and increase the risk of some skin cancers. Sunglasses protect your eyes from glare and discourage frown lines around the eyes. When working in your garden, use sunscreen and wear a hat to keep the sun off your face.

Tool Keepers

Drill a ¼-inch hole in the handle of a garden tool and hang the tool over a headless nail driven into the wall. To get a large number of tools in a small area, space the nails close together. Also paint tool handles orange — the color scientists consider safest for hunting caps and jackets. The color is readily discernible to the eye when you lay a trowel or clippers down somewhere in the garden or grass.

Garden Creatures

Insects

Ants

Ants are often a nuisance in the garden or in houses. They are repelled by pennyroyal, spearmint, southernwood, and tansy. Indoors, repel them with cucumber slices.

If you have ants in your kitchen, julep mint (a spearmint) or tansy planted near the kitchen wall or entrance will help keep them away.

Aphids: Greenfly, Whitefly, or Plant Louse

A most familiar small pest in the garden and on houseplants, aphids come in green to match plant stems or in red or black. They are sucking insects and affect nearly all plants at one time or another. They attack houseplants in late winter when the plants' resistance is low.

The lady beetle and her weird-looking larvae are always on the lookout for aphids and help keep them under control. Another insect preys upon aphids with such voracity that it is named the aphis lion.

Garlic, chives, and other alliums, coriander, anise, nasturtium, petunia, pennyroyal, spearmint, southernwood, and tansy will repel aphids.

Bee Flowers

A bee is said to make three journeys in order to bring one drop of nectar to the hive; 25,000 foraging trips are said to be necessary to gather the raw material for one pound of honey.

Important honey plants are clover, alfalfa, mustard, cabbage, buckwheat, willow herb, cotton, mesquite, goldenrod, acacia, blueberry, willow, maple, linden, locust, pear, plum, apple, and cherry.

Almost all single flowers produce a certain amount of nectar, but the following flowers produce nectar profusely and should find a place in every beekeeper's garden: wallflower, arabis, forget-me-not, borage, all members of the Bellflower or Campanula family, the mauve catmint *(Nepeta mussini)*, heather, heath, honeysuckle, thyme, hollyhock, crocus, scilla, chionodoxa, snowdrop, heliotrope, cleome, lavender, lemon balm, cornelian cherry, daphne, barberry, winter aconite, *Clematis paniculata,* mock orange, sunflower, bearberry, robinia, asclepias, hepatica, *Rhamnus frangula, Limnanthes,* mignonette, phacelia, scabious, stonecrop, and the Michaelmas daisies.

In addition, all the small fruits, including currants, loganberries, raspberries, strawberries, and blackberries, are valuable, and particularly the gooseberry, owing to its early flowering. And after being visited by bees, these fruits will set much better crops.

Bees are not especially attracted to fragrant flowers, and their marked preference for those of blue color, which are so often scentless, bears this out.

Willow flowers, passionflower, sunflower, and the inconspicuous blossoms of the English ivy are said to be intoxicating to bees.

Cutworms

Climbing cutworms crawl up the stems of plants at night to feed, so just because you don't see them doesn't mean they aren't there! Tansy is repellent to cutworms. Or collar stems of newly set plants, letting the cardboard collar extend both above and below soil line for about two inches. Occasionally a plant will be cut off even inside the collar; if this happens, dig down and find the cutworm before placing another plant.

A mulch of oak leaves or tanbark placed in strips in the beds and spread on garden paths will repel cutworms, slugs, and the grubs of June bugs.

Eugenol

A chief constituent of oil of cloves, eugenol is an effective attractant for baiting insect traps. Star anise and citronella grass are also useful for this purpose.

Flea Beetles

This pest is repelled by wormwood, mint, and catnip, or you might try interplanting susceptible crops near shade-giving ones.

Grasshoppers

Unlike bees, grasshoppers damage crops and are of no value in pollinating plants. The biological means of controlling grasshoppers, which are becoming an ever-increasing problem, is nosema grasshopper spore. *Nosema locustae* is a protozoan that specifically attacks grasshoppers and some species of crickets. Dissolve the spore in water and add to a bran mixture, then disperse over the garden or yard area. As the grasshoppers feed, they become infected and slowly die. Research has shown a 50 percent drop in population in a month. Furthermore, nosema is passed on from one generation to the next through the egg mass, and is also transmitted when infected grasshoppers are eaten by healthy ones.

Grasshopper

Ichneumonid Wasps

These are parasites of moth and butterfly larvae. The adult wasps feed on pollen and nectar, and often from puncture wounds made in host larvae.

Insect Predators

Ladybugs and the praying mantis are known for their good work in the flower garden, but did you know that the larvae of the firefly (lightning bug or lampyrid beetle) benefit growers by feeding on slugs and snails? Assassin bugs feed voraciously on caterpillars, Japanese beetles, and leafhoppers. Damselflies eat aphids, leafhoppers, treehoppers, and small caterpillars. Flower and robber flies are excellent pollinators and the larvae eat aphids, leafhoppers, and mealy bugs.

Insects, Pollination by

Many insects are helpful as pollinators. Odor usually repels or attracts them, but color also plays a part. Many insects do not see red (which attracts hummingbirds, for instance) but can see ultraviolet, which we cannot see.

Wasps

The parasitic wasp trichogramma is an efficient destroyer of the eggs of many moths and butterflies, which are leaf eaters in the larval stages. It is also effective against the eggs of cabbageworms and loopers, corn earworm, and geranium budworm.

Encarsia wasps are tiny and parasitic to whiteflies. Aphytis wasps are live controls for scale insects. Fig wasps, which live in caprifigs, carry pollen from the male flowers to the female flowers of the Smyrna figs. The calimyrna, a variety of the Smyrna, is widely grown in California.

Black-eyed peas and other field peas grown widely in the southern states are largely pollinated by wasps. Gather the pods early in the morning while the wasps are still lethargic from the cool of night.

Wasps, often ill-tempered and prone to sting, are very effective against a variety of insect pests. They're helpful as pollinators, too.

Insect Controls

Companion Plants

Many plants are protected from insect damage by the presence of other plants grown nearby. (See Companion Planting with Flowers and Herbs for a list of insect pests and the herbs and flowers that repel them.)

Rotenone, Derris

Long ago the Chinese discovered the insecticidal value of the derris, or tuba root. When the crushed roots, stems, and leaves of derris are thrown into lagoons and streams, fish float to the surface, insensible. Despite the extreme sensitivity of the fish, however, derris in normal concentration is believed relatively nontoxic to domestic animals and man.

Rotenone is an insecticide derived from derris and certain tropical plants. This contact and stomach poison is often mixed with pyrethrum. It can be used on both plants and animals for insect control. It is notably effective against leaf-eating caterpillars, mosquito larvae, and aphids. The addition of oil of teaseed as a synergist increases its toxicity to squash bugs.

Derris is widely used on farms in animal dips to control lice and ticks. Applied to young bean plants, it makes the leaf growth less palatable to Mexican bean beetles.

Devil's shoestring *(Tephrosia virginiana)* is the only native plant that contains rotenone. This is a common weed in the eastern and southern states, and its roots may contain as much as 5 percent rotenone. Rotenone is safely used on all crops and ornamentals, but the period of protection is short.

Ryania

This plant-derived insecticide was discovered in 1943. It is a powder made by grinding up the roots of the South American plant *Ryania speciosa*. Ryania has little effect on warm-blooded organisms but is useful in controlling corn borers, cranberry fruitworm, codling moth, Oriental fruit moth, cotton bollworm, and other insects.

While ryania may not reduce the number of harmful insects present, it protects the crop by making the pests sick enough to lose their appetite. Some species are not killed outright by it but are induced into a state of "flaccid paralysis." Ryania is recommended when there is an unusually large insect infestation and the gardener feels that nature needs a helping hand.

Smoke

Control aphids, ants, and mites in the greenhouse with smoke from oak leaves, which are not poisonous, do not kill soil bacteria, and leave no harmful residue. Dried stems and leaves from canna plants and peppergrass may also be used.

Sprays, Homemade

Here are some insect controls you can easily make yourself from ingredients in the house and garden.

Onions. Red spiders and various aphids, especially those attacking roses, are routed out by onion spray. Grind up onions in a food chopper or an electric blender, add an equal amount of water, strain mixture, and use as a spray. Bury the mash in the flower bed or garden.

Hot peppers. Chop up hot pepper pods (wear gloves and eye protection). Mix with an equal amount of water and a little soap powder to make the materials stick. This makes an effective spray against ants, cabbageworms, spiders, caterpillars, and tomato worms. Dry hot pepper, ground up and dusted on tomato plants, offers protection against many insects. Dry cayenne pepper sprinkled over plants wet with dew is good against caterpillars.

Combinations. Use a combination of several materials as an all-purpose spray. For instance, grind together three hot peppers, three large onions, and a whole bulb of garlic (peeled and chopped). Cover the mash with water and allow to stand overnight. Strain the following day and add enough water to make a gallon of spray. Use on roses, azaleas, chrysanthemums, beans, and other crops three times daily if infestation is exceptionally heavy. Repeat after a rain. Bury mash under rosebushes.

Rhubarb. Boil rhubarb leaves in water and sprinkle on the soil before sowing wallflowers and other seeds as a preventive against clubroot. It is also useful against greenfly and black spot on roses.

Tomato leaves. These have insecticidal value as they contain an alkaloid similar to digitalin and more active than nicotine. An alcoholic extract of this substance is very effective against aphids on roses, pears, beans, and other plants. A spray of macerated tomato leaves soaked in water also frees rosebushes of aphids and eggplant of caterpillars.

Elderberry leaves. An infusion made by soaking elderberry leaves in warm water may be sprinkled over roses and other flowers for blight and also to control caterpillar damage.

Soap. A simple soap spray is often effective against aphids, thrips, mites, and other garden pests. Mix one to two teaspoons of Ivory Liquid, Shaklee's Basic H, Tide, or a small chunk of Fels Naphtha with a gallon of warm water and apply with a plastic squeeze bottle. Be careful of beneficial insects such as ladybugs and mantises, since the soap may harm them also.

Tree Tanglefoot

Tree Tanglefoot is a nondrying, sticky compound that forms a barrier against climbing and crawling insects such as caterpillars and cutworms. It is effective used on trees.

Butterflies

Plant a Butterfly Bush!

The buddleia, or summer lilac, is called the butterfly bush because it attracts monarchs and swallowtails, including the tiger and zebra, with their brilliant coloring.

Many plants that attract birds and bees also attract butterflies, but there are certain flowers, shrubs, and vines particularly loved by these "flying flowers." Such plants are attractive for their nectar.

Butterflies instinctively choose very different plants for egg-laying. These are mostly herbs, weeds, and certain trees. They include umbelliferous plants such as dill and parsley; weeds such as clover, goldenrod, milkweed, and dandelion; and trees such as willow, poplar, birch, and hackberry.

Besides liking flowers whose nectar content is both ample and suitable, butterflies also have color preferences. They have a passion for yellow and purple blossoms, also notable in their likes and dislikes of weeds. Thistles are violet-mauve, clover is mauve to rose-purple, dandelions and goldenrod are yellow.

Butterflies don't care much for roses, particularly white ones, but will rush to the nearest purple lilac bush, preferring the purple to the white. They also like marigolds.

Gardeners who would attract butterflies should choose plants that will encourage butterflies to feed, not breed. Among these garden attractants are wallflower, alyssum, sweet William, sweet rocket, candytuft, mignonette, zinnia, and the beautifully scented phlox flowers. Or grow portulaca; butterflies love it.

As you will note from this selection, butterflies prefer the simpler blooms, some intensely perfumed, to the hybrids that have been bred away from their natural development. For this reason, a butterfly-attracting garden is easy to grow.

A Problem Butterfly

In the strictest sense, butterflies aren't harmful. They cannot bite, chew, or sting. In the butterfly stage, they pollinate many flowers. Even in the caterpillar stage they are seldom numerous enough, in most areas, to do much damage.

One in particular, however, can be a real pest: the white or imported cabbage butterfly. This one is usually found wherever cabbages are grown (also other members of this family such as broccoli, collards, and Brussels sprouts). It is generally so abundant that its eggs, caterpillars, and chrysalids are readily discovered.

This familiar butterfly is white with black dots on the wings and blackish front angles on the fore wings. They flit freely about over fields, meadows, and gardens, sipping the nectar of various early flowers through their long, coiled tongues. From time to time they light upon the leaf of a cabbage or other plant of the Mustard family to deposit their small, pale yellow eggs, which remain attached by a sort of glue.

About a week later the egg hatches into a tiny caterpillar that is very destructive. You will note its presence by the lacing of the leaves. A safe control for these worms is *Bacillus thuringienses* (BT), sold at garden centers under various trade names — Dipel, Biotrol, or Thuricide. Do not hesitate to use it. It kills only these caterpillars; otherwise it is harmless.

Enemies of Butterflies

The worst enemies of butterflies are the flies and wasps that lay their eggs on the caterpillar or inside the body. When the eggs hatch, the larvae eat the caterpillar. Other insects, such as dragonflies and mantids, eat great numbers of butterflies and caterpillars. Spiders catch them in their webs or lie in wait inside flowers. Birds, frogs, toads, and lizards feed upon them.

Butterflies have no strong body parts to use as weapons against attack and are easily killed by their enemies. As a group they survive because of their high rate of reproduction. A female butterfly may lay several hundred eggs during her lifetime. Though only a few live to adulthood, they carry on the species.

Butterflies are helped by protective coloration to escape from their enemies. The anglewings, for example, have bright colors on the upper surfaces of their wings but dull brown or gray underparts. When their wings are folded, only the dull underparts show.

Some butterflies, such as the monarch, feed on milkweeds, which makes them unpleasant-tasting food for birds. And they advertise their bad taste by warning coloration. Other butterflies, such as the viceroy, are protected from attack by having coloration similar to that of the monarch.

Birds

Of all the roles birds play in the garden, the least known is probably pollination. Certain flowers depend upon certain insect friends to carry their pollen from blossom to blossom so they may set fertile seed; other flowers depend upon the hummingbird. Only his tongue, which runs out beyond his long, slender bill and can turn around curves, could reach the drops of nectar in the tips of the wild columbine's five inverted horns of plenty. He also seeks honey from monarda or bee balm, coral honeysuckle, jewelweed, cardinal flower, and many others.

Birds also play a valuable part in disseminating the seeds of many flowers. Mistletoe, for example, is spread by birds scraping their bills on the bark of trees, after they have feasted on its berries.

But flowers are not always kind! The cuckoopint, or spotted arum, of Europe, a relative of our jack-in-the-pulpit, actually poisons messengers carrying her seed; the decaying flesh of the dead birds affords the most nourishing food for her seed to germinate in. Birds help keep the balance of nature by trimming down the insect population. They are caretakers of the ground floor, eating grubs and beetles; they destroy grubs in the bark of trees; and others, like purple martins, catch flying insects.

Landscaping for Birds

For their beauty, their song, and their ability to catch insects, birds are an asset to flower and vegetable gardens. To attract birds to your garden, furnish them with food and shelter. Hedges and dense shrubs, as well as trees, provide birds with nest sites and protection.

Most birds need open water of some kind, such as a conventional birdbath or a small pool with stones in the shallow edge. They drink and bathe, then use the dry tops of the rocks for preening sites.

Birds like variety in their diet — so remember this when deciding what plants to use in your wildlife landscaping. Create a varied pattern by intermingling plant species, sizes, and shapes. Give them a choice of food sources — seeds, nuts, fruits, berries, and flower nectar. Use plantings of annuals such as coreopsis, marigolds, sunflowers, and petunias for additional bird foods.

Some birds are almost exclusively seed eaters; others are "switch-hitters," eating insects, worms, and other animal foods as well as seeds. Among the seed eaters are finches, nuthatches, titmice, sparrows, siskins, towhees, juncos, jays, Clark's nutcracker, and of course, doves, pheasant, and quail.

Depending on your location and altitude, here are some planting suggestions for birdseed: coreopsis, cosmos, sunflowers, verbenas, and thistles as small flowering plants; burnet and croton as dove favorites; trees such as spruce, fir, birch, pines, oaks, and paloverdes. A hackberry or sugarberry tree has red, edible seeds that are relished by birds in late fall and winter.

Native grasses having seeds beloved of birds are bluegrasses (*Poa* species), grama grasses (*Bouteloua* species), bluestems (*Andropogon* species), wheatgrasses (*Agropyron* species), vine mesquite *(Panicum obtusum),* and Indian ricegrass *(Oryzopsis hymenoides).*

Supplementary Feeding

Feeders stocked with fruits and grains are welcome food sources in late winter after fruits from your plantings have been depleted.

To attract wild birds, try a traditional mix of sunflower seed, oats, millet, and yellow corn. Sunflower seed alone is the best all-around food for attracting the greatest number of desirable birds such as cardinals, chickadees, blue jays, grosbeaks, nuthatches, finches, and titmice.

Thistle seed draws large numbers of songbirds where they have not been attracted previously, such as goldfinches, purple finches, pine siskins, and red-polls. Tender, husked sunflower hearts also provide a wholesome food for songbirds such as chickadees, cardinals, finches, and grosbeaks.

If you wish to attract cardinals, try safflower seed. Mix it with sunflower seed at first and soon the cardinals will be won over to it, while the other birds remain indifferent. Then you'll have a feeder strictly for these colorful birds.

Hummingbird Flowers

In our western garden alone there are 15 different species of tiny iridescent hummingbirds, the ruby-throated being the only one widespread in the East. Hummingbirds have excellent color vision and are easily attracted by bright red flowers, to which they fly from great distances. However, once in your garden, they will visit flowers of any color in their search for nectar and small insects.

Without feathers, the smallest of the hummingbirds is no larger than a bumblebee. This bird's long, slender bill is especially suited for sucking nectar from deep-throated flowers such as honeysuckle and the trumpet flower.

Hummingbird flowers are long, tubular, contain copious nectar, and are often borne sideways or drooping rather than upright. Hovering before the flowers, the tiny creatures insert their long bills and tongues while whirring their wings more than 3,000 times a minute as they feast.

Good flower choices for hummingbirds also provide color all season and include: red columbine *(Aquilegia elegantula);* Indian paintbrush *(Castilleja integra),* blooming in the spring; scarlet-bugler *(Penstemon barbatus);* skyrocket *(Ipomopsis aggreta),* summer; and hummingbird trumpet *(Zauschneria latifolia)* in the fall. Some species, such as Indian paintbrush, scarlet hedge-nettle *(Stachys coccinea),* and autumn sage *(Salvia greggii),* begin blooming in early spring and are stopped only by fall frosts. Other possibilities include desert beardtongue *(Penstemon pseudospectabilis),* shocking pink flower; scarlet runner bean, very showy scarlet flowers; scarlet larkspur, red-orange flowers; toadflax, violet to magenta; Rocky Mountain columbine, blue and white; *Penstemon polmeri,* pink to salmon pink; and foxglove, purple flowers.

Animals

Cats

Although cats sometimes do catch birds, their hunting instinct also leads them to keep the garden clear of snakes, mice, rats, grasshoppers, and tarantulas.

Cats that rarely have the opportunity to go outside enjoy greenery to nibble on. Oats fulfill this need, providing a safe, healthy distraction from nibbling on houseplants, some of which may be poisonous. Catnip, a perennial mint, is also a favorite of felines, who are stimulated by its leaves.

Grow catnip or baby blue-eyes as a treat for your cat. And if the cat claws furniture, break this habit by rubbing crushed rue on the furniture; the cat will leave it alone. Caution: *Rue gives some people dermatitis.*

Circus in Town?

Check around; you may find exotic animal manure available for the taking. If fresh, it's a valuable repellent for animal pests. Let it age a bit before using around plants, or dig it in freely between rows. Bengal tiger and lion manure may be just what you need to make your garden a roaring success!

Dog-Gone!

Man's best friend can be a nuisance sometimes. He can leave yellow patches on the lawn, ruin shrubs, and dig in your best flower bed. Mothballs or naphtha flakes around the beds will discourage him, but shouldn't be used where small children can pick them up. Or pound small sticks a foot or so apart in the region you're trying to protect.

Rabbits, Cottontails

Their name comes from the fluffy, snow-white underside of the tail. They like to hide in heavy thickets or dense grass. Though often seen in daytime, they usually come out at night to gather their food. When there are too many of them, they can become serious pests by eating growing hay, vegetables, grapevines, and young fruit trees. And they also like to eat young flower plants. If you find your plants being eaten and no trace of insects, cottontails may be infesting your garden by night.

Onions, a thin line of dried blood, or blood meal sprinkled around the edges of the garden may discourage them. Or try powdered aloes, wood ashes, ground limestone, or cayenne pepper.

Squirrels

If squirrels dig up your flower bulbs, lay a section of chicken wire on the soil surface of the planted area. Secure with rocks around the edges. This also discourages cats, which like to dig in newly cultivated soil.

Protect trees from squirrels with a guard around the trunk. Encircle the tree with a slippery, smooth metal, shaped in the form of a downward cone. Be sure it is wide enough to prevent squirrels from jumping over it.

Rabbits, cute as they are, can level both flower and vegetable gardens during a one-night visit. They're hard to discourage, but try one or some of these: dried blood, blood meal, cayenne pepper, or wood ashes.

More Garden Creatures

Frogs

Toads and frogs are avid consumers of garden pests. It is estimated that a toad eats up to 10,000 insects in about three months and about 16 percent of these may be cutworms. It also gobbles grubs, crickets, rose chafer, rose beetles, squash bugs, caterpillars, ants, tent caterpillars, armyworms, chinch bugs, gypsy moth caterpillars, sow bugs, potato beetles, moths, flies, mosquitoes, slugs, and sometimes even moles.

In spring, gather frogs for your garden from around the edges of ponds and swamps. Pen them in for a few days, otherwise their homing instinct may urge them to leave. Give them some shelter such as a clay flowerpot turned upside down with a small hole broken out of the side. Bury the pot in a shady place several inches in the ground. And don't forget to give them a shallow pan of water.

Goldfish

If you have a pool in your garden, stock it with fish. Goldfish are excellent for consuming mosquito larvae, and so are the small topminnows called mosquito fish, *Gambusia affinis.*

Snails and Slugs

These land-based mollusks have grayish, wormlike, legless bodies, ½ to 4 inches long when fully grown. They hide in damp, protected places during the day. At night they chew up leaves, leaving a glistening trail of slime. Inverted cabbage leaves make good traps for both slugs and snails; or spread wood ashes on the ground. Toads, which eat them, are good garden aids.

Snakes

The harmless, so-called "garden" variety of snake catches and kills many injurious insects and is itself not poisonous. Protect it. In the Southwest, be very careful around berry patches, which are attractive to rattlesnakes. Tarantulas, the big hairy spiders, are also attracted by berries.

Sow Bugs or Pill Bugs

These aren't insects but crustaceans, related to the shrimps and lobsters. They have oval, dark gray, flattened bodies, seven pairs of legs, and are up to ½ inch in length. They hide under logs, boards, or crop refuse, and in other damp places. When disturbed, they roll up and look like pills. They feed — and how they feed! — on tender parts of plants and newly emerged seedlings. Look for and eliminate

Snakes can be destructive, but most of them are friends of the gardener, feeding on abundant insect populations.

their hiding places. Toads, including the horned toad (really a lizard), are helpful.

Spider Mites

Spider mites attack many flowers, being particularly troublesome on columbine. A spray made from onions controls them (see *Sprays, Homemade,* in this chapter). Experiments at Purdue University made use of an old-time favorite, a combination of buttermilk and wheat flour, to destroy spider mites by immobilizing them on leaf surfaces, where they then "exploded."

Spiders

Just because the note on the spray can says KILLS SPIDERS, it doesn't mean that you should. Spiders make good predators and only two common species, the black widow and the brown recluse, are really to be feared.

Spiders are rather wonderful — the nimble crab spider, for instance, named for its ability to scurry both sideways and backward. The little hunter can turn white, pink, or yellow to blend with vegetation. In a mini-jungle of stalks and stems, you may see a green lynx spider snatching up a victim as it trails a dragline behind it. This is a safety thread, anchored at intervals, which most spiders put down as they move about.

Spiders are particularly helpful during a heavy infestation of grasshoppers, killing large numbers by trapping them both in their aerial webs and on the ground.

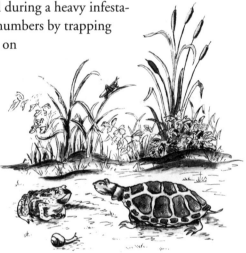

Toads

Toads are very helpful in the garden for catching and eating unwanted insects. They work long hours for low pay. If you cannot find any, they can be purchased commercially.

Tortoises

These turtles live in arid regions. They are large, timid, harmless animals. But they do eat plants and may ruin low-growing tomatoes by taking a bite out here and there. If you find one in your garden, do not kill it; remove it to another area.

Toads, like snakes, work for the gardener by eating insects. You can introduce toads to your garden, and they'll remain if they have lots to eat and some shelter, such as a piece of a clay pot.

Growing Wildflowers from Seed

Wildflowers **are truly** wonderful materials for the gardener, especially the mixtures that can be grown from seed. They are usually labeled by climate or geographical area and contain between 6 and 12 different kinds of flowers. Many such mixtures are available from catalogs and garden centers.

Wildflower seeds may be scattered on the ground, but it is best to give nature an assist and rake them in lightly to provide some protection from wind and rain. For better results, till the soil and cover the tiny seeds with a thin layer of peat moss. Keep the seeds moist for about six weeks.

On steep slopes where moisture is difficult to retain, sow the seeds into a top covering of very coarse gravel or lava rock. The seeds will sprout in between these materials, which will help to keep the soil moist and to hold the small seedlings in place, thus giving their roots a chance to take firm hold.

Temperature

Most wildflowers germinate readily in a temperature range of 60°–75°F. Temperatures higher than this may be harmful to some species. This temperature sensitivity is nature's way of preventing seeds from germinating during hot, dry periods when it would be difficult for the seedlings to survive.

Plant hardy perennials during spring or fall for best results. Seeds should be planted in a protected area to minimize the danger of being washed or blown away. Plant late enough in the fall to ensure that germination will not take place until the following spring, or early enough so that seedlings are well established before the first frost. Plant in spring after danger of frost has passed. Get the seed in the ground if you can before a rain, or water the seeds so that they have sufficient moisture to germinate.

Dormancy

Seeds that fail to germinate under favorable conditions are said to be dormant. This state of dormancy is not accidental; plants survive in nature because of certain built-in timing mechanisms that delay germination until seedlings have the best chance for survival.

Some seeds will not germinate if exposed to cold temperatures. This causes a delay in germination, most usually until spring, when rainfall and other conditions in the environment are favorable. Wildflowers having "cold-temperature dormancy" may be planted outdoors in late fall, or be treated by a procedure called moist-chilling wherein seeds overwinter in your refrigerator for one to three months. Here is how this is accomplished:

Soak seeds that respond to moist-chilling in water at room temperature for 12 to 24 hours. Then mix them with a sterile, moistened medium such as sphagnum peat moss, vermiculite, or sand. Place the medium in a plastic bag or similar container that is not airtight. Store this in the refrigerator at 40° to 50°F, not in the freezer, for three to six weeks. Keep the medium moist but not wet. When the chilling period is completed, sow seeds at once at relatively cool temperatures.

Seeds that require only three to four weeks of moist-chilling may be germinated in a greenhouse if nighttime temperatures are in the range of 40°–50°F.

Generally speaking, if this type of treatment is necessary, the packet will list the instructions. Most wildflower seeds do not need such exposure to cold temperatures and will sprout without special treatment.

Mass Plantings

If you would like to make mass plantings of wildflowers, here is a simple way to achieve good results:

Till the soil to a depth of six to eight inches. The seedbed should have a loose, crumbly texture and good drainage. You can improve the air- and water-holding capacity of the soil by mixing in peat moss or other available organic material. Broadcast the seeds evenly and cover with a thin layer (not more than ¼ inch) of peat moss. If peat moss is not used as a top covering, rake the seeds lightly into the soil. If a few seeds are not entirely covered, don't worry about them; it is best if the seeds are not deeply planted.

Use a fine spray of water to moisten thoroughly. Keep the planting evenly moistened for four to six weeks; thereafter, waterings may be gradually reduced.

You may also sow seeds into a single layer of coarse gravel or lava rock (1- to 1½-inch size). This is a good way to plant steep slopes or areas difficult to keep moist. The seeds germinating in the cracks and crevices will be in contact with moist soil and also be protected from the elements. If natural rainfall is the only source of moisture, plant seeds in the spring just before anticipated periods of rain.

Dry Areas

If you plan to plant a dry area, buy a mixture containing annuals, biennials, and perennials, most of which will sprout in 10 to 21 days at a temperature of 55°–70°F. While such a mixture is best adapted to dry climates, most of the flowers will adapt to moist climates in sandy, well-drained soil. Perennials will survive cold winters in northern climates. Such a mix might contain baby's breath, chicory, coneflower, cornflower, wild blue flax, gaillardia, penstemon, poor-man's-weatherglass, California poppy, prairie aster, and yarrow.

Moist Climates

The following mixture is best suited for moist climates, but will survive in dry climates if watered regularly. Recommended are baby blue-eyes, columbine, coreopsis, dame's rocket, larkspur, ox-eye daisy, scarlet flax, and wallflower. These perennials will survive cold winter climates. In mountainous regions above 8,500 feet elevation, there is usually ample moisture for this mix.

Harvesting Seed

To save seed of your wildflowers, break off stalks or seed heads, taking care not to disturb the root system. Timing is critical; if seeds are harvested too early, their viability may be seriously impaired. A change in color (often from green to brown or black) and a tendency to disperse seed are reliable indications of maturity. After removing your plant material, dry it thoroughly and either crush or shake to remove the seeds. Clean by sifting your seeds through a series of screens to remove dirt, chaff, and other unwanted material.

Wildflowers Adaptable to Large Areas

Most of these wildflowers are particularly well suited for restoration of large areas of land. They are easy to grow and, in most instances, highly adaptable to different climates and soils. These include: sweet alyssum *(Lobularia maritima)*, prairie aster *(Aster tanacetifolia)*, baby blue-eyes *(Nemophila menziesii)*, baby's breath *(Gypsophila elegans)*, black-eyed Susan *(Rudbeckia hirta)*, catchfly *(Silene armeria)*, chicory *(Cichorium intybus)*, columbine *(Aquilegia caerulea)*, prairie coneflower *(Ratibida columnifera)*, purple coneflower *(Echinacea purpurea)*, lance-leaved coreopsis *(Coreopsis lanceolata)*, plains coreopsis *(Coreopsis tinctoria)*, cornflower *(Centaurea cyanus)*, ox-eye daisy *(Chrysanthemum leucanthemum)*, dame's rocket *(Hesperis matronalis)*, wild blue flax *(Linum lewisii)*, scarlet flax, *(Linum grandiflorum* var. *rubrum)*, gaillardia *(Gaillardia aristata)*, firewheel gaillardia *(Gaillardia pulchella)*, gayfeather *(Liatris spicata)*, gilia *(Gilia rubra)*, and rocket larkspur *(Delphinium ajacis; Consolida ambigua)*.

Indoor Pleasures

Houseplants

Cosmetic care of indoor plants also helps keep them healthy. Remove dead or old flowers and yellowed leaves; these can harbor and encourage insect and disease problems.

Wash foliage periodically. To wash off your houseplants, put them in the shower, turn on a gentle, tepid spray for a minute, then leave them a few hours so excess moisture can drip off. You'll be surprised to see how this perks up plants, especially ferns. Dust and grime block out light and clog the stomata cells, which allow the transfer of gases from plants to the atmosphere. Showering or syringing also helps reduce some insect populations such as spider mite and mealybugs, and the cooling effect stimulates growth.

However, be cautious of syringing espicias, gloxinias and most other gesneriads, and succulents when water is cold; spot damage will occur on leaves. Time your hose-down so water will not be on your plants at night, or fungal disease will result, especially during cool months. Collect and use rainwater if your tap water is high in iron, carbonates, or other dissolved minerals.

Foliar Feeding

Spraying or applying fertilizer to plant foliage is effective with houseplants as well as outdoor plants. Take care not to discolor or otherwise damage home furnishings when you spray. Apply only at recommended concentrations and when plant is not in its rest period.

Propagate spider plant by removing a small "spider" and planting it separately.

Starting a burro's tail plant is easy. Just poke one of those round leaves into a pot of soil.

It's called dumbcane because if you bite its roots, you will be speechless for days.

The dracaena plant has leaves much like those found on a palm tree.

Isolation Ward

Place a new pot plant somewhere by itself for a week or so before you put it with your other plants. This will give you a chance to ensure that it is free of insects or disease without running the risk of infecting your other plants.

Kitchen

Use flowers to brighten your kitchen. Put them on counter space with over-head lights or under a window. Top off a room divider cabinet with flowers. Light, humidity, and good ventilation are usually in abundant supply, and the proximity of the kitchen sink encourages good watering habits. Keep your green friends well away from cooktops and ovens, where heat and fumes may damage them. Bathrooms provide another opportunity for humidity-loving plants. Choose moisture lovers such as devil's ivy, English ivy, arrowhead vine, hollyfern, and baby's tears. Avoid plants such as cacti that need dry conditions. Plants enjoy a sudsy bath; wash them with a little mild soap and cool water.

Provided you have a fairly good light where your planter is situated, grow a variety of begonias, spider plants *(Chlorophytum)*, ivies, wandering Jews, ferns, and herbs — and of course grow such vines as grape ivy and philodendron. Foliage plants will give you more year-round satisfaction than flowering kinds. Try a selection of dieffenbachias, aspidistras, snake plants, ferns, dracaenas, pandanus, and coleus.

Layering Aid

When air-layering plants, place wet sphagnum moss or other rooting medium in old nylon hose to wrap around the prepared spot on the plant. Wrap again with a plastic bag and tie it down. The nylon hose keeps the rooting material in place and the roots grow right through it.

Lighting Hint

The color of house walls affects light intensity for indoor plants. Flat white, not glossy or semiglossy, is the most efficient reflector of available light.

Mistakes to Avoid

Here are some suggestions for preventing problems with houseplants:

Overfeeding. Don't fertilize houseplants too often. Once a month with a dilute liquid fertilizer is sufficient. Remember, don't fertilize a plant to make it grow; fertilize it because it is growing.

Overwatering. Underwater rather than overwater. More plants are killed by overwatering than by anything else. A dry surface is a poor test of water needs because the indoor atmosphere dries the surface quickly.

Poor lighting. Proper lighting is difficult to achieve in city homes and apartments. The best way to overcome this is to grow most plants under the new full-spectrum fluorescent lights. Flowering houseplants must have light, so reserve the sun-filled windows for them. Foliage plants prefer indirect light without sun. Only a few can get along in dark hallways.

Improper humidity. Proper humidity is very important. Most homes lack humidity in the winter due to radiator and heating units that dry the air. A humidity of between 50 and 60 percent is best for most plants.

Too much heat. Most homes are warmer than the recommended temperature for houseplants. A cool room is much preferred to a warm one for plant growth. Plants require air circulation even in cold weather, but avoid cold drafts or air from central heating systems blowing directly on them.

Remember that plants are not like animals or people. They cannot refuse the food given them, nor can they move to a more favorable location.

Wick Watering

When you vacation, provide your larger container plants with wicks leading from the pot to a water supply in a coffee can fitted with a plastic lid. Punch a hole in the lid, then thread the wick through. Lid cuts down on evaporation so water supply lasts longer.

Cut Flowers

Cutting Garden

In an out-of-the-way corner, plant a cutting garden so that there will be fresh flowers for the house without the necessity of robbing the display flower beds. No need to pay lots of attention to design or aesthetics — simply grow neat rows of those annuals that bloom abundantly in colors and forms you want for decoration.

If your color scheme calls for pinks and blues, raise larkspurs, Canterbury bells, asters, bachelor buttons, felicia daisies, and stock. Add some dusty miller for its gray foliage; it's most compatible with pink tones.

For vivid reds, yellows, and oranges, grow marigolds, plumed celosia, red-hot poker, geraniums, gloriosa daisies, and gazanias. The taller varieties are best. Coleus make a fine foliage filler with these flowers.

Poppies, both the Shirley and the Iceland poppies, are great additions to mixed bouquets. They are long lasting if you sear the stem ends when you cut them.

For airy filler, grow some annual baby's breath or dill. And plant a few rows of strawflowers, statice, and bells of Ireland to cut and use fresh or dried in your home during the winter.

If you only have space for a tiny cutting bed, try tall zinnias and snapdragons. Their white, yellow, orange, red, and pink colors blend well and their forms contrast nicely.

Cutting Pointers

A Cornell University extension bulletin gives the following advice:

1. Cut the flower stems. A freshly cut stem absorbs water freely. Use a sharp knife or shears and cut either on a slant or straight across.
2. Follow special procedures for special cases. Some flower stems exude a milky fluid that plugs their water-conducting tubes. To prevent this, place about ½ inch of the stem in boiling water for thirty seconds, or char the end of the stem in a flame.
3. Remove excess foliage and those leaves that will be below water. Excess foliage increases water loss; submerged foliage decays and hastens fading.
4. Place the stems in water at 110°F. Warm water moves into the stem faster and more easily than cold water.
5. Use a commercial flower food in the water. These foods combine sugars, acidifiers, and a mild fungicide to lengthen the life of cut flowers.
6. Wrap a piece of paper or plastic around the flowers after you have put them into warm water. This will prevent rapid air movement over the flowers and reduce water loss. After the flowers become crisp (about two hours), you may arrange them and they will continue to take up water. Sometimes wilted flowers can be restored by repeating this treatment.
7. Wash vases with soap and water after each use to remove bacteria. When bacteria multiply, they can often clog the water-conducting tubes of the flower stems.
8. Avoid excessive heat. Do not place flowers in direct sunlight, over a radiator, or in a draft.
9. Double the life of your flowers by placing them in a cold room or refrigerator at night, or when you are not at home.
10. Do not mix flowers with fruits or vegetables. Many fresh fruits and vegetables produce enough ethylene gas to shorten flower life.

Sipping-Straw Stilts

When your cut flowers have stems too short for a tall vase, insert the stems into plastic drinking straws, then cut them to the length you want.

Transporting Cut Flowers

Carry cut flowers such as iris in containers made from beverage cans. Punch six or seven holes in the top with a can punch, partially fill with water, and insert the stems. The can holds the flowers upright.

Some usual and unusual flowers for the cutting garden

Drying Flowers for Lasting Beauty

Dried arrangements brighten a home or office during the cold months of fall and winter. During the fall, gather weeds, vegetables, fruits, flowers, and foliage, as well as dried grasses, from the roadside, market, and garden. There is an abundance of material to select from. By treating this plant matter with certain special agents, you can preserve its beauty and color almost indefinitely.

Many plants will dry naturally as part of their life cycle. Tall brown stalks of mullein, teasel, thistle, heracleum (cow-parsnip), and nonpoisonous sumac, cattails, and dock may be used without treatment if picked when dry. Dip cattails, however, in undiluted shellac to keep them from shattering.

Look for interesting pods on the ground beneath black locust. Sweet gum balls and cones of needled evergreens are attractive subjects. Also save some dried okra pods from the late garden.

Yarrow from the garden dries naturally, as do seed clusters of ornamental onions or leeks, but catch them before they start to deteriorate. Pick such materials a little prematurely; they can finish drying in the house. Hang them from coat hangers in your attic or in an unused room, or simply prop the stems in a deep, empty container.

Method for Hanging

Group three or four stems together and tie tightly. This is necessary because stems lose moisture as they dry, shrinking in size, and may loosen enough to slip out. Elastic bands or twist-ties are better than string to keep materials bound. Hang thick stalks such as mullein and large stems such as cockscomb singly. Suspend the bunched materials or stalks upside down; this keeps the stems straight and the flower heads upright. When hanging flowers, remove the foliage.

Hang the materials in any manner that will allow free passage of air to all surfaces. Bunches or stalks may be hung on a line as you would clothes on washday, or on a rack. You will need less space if you attach three or four bunches to a wire coat hanger. Clothespins are handy for attaching bunches to a line or hanger.

Choose any warm, dry spot for hanging, provided it has free circulation of air. Use a kitchen, garage, attic, or shed if it is convenient. Don't shut the plants up in a closet or expose them to direct sunlight while they are drying.

Weather conditions at time of drying determine the number of days needed, but generally the majority of plants will dry in 8 to 10 days.

Plants that can be successfully dried indoors by hanging include the everlastings listed in this chapter, as well as acacia, artemisia, bird-of-paradise, rubber plant leaves, magnolia leaves, bells of Ireland, cacti, ornamental grasses, palm, pepper berries, nandina berries, snowball hydrangea, and sunflowers (with petals removed). Globe thistle, liatris, and Queen Anne's lace can be dried by hanging but retain better color if buried in a drying agent. Many dried materials will last much longer if sprayed a time or two with hair spray.

Drying Flowers with an Agent

Fragile garden flowers dry best buried in a special agent such as silica gel, sold by craft suppliers under various brand names. Follow the supplier's directions.

Alternatively, you can make your own drying agent by mixing together equal parts of borax and yellow cornmeal, or use dry sand. Proceed as follows:

Pick your flowers on a dry day, selecting only those in good condition, preferably just before maturity. Process without delay.

1. Cut stems to within an inch of flower heads, and strip off any remaining foliage.
2. Make a false stem by dipping the end of a length of 22-gauge wire in white glue. Insert this into the base of the flower head close to the stem and tape the two together.
3. Line a shallow box of suitable size with waxed paper.
4. Prepare the drying mixture of borax and cornmeal. Add three tablespoons of uniodized salt per quart to the mixture if you want better color preservation.

5. Cover the bottom of the lined box with a half-inch layer of mixture.
6. Place the flowers face up in the box, bending the wires far enough below the heads so they lie flat. Mound up the mixture beneath the flower heads to cushion.
7. Sift the mixture gently between petals, adding gradually until the flowers are just covered but not deeply buried. Do not crowd and do not dry more than a single layer of blossoms at a time.
8. Leave the box uncovered. Check in six to seven days. Flowers should not be left in the mixture when dry.
9. When drying is complete, gently brush away the mixture. Then slide your hand carefully under each head and lift it on your out-stretched fingers. Place the flower on top of the mixture and allow it to remain for at least another 24 hours to firm up the petals. Without this treatment, the petals will shatter. When the petals are completely cured, spray them lightly with a plastic coating for permanence.
10. Keep your dried flowers in closed boxes on tissue paper until you are ready to use them.
11. Store the drying mixture in tightly covered tins to be reused.

Flowers to dry by burying include: acacia, China aster, bells of Ireland, celosia, daffodil, dahlia, delphinium, echinops, everlastings, gladiolus, liatris, lilac, lily, marigold, peony, Queen Anne's lace, snapdragon, stock, tulip, wand-flower, and zinnia. Roses may be dried if picked when only about two-thirds open; if full blown, they will fall apart. Also try drying the buds of small "sweetheart" roses, especially nice for potpourri jars.

Foliage

It is possible to preserve lovely autumn foliage with glycerine. Leaves will achieve a rich brown shade but still remain soft and pliable. If the foliage has been in water before processing with glycerine, the method may not be successful, so keep this in mind when making your selections.

Types of foliage that can be treated successfully include those of house-plants, as well as garden and florist materials. Here are some you may wish to try: acuba, aspidistra, beech, boxwood, cocculus (snailseed), copper beech, elaegnus, euonymus (*Euonymus alatus* and *E. japonica*), ivy, laurel, leatherleaf viburnum, leucothe, magnolia (*Magnolia grandiflora* and *M. virginiana*), mahonia, papyrus, peony, plum, red maple, sorrel tree, winter hazel.

There are no hard-and-fast rules as to what foliage can be preserved in glycerine, but it is best to use leaves or branches that absorb water freely and are entirely crisp and fresh.

Make a solution composed of one-third glycerine to two-thirds water. Fill a container with this to a depth of four to five inches. Slash the stem of the leaf or branch with a knife or mash it with a hammer for about one inch at the cut end so that absorption will be more complete. After placing the stem or branch in the solution, allow it to remain until saturated. This is easy to determine, as the color of the leaves will change. The foliage absorbs the solution more readily during the warmer months.

Store the container in a dark, cool place for about three weeks. When you notice beads of glycerine on the leaves, absorption is complete. Remove the branches and hang them upside down, allowing the solution within the stem to work down to the tip.

Adding a few drops of chlorine bleach to the mixture will usually prevent mold from forming. The solution is reusable.

Everlastings

It's easy to have colorful cut flowers year-round with the simple-to-dry kinds known as everlastings. Cut your material before the flower is fully open, remove the leaves, and hang heads-down in an airy location. These are lovely in arrangements and used in framed pictures and other crafts. Here are some suggestions:

Strawflower *(Helichrysum)* is an easily grown annual in a delightful range of colors from white and pastels to deep reds and yellows. It grows about 30 inches high, and can also be had in dwarf varieties.

Ammobium alatum, a hardy annual, has silvery flower heads.

Gomphocarpus fruticosus has brown to greenish yellow fruits on three-foot stems. Use this annual, which fruits in August, for both flowers and arrangements.

Statice is available in both annual and perennial varieties. Use fresh or dried for light, airy bouquets.

Echinops, or globe thistle, is a splendid everlasting but does best dried with an agent. Globe thistles in shades of purple grow wild in many regions.

Xeranthemum annuum has papery double flowers in white, purple, or mixed shades. *X. anaphylis* has pearly white flowers and gray foliage. Do not pick until the flowers reach the papery stage.

Helipterums, sometime sold under the names of rhodanthe and acroclinium, are among the prettiest of the immortelles, and are easy to grow. Pick the flowers as soon as they are open and, again, dry head-down. Acroclinium (sunrays) has rich shades of salmon, apricot, pink, rose, and cerise with white and creamy tones. Pick in bud to dry for winter bouquets, or use as fresh cut flowers. Plants branch and bloom freely and grow to a height of 24 inches. *Helipterum sanfordii* has silvery foliage and papery yellow flowers. *Helipterum rhodanthe* has showy, nodding, 1½-inch flower heads of handsome rose pink.

Globe amaranth *(Gomphrena globosa)* will thrive in any soil and stands drought well. It retains its form and color in drying.

Amaranthus caudatus, or love-lies-bleeding, is very pretty.

Catananche caerulea or Cupid's dart, with lovely blue flowers, must be picked and dried as soon as the flowers open or they will fade.

Didiscus caeruleus has many lavender-blue flowers on long stalks.

Physalis, the old Chinese lantern, and lunaria, or honesty, are excellent in mixed, dried bouquets.

Bells of Ireland *(Moluccella laevis)* has wonderful 18-inch sprays of tiny flowers with large green calyxes. It is as pretty and green in a summer arrangement as it is silvery and dried in winter.

The yarrows (achilleas) and the silvery sprays of lamb's-ears *(Stachys lanata)* should be dried upside down.

Wood rose *(Ipomoea tuberosa)* is a "must have"! The "wood roses" are the dried flower calyx (seed cases) of a yellow-flowered perennial morning glory native to the West Indies and other tropical regions. It blooms the second year when grown from seed. The five so-called petals are usually the sepals rolled back from the central budlike ball. The wood rose looks like a rose carved out of wood, stiff and polished to a beautiful satin brown. These "roses" make spectacular corsages and are lovely in dried arrangements.

Dyeing with Nature's Colors

Why use natural dyes? First, because they are so beautiful, and second, because of the wonderful feeling it gives you to say, "I did it!"

Natural dyes can be used on many types of material: yarn, cloth, macramé objects, crochet work, tie-dye fabric — silk, wool, cotton, jute — sometimes even wood. However, you will have your best results with cloth or yarn made of natural material such as wool or cotton. Experiment with others if you like, but try a sample first.

Some natural dye colors will be fast, others less so. Colors can be repeated, but don't count on the results being exactly the same; sometimes even commercial dyers have problems. Quantity dyeing is possible if large enough quantities of natural dyestuffs are available and your container is large enough.

Do all your dyeing in enamel kettles. Aluminum, tin, and iron pots change colors. Also, do not use the mordants (mentioned later) in pots that you are using for cooking because some of these are poisonous. Keep a separate pan for dyeing and keep mordants out of the reach of children. Actually, many of the flower and vegetable dyes do very well without mordants, but the colors will not be so permanent and sometimes not so bright.

Dyes from the Garden and Kitchen

There are probably hundreds of flowers, both garden and wildflowers, that can be used in dyeing, including coreopsis *(Coreopsis auriculata* and *C. calliopsidea)*, dock root *(Rumex)*, goldenrod *(Solidago)*, goosefoot *(Chenopodium)*, hedge-nettle, betony *(Stachys)*, wild geranium *(Geranium robertianum)*, red-flowered orchid cactus *(Epiphyllum)*, pansy *(Viola tricolor)*, pearly everlasting

(Anaphalis margaritacea), and iris *(Iris).* For an attractive yellow-green, try sunflower seeds. After boiling them, spread the seeds outdoors somewhere and let the birds have a feast. (See the chart with this chapter for further possibilities.)

Fruits and vegetables from your garden can also be used. Many vegetables that make good dye can be served at the table and the cooking water saved for use as the dye bath. Overcook spinach just slightly and it becomes a fancy puree for the table and a lovely green dye for your wool. Purple cabbage cooked for one hour is still edible and the broth is left for dyeing. From the cabbage you will derive several shades of green, depending on the size of the cabbage and the quantity used.

Save the water from boiling your beets or beet tops. It will dye your fabrics pink or yellow-green. Beet dyes are fugitive and the color may fade a little, but the material will still be attractive.

Oranges are a real treasure. Use the orange juice or the pulp, boil the peel for one hour, and dye your yarn or cloth a bright orange!

Blackberries, huckleberries, blueberries, strawberries, and raspberries all produce delightfully strong colors. For brightest purple try the raspberries; the equivalent of two 10-ounce frozen packages will dye about half a pound of yarn. Frozen grape juice gives a lively purple and is easy to use. The bottled grape juice gives an even darker shade. Soak a box of currants overnight and simmer for a pearl gray or lavender color. For a lovely rose to lavender color, try cranberries — and use the berries with sugar for sauce or preserves.

Any of the nut hulls — particularly those of walnuts — make good dyestuffs, and the nut meats are used in cakes or cookies. Or look in the barbecue section of the supermarket for hickory chips and soak these overnight for the same rich brown that walnuts and hickory nuts give.

Cinnamon, turmeric, ginger, saffron, paprika, curry powder, and mustard give vivid dyes in yellows and reds. Experiment with oregano and chopped chives for other colors and effects.

Instant tea or coffee is quick acting and gives interesting shades of tan or brown. Boil coffee grounds in a cheesecloth bag with wool for a rich chocolate brown. Rose-hip tea produces a rosy tan that is delightful.

The canned-goods shelf holds possibilities too. Canned spinach, beets, okra, and blueberries give pretty colors when simmered half an hour, including the liquid in the can. Strain out the vegetables, drop your thoroughly wet wool into the dye pot, and you will have enchanting color. Try pie cherries for a soft rose.

If you achieve a color that is too pale or doesn't please you, overdye it in another dye bath. The color will probably come out even more interesting.

Mordants for Fast Colors

Mordants are a must if you plan to use your dyed material in an article that will be washed frequently. A mordant is a mineral salt that binds the color, making it sunfast and washfast. If mordanting seems a bit difficult, use a half-cup of white vinegar or lemon juice or one tablespoon of salt in the dye bath. The material should then be washed gently by hand rather than machine-washed.

Dyer's mordants may be purchased at a drugstore, a chemical supply house, or, occasionally, at a health food store. To use them, mix the prescribed amount of the mordant crystals in a jar with about a cup of water. Shake them well to dissolve the mordant and add the solution to the dye bath. The easiest ones to find and use are:

Alum (potassium aluminum sulfate). This does not change the color of the dye but binds the color to the material. Use with cream of tartar (found in the spice section of the supermarket). The quantity for one-half pound of yarn is two teaspoons of alum and one teaspoon of cream of tartar.

Chrome (potassium bichromate). This brings out greens and yellows. Mix one teaspoon of chrome and one teaspoon of cream of tartar for one-half pound of yarn. Cover your dye pot, because chrome is weakened by exposure to light.

Copper sulfate (blue vitriol). Copper sulfate intensifies green dye. Use one teaspoon to half a pound of wool.

Iron (ferrous sulfate or rust). This "saddens" or darkens colors. The effect may be had by boiling a handful of rusty nails in a cheesecloth bag.

Tin (stannous chloride). Tin is good for brightening colors. It may be added to an alum bath during the last half of the cooking process to pick up bright color. Rinse in soapsuds after dyeing to keep tin from hardening wool.

Experiment for surprises. Sometimes a plain household ammonia rinse will give a unique shade. A lovely, soft rose from cranberries changed to a bright chartreuse after this treatment! After mordanting, wash your cloth or wool in a washing machine.

The Basics of Dyeing

Here are the basic steps for dyeing half a pound of material — for more, just multiply:

1. If using skeins of wool, tie them loosely in two places so they will not tangle — ditto for dyeing thread.

2.   Soak skeins or cloth in water for at least an hour to keep wool from streaking or blotching in the dye bath. This also helps the dye to absorb more evenly.

3.   Put the dye bath (your vegetable, flower, or fruit broth) into an enamel pan. Add sufficient water to make three quarts. Add the material and simmer one hour, or until the desired color is achieved. Remember that colors look darker when wet and allow for this. Keep the material submerged by poking with a wooden dowel or spoon. Wool is light and tends to float. Do not stir yarn or it will tangle. *Note:* If using a mordant, dissolve it in a jar with a cup or so of water, shaking to mix well. Pour this into the dye bath and stir well before adding the yarn or cloth.

4.   Remove the material when the desired color is reached. Pinch a little with your finger to get some idea of the color when dry. Rinse in hot water about the temperature of the dye bath (a change of temperature may shrink or mat wool). Rinse until the water is clear and hang in a shady place for drying. If you mordant with tin, rinse in soapsuds and then rinse out the soap. Each rinse should be a little cooler than the one before. Gently squeeze out water, never wring. A commercial fabric softener used at the end of rinsing helps to make wool soft and fluffy.

As you get more experienced in dyeing, you may wish to try for variegated effects. Try dyeing half a length of a skein by placing a stick across the dye pot and letting half the skein hang in a cranberry bath, the other half length in a grape juice bath. Let each simmer the required amount of time. Remove and rinse. You will have lovely soft colors that blend well with each other. Other combinations give equally interesting results. Try two shades of green or brown, yellow, or orange.

Dyeing with nature's colors is fascinating and satisfying, and the colors you create will be uniquely yours. With these beautiful yarns and fabrics you can go on to make clothing or decorative objects. If you have dyed wool yarn, for instance, use it for knitting, weaving, crochet, or needlepoint.

For a soft shade of rose, use beets for dyeing.

Dyes from Nature

Here are some suggestions for using nature's colors. Most of these work best with wool. Where indicated by a "w/c" you may also dye cotton:

COMMON NAME	SCIENTIFIC NAME	PLANT PART USED	DYE COLOR
Acacia	Acacia sp.	flowers	Yellow or gray, maize yellow to light golden brown
Althea shrub or Rose of Sharon	Hibiscus syriacus	pods	Moss green or tan Medium to dark blue
Anemone, blue	Anemone sp.	flowers	Teal blue or light green
Bottlebrush	Callistemon sp.	flowers	Tan to greenish beige
Brassbuttons	Cotula coronopifolia		Deep brassy gold
Butterflybush	Buddleia davidii	flowers	Orange-gold or gold-green or golden brown — wool or jute
— in iron pot		leaves and stems	Olive green
Cactus	Opuntia robusta	purple fruit, steeped	Various greens or black
Camellia, red, in iron pot	Camellia sp.		Magenta to rose
Camomile	Anthemis nobilis		Medium gray to dark gray
Canterbury bells, purple	Campanula medium		Various gold yellows, aromatic
Chrysanthemum, maroon	Chrysanthemum spp.	flowers	Medium green or pale blue
Daffodils, yellow	Narcissus pseudonarcissus		Variations of gray-turquoise w/c
Dahlia	Dahlia pinnata		Bright yellow or deep gold
Daisy, gloriosa, black-eyed Susan, brownish	Rudbeckia spp.	seed heads	Bright orange
Morning glory, bindweed	Convolvulus arvensis		Bright olive green to dark green
Mulberry, black,	Morus nigra	berries	Dull green or khaki green to yellow Intense red-violet to dark purple or purple, wool and jute

COMMON NAME	SCIENTIFIC NAME	PLANT PART USED	DYE COLOR
Dock	*Rumex* spp.	blossoms	Rose beige to terra-cotta w/c
		root in iron pot or with nails	Dark green to brown or dark gray w/c
Dodder and bits of pickleweed	*Cuscuta* sp. and *Salicornia* sp.		Yellow or ocher
Elderberry, blue or black, one pot and mordant method	*Sambucus* spp.	berries	Mauve
Eucalyptus, blue gum	*Eucalyptus globulus*	leaves	Deep camel tan
		leaves in iron pot	Light to dark green or charcoal gray w/c
Fennel	*Foeniculum vulgare*	flowers, leaves	Mustard yellow or golden brown, aromatic
Flax, New Zealand	*Phormium tenax*	flowers	Brown
		seedpods	Bright terra-cotta
Foxglove, purple	*Digitalis purpurea*	flowers	Chartreuse
Geranium, red	*Pelargonium hortorum*	leaves	Dark purple to gray w/c
Goldenrod, in iron pot	*Solidago* spp.	flowers (fresh)	Mustard, tan-orange, or brown-olive
Goosefoot, in unlined copper pot or with cupric sulfate	*Chenopodium* sp.		Dark green or green-gold
Grape, Concord-type	*Vitis labruscana*	skins and ferrous sulphate	Dark blue
Hawthorn	*Crategus* sp.	blossoms	Variations of yellow-green or gold-brown
Hedge-nettle, Betony	*Stachys* sp.		Chartreuse green
Herb Robert, wild geranium, red robin	*Geranium robertianum*		Light golden brown to rich brown
Hibiscus, red, and tin	*Hibiscus* spp.		Purple

Hollyhock, red, in iron pot with tin crystals	*Althaea rosea*		Brown
Honey bush, and tin crystals	*Althaea rosea*		Wine color
Indigo, blue, in pot	*Melianthus major*		Violet
Iris, dark purple	*Indigofera tinctoria*	leaves	Blue
Iris, purple, fleur-de-lis, and tin crystals	*Iris* spp.		Various violet blues
Klamath weed, and ammonia	*Iris germanica* and other *Iris* spp.		Various dark to light blues
Knotweed, doorweed, matgrass	*Hypericum perforatum*		Mustard gold or raw siena
Ladies' purse, yellow	*Polygonum aviculare*		Creamy yellow, brighter yellow or brassy yellow
Laurel, California, bay tree	*Calceolaria angustifolia*		Maize yellow to gold or deep orange, wool and jute
Lichen, brown, Rock oyster lichen	*Umbellularia californica*	flowers	Greenish beige, aromatic
Lilac, purple	*Umbilicaria* sp.		Magenta violet, aromatic
Lobelia, blue, in copper pot	*Syringa* spp.		Light green or light blue-green
Lupine, purple	*Lobelia erinus*		Pastel green
Manzanita	*Lupinus* spp.		Bright yellow-green or dull green
Marguerites, yellow, Paris daisy	*Arctostaphylos* spp.	leaves	Deep camel or rose buff w/c
Marigold, with tin crystals	*Chrysanthemum frutescens*		Gold or mustard-green
Meadow rue	*Tagetes* sp.	flowers	Yellow-orange, gold, or dull green
Milkweed, showy, and cupric sulfate or unlined copper pot	*Thalictrum polycarpon*	leaves/flowers	Bright yellow, fragrant
	Asclepias speciosa		Moss green or brass green
Morning glory, bindweed	*Convolvulus arvensis*		Dull green or khaki green to yellow

COMMON NAME	SCIENTIFIC NAME	PLANT PART USED	DYE COLOR
Mulberry, black	Morus nigra	berries	Intense red-violet to dark purple or purple, wool and jute
Mule ears	Wyethia augustifolia		Gold to brass
Mullein, and ammonia	Verbascum thapsus	leaves/stalks	Bright yellow or chartreuse
Nicotiana, maroon, and cupric sulfate	Nicotiana sp.		Gray-green
Nightshade	Solanum sp.		Bright yellow or dull gold or various khaki greens
Oleander, dark pink	Nerium oleander		Light gray-green or medium gray
Olives, raw	Olea europaea		Variations of maroon
Onion, red	Allium sp.	skins	Gold to henna red to maroon w/c
Onion, yellow	Allium sp.	skins, in iron pot	Yellow-green
Osage orange	Maclura pomifera		Intense greenish yellow or deep burnt orange
Owl's clover	Orthocarpus spp.	extract	Lemon yellow or mustard or ocher
Pansy, dark blue, steeped	Viola tricolor		Blue-greens
Penstemon, red, one pot and mordant method	Penstemon sp.		Medium brown
Petunias, purple, and English walnut	Petunia hybrida and Juglans regia	leaves	Light khaki green
Petunias, red, and marigolds	Petunia sp. and Tagetes sp.		Various dark greens to brown
Pigweed	Amaranthus sp.		Moss green or brass or pale yellow
Pine needles, in iron pot	Pinus sp.		Olive green, aromatic
Plum, dark red	Prunus sp.	leaves, and tin crystals	Violet to purple or lavender
Poinsettia	Euphorbia pulcherrima	leaves	Greenish brown
Primrose, dark red, in iron pot	Primula sp.		Greenish yellow or bright avocado
Rabbit brush	Chrysothamnus sp.		Lemon yellow or gold copper

Common name	Botanical name	Part / process	Color
Ragwort, tansy-ragwort, stinking Willie	Senecio jacobaea		Bright yellow or brassy gold
Redwood, California	Sequoia spp.	bark	Tan or light golden brown to terra-cotta
Rhododendron	Rhododendron spp.	leaves, in iron pot	Gray-green
Rosemary	Rosmarinus officinalis	leaves, flowers	Various yellow-greens
Rudbeckia	Rudbeckia sp.		Bright chartreuse to dark green
Sagebrush	Artemisia tridentata		Various tan-golds, brilliant yellow, or yellow
Salal	Gaultheria shallon	berries	Dark blue
Santolina, lavender cotton, French lavender	Santolina chamaecyparissus	berries, and cupric sulfate	Various dark greens / Siena gold or yellow
Scabiosa, purplish, pincushion flower	Scabiosa atropurpurea		Bright green or dull dark blue
Self heal, Heal-all	Prunella vulgaris		Bright olive green
Silk oak	Grevillea robusta		Intense canary yellow or olive green
Snapdragon, dark reddish	Antirrhinum majus		Pale green or tannish gold
Spicebush, and cupric sulfate	Calycanthus occidentalis	on plant fibers	Light brown
Stock, purple	Matthiola incana		Blue or turquoise
Tarweed	Hemizonia luzulaefolia		Golden yellow or light yellow; aromatic w/c
Tea, black	Thea sinensis	leaves	Rose tan or gray or black
Tea, sassafras	Sassafras albidum	bark	Light terra-cotta to orange tan
Twinberries, and tin crystals	Lonicera involucrata		Gray
Walnut, black	Juglans nigra	leaves	Cinnamon to dark brown or tan to brown; wool, cotton, jute
Woodruff, sweet	Asperula odorata		Soft tan or gray-green
Woolly aster, seaside	Eriophyllum staechadifolium		Bronze gold to golden brown
Yarrow	Achillea millefolium and spp.	flowers	Yellow to maize or dark green
Yarrow, in copper pot	Achillea millefolium and spp.	leaves	Chartreuse to tan-greens

Beautiful Easter Eggs, Naturally

Coloring eggs at Eastertime is a very old tradition practiced in many countries. The methods have varied, but none is more lovely or simple than the old German custom of employing natural materials. Perhaps best of all, in these days when we are again becoming ecology-minded, these eggs may be eaten without worrying about their wholesomeness or their effect upon the system. And many of these materials are right in your own flower or vegetable garden, on your lawn, or in the woods or fields near your home.

Save the outer skins of onions. Carefully peel these off as they dry and darken. Store them in a mesh bag, using a bag of fairly close weave so small particles will not be lost. If you have a good supply of both yellow and red onions, save the skins separately for greater variation of color. Do not cook them together, for the results will not be attractive.

Rainwater (or melted snow) makes the best onion-skin broth. Catch this in a glass or enamel vessel and store it in advance. Well-washed glass or plastic vinegar jugs are handy for this purpose.

Make a broth by simmering the onion skins gently for an hour or until the color of the water is quite deep. Let cool to room temperature but do not remove the skins.

While the broth is cooling, remove the eggs you will use from the refrigerator so they, too, will be brought to room temperature; cold eggs may crack in the boiling process and spoil your efforts. Choose white eggs as large as possible. Some shells will not take up color as well as others, but this does not often happen.

Find an old sheet or several old pillowcases; those that are ready to be discarded are best, as thin material absorbs well and permits the color of the skins to pass through to the egg. Tear the cloth into long strips, one inch wide and one yard long. If the material is still strong enough, tear the salvages into strips about a quarter-inch wide. If not, have ready a spool of thin, soft white twine for use in tying the wider cloth securely after the eggs are wrapped, or use sewing thread.

While the onion skins are cooking and the eggs are warming up, take your garden basket outdoors in the warm spring sunshine and see what you can find. This will depend on the Eastertime weather and on your climate zone.

Grape hyacinth makes a lovely delicate imprint; often the blue color is transferred to the egg as well.

Dandelion heads, carefully cut so they will lie as flat as possible, impart their own yellow color, and pink japonica and rose petals leave their own lovely hues. Hunt in the lawn or in a nearby field for young yarrow plants. Their fine, fernlike leaves leave an exquisite tracery. Clover leaves and ferns are lovely.

Do not overlook the decorative possibilities of dried grasses left over from winter and still holding their shape. Consider weeds with interesting outlines; some of these make markings on the eggs as pretty as cultivated flowers and plants.

Do not gather too much at a time. Some of your plants or flowers may wilt or curl before you can use them. You can always go back for more. Try, at least in your early attempts, for flowers and leaves that will lie as flat and close to the egg as possible. These leave a more definite imprint.

Now, lay a large soft bath towel on the table over which you will work. Have a pair of sharp scissors handy for cutting cloth or plants as you need them. If you are right-handed, hold an egg in your left hand, slipping the cloth strip under the egg slightly so you can grasp it with your fingers. Lay a bit of fern, leaf, or flower on the cloth and fold it upward so that it is pressed securely against the egg.

As you lay each bit of flower or fern against the egg, pull the cloth over it and hold firmly. Then put on another flower or leaf, continuing in this manner until the egg is completely covered. Give a half-turn twist to the cloth when you have gone around the egg once (preferably lengthwise) so that you may also place a bit of plant on the ends. Do not be dismayed if you find this procedure awkward at first. With a little practice, even children become adept. You may not be able to cover your first few eggs completely with flowers, nor is it even desirable to do so, for the contrasting brown is what makes the eggs so pretty.

After the egg is wrapped with the inch-wide strip of cloth, gently tighten the wrappings by going over them once more with the narrow cloth or twine. This is to prevent the covering from coming off in the coloring bath.

Use a slotted spoon to insert the eggs gently in the warm broth. Make sure they are well covered. For a four-quart saucepan, three to five eggs at one time are all you should try to cook. After the eggs have been placed in the broth, cook them as you would any hard-cooked eggs. Heat the broth slowly, letting it simmer for eight minutes so that the shells take up as much color as possible.

When the time is up, take the eggs out one at a time with your slotted spoon. Flick any clinging onion skins back into the saucepan. Place the eggs in water that is at room temperature or slightly warmer, and allow them to cool until they can be conveniently handled.

After a few minutes, change the water to cool the eggs more rapidly, or add more cool water. Or have two pans handy and just slip them into the other one as a new batch is made.

The wrappings should begin to slip off easily, but if necessary, untie them, pull off the cloth, and discard. (If you are pressed for materials, you can rinse them out in clear water, hang them up to dry, and reuse.)

After the wrappings have been removed, place the eggs on a couple of layers of absorbent paper to dry thoroughly. While they are still warm, add a bit of glamour by rubbing them with cooking oil, one that is not sticky. Use a soft cloth for rubbing. You will be delighted with the added shine, which enhances the beauty of the coloring and the brown or reddish brown background.

These eggs, with their lovely, shadowy imprints, are perfect when used as centerpieces in low bowls or trays, or in a pretty, brightly colored basket.

If you wish, write names on these "flower eggs" with a wax pencil instead of, or in combination with, the flowers before cooking them in the broth. You may also cut out small pictures of thin (easily bendable) cardboard or heavy paper and wrap them on the eggs along with the grasses or leaves. Tiny bunnies and chicks are special favorites.

You need not have any qualms whatsoever about letting youngsters enjoy these eggs. Even if an egg should crack in the cooking process and a little color get on the egg, it is perfectly harmless.

The eggs can be made several days in advance of the time they are needed. After they have been cooked, return them to the egg carton and store them in the refrigerator. They will keep just as well as any other hard-cooked eggs. The oil film may dull a little when the eggs are cold but it will quickly become glossy again when they are taken out and returned to room temperature.

Many other natural materials can be used for coloring eggs. Some people use beet juice or even coffee grounds. In Russia the pasqueflower, *Anemone pulsatilla,* which imparts a green color, has been used to color Paschal or Easter eggs. In England, furze or gorse, a shrub with yellow flowers, has been used. Perhaps you will be inspired to experiment with other flowers and plants from your own garden.

Cosmetics and Fragrances

Beauty Preparations from the Garden

Hungary Water

Queen Elizabeth of Hungary, an eternally youthful beauty, attributed her marvelous looks to an herb tonic that became known, in her honor, as Hungary Water. Here is how it was made:

HUNGARY WATER

12 ounces rosemary
1 ounce lemon peel
1 ounce orange peel
1 ounce mint
1 ounce balm
1 pint rose water
1 pint spirits of wine (pure alcohol, grain alcohol, or vodka)

Mix together and let stand for several weeks. Then strain and use the liquid to rub into the skin after bathing.

This recipe, too, is reputed to be that of the queen. This tonic lotion was once made and used by ladies everywhere. Not only was it used for perfumery, but also a few drops taken internally were recommended for nervous ailments and mental depression. Here is the recipe:

QUEEN OF HUNGARY'S WATER

2 tablespoons dried rose-
mary flowers
1 nutmeg, grated
2 teaspoons cinnamon
1 tablespoon sweet cicely
leaves (if available)
1 quart pure alcohol
(grain alcohol or
vodka)

Pulverize all the dry ingredients (a mortar and pestle is helpful) and mix well together. Add the alcohol. Let the mixture steep for ten days. Then strain off and bottle. Apply on cloths wrung out in cold water, and place over forehead to allay headaches and soothe fevers. With fevers, also apply to the pulse of the wrists.

Roses for Beauty

Gather roses (wild or old-fashioned roses are best) when dew has dried but before the sun becomes warm. The green or white base of the petals, known as the heel, should be clipped off, as this has a bitter taste. Press petals between two sheets of paper toweling to absorb moisture.

Glycerine and rose water, beloved of nineteenth-century ladies and responsible for many a beautiful skin well into old age, is again becoming popular; several of the leading cosmetic firms are now offering it. Other preparations such as Rose Milk are widely advertised. Here is a recipe:

ROSE HAND LOTION

Soak ¼ ounce of tragacanth in water for four to five days. Mix 2 ounces of glycerine with 1 ounce of alcohol and add to the strained solution of tragacanth with ¼ to ½ ounce of rose water and 1 pint of water. If lotion needs thinning, add more water.

Rose water. Rose water may be purchased at herb or specialty food shops. But if you want to make your own, you can easily do so.

ROSE WATER

1 teaspoon rose extract
12 tablespoons distilled
     water

Measure carefully and use only distilled water. Mix liquids thoroughly and bottle, storing in a cool, dark place.

Rose vinegar. This can be added to warm water for a hair rinse after shampooing, or a cupful can be used in bathwater. It can also be wrung out of a cloth and placed on the forehead as a headache remedy.

ROSE VINEGAR

1 pint white vinegar
1 cup fragrant rose petals
   Pinch of rosemary or
      lavender

Boil the vinegar and pour it over the rose petals. Add the rosemary or lavender. Cover tightly, and let stand for 10 days. Strain and pour into sterilized bottle.
  Cook only in stainless-steel, enamel, or glass pans and stir with a wooden spoon.

Rose facial mask. This treatment is especially helpful for oily skin. The ingredients are: ⅔ cup finely ground oatmeal, 6 teaspoons honey, 2 teaspoons rose water. Blend oatmeal and honey until well mixed. If desired, add more honey to make a smooth paste, blending it with rose water. Spread over clean face and neck. Leave on for 30 minutes. Best results will be achieved if you lie down and relax. Using a soft washcloth and warm water, remove and follow with cold water or astringent.

Rose soap. Save odds and ends of leftover hand soap and grate or cut up finely. Add hot water that contains about 6 drops of rose oil (see *Fragrant Delights,* below), using enough to cover. Place over a low flame until the soap dissolves. Pour into a clean cream carton to a depth of 1 inch and set aside to harden.

Skin Care

Elder flowers added to steam baths will clear and soften the skin. Freshly crushed leaves or freshly pressed juice of lady's-mantle *(Alchemilla vulgaris)* is helpful against inflammation of the skin and acne, as well as freckles. Externally used lime flowers *(Tilia)* stimulate hair growth and are a fine cosmetic against freckles, wrinkles, and impurities of the skin. Aloe vera is now widely used in many skin preparations, and jojoba preparations are also becoming popular.

You can grow the very versatile luffa gourd for washcloths and bath sponges. This beauty treatment is centuries old in the Orient.

Use the oil of sesame seeds or the juice of lemon and cucumber to soften and whiten the skin. Wheat germ oil and liquid lecithin (from soya beans) are believed helpful against lines and wrinkles.

Fragrant Delights

Eau de Cologne

This spirituous preparation contains oils of rosemary, citron, orange, bergamot, neroli, and geranium. It has been produced since 1700 and is very useful for freshening a sickroom.

Incense

Incense is predominantly of plant origin, a mixture of sweet-smelling gums and balsams. It burns with a delicate fragrance. The early Egyptians burned it at religious ceremonies; the Greeks and Romans and later the early Christians adopted this practice. The burning of incense is still part of the ritual of the Eastern Orthodox Church, the Roman Catholic Church, and some Episcopalian churches. Buddhists also burn incense at religious ceremonies. And it is often burned in homes to give fragrance to a room.

Incense ingredients of ancient civilization and the early Christians were: *Frankincense gabanum,* myrrh, mastic, rosemary, opopanax, and storax.

Incense ingredients of oriental nations were: cinnamon, cloves, camphor, dragon's blood, galbanum, sandalwood, and star anise.

Leaf Odors

Leaves hold their aromatic scent far longer than flowers. Often they are sweeter in a dried state than when fresh. To release the odor of herbs and leaves, grind them in a mortar using a pestle. Mortars and pestles can be found in specialty cookware shops, and sometimes in herb or health food stores.

Moth Repellents

If you detest the odor of commercial moth repellents, try this one from

Euell Gibbons's *Stalking the Healthful Herbs*. You'll need one pound pine
needles (the needles of western pinon pine are best, he advises), 1 ounce
cedar shavings, and ½ ounce of shavings from the root of sassafras.

Line a drawer with paper, sprinkle in the mixture, and cover with a
thickness of cloth, something like a piece of an old sheet or a thin bath
towel, fastening it firmly in place with thumbtacks. Store your woolens on
top and they will not only be protected from moths, but also have a clean,
fresh fragrance when you take them out to wear. Feverfew, sage, tansy, and
members of the Artemisia family contain camphor and are also moth repellents.

A wide variety of plants have been used to repel moths, including oil of
cade *(Juniperus oxycedrus)*, lavender, costmary, wormwood, and clove; leaves
of fennel, patchouli, sweet flag, fern, bracken, and rosemary; flowers of the
male breadfruit tree; black pepper; Irish moss, citron, alcoholic solution of
coumarin and hemp; extract from broom seed, cichona, lupine, tung oil,
and elecampane. The wood of cedar has long been recognized as a moth
repellent.

In addition to serving as moth repellents, botanicals have been found
useful against other insects that destroy cloth. These include camphor and
powdered clove against carpet beetle larvae. Clothing has been treated with
a soapy emulsion of anise oil or bayberry oil to ward off insects.

Pillows

Flowers and herbs for scented pillows were once very popular. The delicate
fragrance of herbs or blossoms is released when pressure is put on the
pillow. The herbs may be mixed with the pillow stuffing, used entirely as a
stuffing, or put into sachet bags and placed inside the pillow. Scented pillows can be made from: calamus, lavender flowers, lemon verbena, meadowsweet, orrisroot, rosemary, rose geranium, sweet fern, or woodruff.
Pillows stuffed with white pine needles are delightful. (See also *Allheal* in
the Flower Lore chapter.)

Pomander

Take a small, thin-skinned orange and press whole cloves into it until the
surface is entirely studded. Roll the orange in powdered orrisroot and powdered cinnamon, patting on as much as possible. Wrap in tissue paper and
place in a dry, well-ventilated area for several weeks. Remove paper, shake
off surplus powder, and the pomander is ready for use. Hang by a ribbon in

a closet where it will share its fragrance and aroma for many weeks. The mock orange *(Philadelphus virginalis)* is also used for this purpose.

Potpourri

There are many recipes for potpourri. This is one of the most delightful.

Gather as many as possible of the following kinds of scented flowers as they become available: petals of the pale red and dark red roses, moss roses and damask roses, and acacia; heads of pinks, violets, lily of the valley, lilacs (blue and white), orange blossom and lemon blossom, mignonette, heliotrope, narcissis, and jonquils; a small proportion of the flowers of balm, rosemary, thyme, and myrtle. Spread materials out to dry.

As the flowers become fully dry in turn, put them into a tall glass jar, with alternate layers of coarse salt (uniodized) mixed with powdered orris-root (use two parts of salt to one of orris). Pack the flowers and salt-orris until the jar is filled.

Close the jar for one month, then stir all up and moisten with sufficient rose water (see the recipe in this chapter) to penetrate to the lowest layer. Cap with a muslin cloth tightly tied, and use in cotton bags when wanted to scent drawers, linen closets, and clothes hangers.

Rose, Attar of

A tiny, one-ounce copper vial of greenish yellow fluid — the essence of roses used in the world's most expensive perfumes — is more valuable than gold! "Treated like a magic potion," according to Cyril Williams, a British perfume expert, "it's kept locked in bank vaults and fireproof, temperature-controlled safes. Small containers are insured for thousands of dollars."

The precious liquid concentrate (it takes over 100,000 roses to produce just one ounce) comes from the unique Valley of the Roses, where soil and climate have combined to make the finest rose scent in the world.

The rose grown in the Kazanlik Valley, Bulgaria, for the purpose of making attar of roses is *Rosa damascena trigintipetala*. It grows three to four feet tall and has one annual flowering. It has semidouble, rose red, 3½-inch flowers with stiff yellow stamens. This rose also makes wonderful potpourri.

The Turks brought these roses from Damascus when they conquered Bulgaria nearly 600 years ago. When they departed in 1878, they left them behind. "From a distance the fields look like a pink sea," said Valentine Ruskov, a Bulgarian trade attaché in London. "The Turks used to take baths in rose-scented water and before long the distillation of attar became a cottage industry." Ruskov explained that the roses are harvested in May and June before daylight, "so the sun doesn't dry the petals, which are boiled to remove the essence." He went on to say, "Other countries have tried to duplicate the essence, but have not been successful." For home use, try the following:

Rose oil. Steep rose petals in a bland oil, such as mineral oil (or purchase essential oil of rose from a craft supplier or health food store). The petals may also be put into a crock and covered with water. Keep in a warm place and a little oil will rise to the surface. Collect it on a piece of dry cotton and squeeze into a bottle. This oil is attar of rose.

Rose Jar

The great rose for making potpourri is also the rose used for attar of roses, *Rosa damascena trigintipetala.* It is available in this country. Plant garlic or onions with your roses; they are not only protective but actually also increase rose fragrance when grown nearby.

Roses are the most fragrant in the sunniest, most protected spot in the garden. It is there that they develop their essential oils in the highest degree. Collect the flowers before the sun is high, on a dry day after two or three days of dry weather. Never use inferior, rain-soaked blossoms or those that have been open for a few days. Also, fragrant oils will not be present in the petals of flowers that have been in the house for a week.

Gather damask rose petals when the roses are blooming abundantly. Pack them in a glass jar that has a tight cover. The addition of tiny pink buds of 'De Meaux ' will make the final product prettier and more highly scented. Between every two-inch layer of petals sprinkle two teaspoons of salt. (Use common uniodized salt.) Add more layers of petals and salt each day until the jar is full. Keep in a dark, dry cool place for one week. Then spread the petals on a paper towel and loosen them carefully.

Mix the following ingredients thoroughly and mix well through the petals in a large bowl: ½ ounce violet-scented talcum powder, one ounce orrisroot, ½ teaspoon mace, ½ teaspoon cinnamon, ½ teaspoon cloves, four drops oil of rose geranium. Add the following very slowly: 20 drops eucalyptus oil, 10 drops bergamot oil, two teaspoons alcohol. Repack the mixture in the jar, cover tightly, and set aside for two weeks to ripen. It will then be ready for distribution into rose jars, which make wonderful birthday or Christmas gifts.

Some of these ingredients are readily available at most supermarkets, but you may have difficulty finding others. Indiana Botanic Gardens and Nichols Garden Nursery are possible sources, as are health food and herbal stores.

Traditional Remedies from the World of Plants

Arthritis

Eating the right fruits, vegetables, and seeds sometimes helps alleviate the pain of arthritis. These include: alfalfa, tea brewed from alfalfa seeds, asparagus, celery, cherries, collards, fennel, gooseberries, kale, lemon juice, lettuce, limes, melons, molasses, mustard greens, oranges, spinach, sunflower seeds, tangerines, and watercress.

Eyes

Various Native American tribes developed herb and flower remedies for sore or strained eyes. Plants were often named according to the way they were used. The prairie zinnia *(Crassina grandiflora)* was known as Put into Eyes because the Zuni crushed the flowers in cold water and used the strained liquid as an eyewash. Wash Eye Tea is a Native name for the wahoo *(Euonymus atropurpurea)*.

Several tribes made infusions for sore eyes from either St.-John's-wort or St.-Andrew's-cross. Other mild infusions were made of any one of the following: alder, bark, bearberry leaves, yarrow herb, chickweed herb, black-

---

STREWING HERBS

In northern countries, before rugs were commonly used, the floors of castles and churches were strewn for warmth with various organic materials such as rushes. Herbs, called strewing herbs, were popular, and lavender, thyme, Acorus calamus, the mints, basils, balm, hyssop, and santolina were widely used. Marjoram, believed to be an antiseptic, was scattered over church floors at funerals.

berry root, black oak bark, chokecherry bark, or bark of buttonbush. Ginseng root was also used for sore eyes, the pounded root being soaked in cold water and then strained.

In the South, buds of sassafras were gathered and placed in cold water; the mixture then was allowed to stand several hours in the sun. The glutinous substance formed was used in treating sore eyes.

Herbalist Jethro Kloss recommends a poultice of slippery elm applied (cold) to the eyes to relieve inflammation. Other herbs he recommends for sore eyes are rosemary, borage, chamomile, chickweed, elder, fennel, goldenseal, hyssop, rock rose, sarsaparilla, sassafras, witch hazel, wintergreen, yellow dock, plantain, tansy, white willow, and angelica.

Fatigue

The Aztecs breathed flower fragrances to ease fatigue. They also recognized melancholia and loss of memory as diseases. The fragrance of flower concentrates and other ingredients calculated to retain the delicate aroma were used in body massage. A very similar preparation of flowers was also taken internally.

Ginseng *(Panax quinquefolium)*

Ginseng is the most expensive botanical in the entire vegetable kingdom and surpasses even the truffle as a precious aphrodisiac. Ginseng has been known and prized in the Orient for centuries. People believe that ginseng promotes long life and virility, and have used it as a cure for many ills. Americans who use the root praise it for its tranquilizing qualities. Recently, clinical and biochemical studies have found that ginseng has a beneficial, estrogen-like effect on women.

Ginseng

Ginseng also stimulates the nervous system, making one feel more active, more aggressive, more interested.

Ginseng, Siberian *(Eleutherococus senticosus maximus)*

The plant is so called because *senticosus* means "prickly" in Latin. One day, it is said, a young Russian doctor named Gorovoy noticed deer greedily eating the leaves of a thorny plant commonly found growing wild in the Russian

Far East. It belonged to the Araliaceae and shortly joined the other araliaceous medicinal plants on trial in the laboratory. It outshone them all, rivaling or even surpassing ginseng itself. It was found to be a first-class tonic plant medicine, greatly increasing stamina in long-term administration.

Although similar in pharmacological effect, *Eleutherococus* was found to have advantages over ginseng. Under the stress of hard physical work, both men and animals were found to receive greater stimulation for longer periods with *Eleutherococus* than with ginseng. In hyperactive individuals it seems also to possess some calmative effect.

Actually, the name Siberian ginseng is a misnomer, for it is an entirely different plant, though having much the same effect. It is sometimes called eleuthero to make the distinction. Its qualities were not discovered until 1962 and there is no mention of it as a Russian folk medicine. It is an example of that rare species, a new national plant medicine discovered by modern research. Since the plant grows abundantly, it is far less expensive to buy than the rarer ginseng.

Hay Fever

Knowing what and when to avoid is helpful. The eucalyptus tree spreads its misery from January through September. March, April, and May are particularly rough periods for those allergic to sycamore, English walnut, and live oak. Springtime also brings the cottonwood fuzz. Bermuda grass can keep you down from March through November. April and May are the toughest

---

BENIGN AND EVIL HERBS

Down through the centuries, some plants were thought to have a benign effect while others brought evil in their wake.

The "good" plants were southernwood, rosemary (effective against witchcraft), lavender (against the evil eye), bracken, ground ivy, maidenhair fern, dill, hyssop, agrimony, and angelica. Yellow and green flowers growing in hedgerows were believed to be especially disliked by witches.

Other herbs had the opposite effect. The herbs to call up evil spirits were vervain, betony, yarrow, and mugwort. St.-John's-wort was used to exorcise them.

How herbs were used made a lot of difference, as did the combinations. It was believed that if coriander, parsley, hemlock, liquid of black poppy, fennel, sandalwood, and henbane were laid in a heap and burned together, they would call forth a whole army of demons.

grass months, with pollen from fescues, rye, and Kentucky blue keeping your eyes watering. Johnson grass hits later, from May through August.

Weeds of all types pollute the air, starting in May and running through October. Ragweed's worst two months are August and September — and don't blame the innocent goldenrod.

Besides flowers, trees, weeds, and grasses, there are some common year-round environmental allergy-producers, including cat hair, cattle hair, chalk, dog hair, glue made from animals, horse hair, house dust, newspaper, sheep wool, tobacco, and feathers. Foods that are most often allergy-producers are wheat, celery, chicken, cow's milk, chocolate, eggs, oranges, peanuts, strawberries, tomatoes, and cantaloupe.

Headache

The Romanies have a number of interesting flower and herb remedies:
1. A few pieces of willow bark boiled in a pan of water is helpful. It contains salicylic acid, the ingredient found in many over-the-counter headache medicines.
2. For nervous headaches, a tea made from the flowery tops of rosemary with boiling water is soothing.
3. A tea made from a few dried lime flowers cures a headache in about half an hour. Take hot, then lie down for thirty minutes and relax.
4. For a severe headache, put a pinch of dried marjoram into a teacup. Half fill it with boiling water, cover and allow to draw, and drink while hot.

Herbal Remedies, Types of

The information given below is not intended to replace a physician, but for those interested in herbal remedies, some simple definitions may be helpful:

Alteratives improve nutritive processes gradually, normally, and naturally. Take in the form of tea. Peppermint tea is a "for instance"; it has been used for relieving colic in babies or minor bloat in children and adults.

Antispasmodics reduce involuntary contractions often arising from nervous causes. *Anthemis nobilis,* or true camomile, is notable for giving relief. Camomile flower tea has been famous since the days of the pharaohs and was as popular in past times as aspirins are today.

Carminatives and aromatics are usually herbs with a spicy scent and pungent taste useful for expelling gas from the stomach and thereby reducing flatulence. Mint, a mild carminative, has often been chewed after dinner. Other herbs traditionally used separately or together are anise and caraway, cloves, dill, ginger, and other aromatic spices. Their delicious fragrances also provide a lift to our spirits.

Demulcents soothe the intestinal tract and are usually of an oily or mucilaginous nature. Olive oil is a natural demulcent. Emollients, similar in meaning, are used to soothe the skin rather than internal membranes, often allaying the pain of irritated parts. Irish moss and slippery elm are considered both demulcent and emollient.

Diaphoretics produce sweating. Sweat baths have been used by many peoples over the centuries (the Finnish sauna, in which water is thrown on heated stones, is a familiar example). Tea of yarrow *(Achillea millefolium)* induces sweating and formerly was used as a cold remedy. Dried elder flowers and mint are both believed to be helpful when added to the brew.

Diuretics stimulate the secreting cells or nerves of the kidneys, increasing the flow of urine. Herbs valued as diuretics are dandelions and juniper berries; lemon juice and milk are also mild diuretics.

Expectorants help in the expulsion of mucous secretions from the air passages and are used to clear phlegm that accumulates in the lungs and windpipe. Yerba santa, red clover tea, and valerian are examples; many more herbs are also considered helpful.

Febrifuges are agents that reduce fevers. Dogwood and boneset, sometimes called feverwort, were used for this purpose.

Laxatives are taken to relieve a temporary condition of constipation, but any plants that are cathartic in action should be used with care. Dandelion greens are a tonic and mildly laxative.

Nervines act upon the nervous system to overcome irritability. The most notable plant for this purpose is valerian.

Sedatives help to quiet the nervous system without producing narcotic effects. The bark of the wild black cherry is added to cough medicines because of its sedative action.

Stimulants quicken vital action and digestion, raise body temperature, and increase general

Sage, one of the easiest herbs to grow, is commonly listed both for cooking and for medical uses. Its name comes from the Latin salveo, *meaning "to save or heal." Recent research suggests that it should not be taken internally for prolonged periods, however.*

awareness. Culinary herb stimulants are anise, pepper, cinnamon, cloves, dill, ginger, horseradish, nutmeg, peppermint, and sage. Medicinal herbs include horehound, hyssop, lavender, lobelia, marjoram, and spearmint.

Stomachics improve stomach activity and stimulate appetite. Spearmint is an excellent example. Chokecherry, often used for making brandy, is another.

Tonics tone up our bodies and give us a feeling of well-being. They are often referred to as bitters. Camomile has been used in this way, and so have feverwort, chicory, goldenseal, and *Verbena officinalis.*

High Blood Pressure

Fruits and vegetables thought to be helpful in reducing high blood pressure are: broccoli, carrots, cauliflower, celery, cherries, cranberries, cucumbers, endive, fennel, garlic, grapefruit, guavas, kumquats, melons, oranges, peaches, pears, peppers, pineapples, pomegranates, raspberries, spinach, strawberries, tangerines, and turnip tops.

Hoarseness

This is a Romany remedy: Take a good-sized turnip, wash it well but do not peel. Then cut a piece from the bottom so that it will stand upright, and cut it downward in four equal slices. Fit the turnip together again to stand up in a deep dish or soup plate, having first added a layer of honey between the slices.

When the turnip has been left standing for an hour or two, a thick syrup from the turnip juice and the honey will have formed in the bottom of the dish. This can be taken a spoonful at a time.

Tranquilizers, Nature's Own

Pleasant at any time, herbs are particularly appropriate at times of emotional stress. Herbs believed to be exceedingly soothing to the nervous system are camomile, valerian, rosemary, and lavender.

For an herbal bath, put the herb or herbs on a muslin square and tie them up like a hobo pack. Toss the packet into the bath as the water runs in and allow to steep for at least 10 minutes. Also good are pine needles, fresh from the tree, wrapped and used like the herbal bath bags. And, while you are relaxing, drink a cup of warm camomile tea, one of the oldest nerve-calming teas beloved of herb enthusiasts — far better for you than tea or coffee. Verbena tea is also highly thought of.

In his book *Back to Eden,* Jethro Kloss has some additional suggestions: celery, dill, fitsroot (skullcap with goldenseal and hops), lobelia, motherwort, origanum, pennyroyal, red clover, rosemary, rue, sage, spearmint. St.-John's-wort, thyme, verbain, wild cherry, wood betony, blue violet, sanicle, buchu, red sage, catnip, peppermint, marshmallow root, and mugwort (used in an antispasmodic tincture for quick results).

Warts

A number of plants are credited with eradicating warts. A Romany remedy is the thick white juice exuded by milkweed plants. Other traditional cures include the white, milklike sap of dandelions and the milky sap of figs.

More Projects for Plant Lovers

Dolls

In colonial times corncob dolls were enchanting little toys that children loved.

Shell off the corn and dry the cob with the shucks left on. Then pull the shucks up and back for the "hair." Slit the shucks and make them into braids; or they may be curled by holding a strip of slit shuck between thumb and a knife and pulling the shuck through, just as ribbon is curled. Try decorating a small Christmas tree with tiny dolls made from midget corn.

When digging potatoes, watch for those with unusual shapes; they often lend themselves to roly-poly comic characters or animals. Carrots with a little trimming can be made into dolls as well. Dolls with apple heads have been made for centuries; some of them are truly works of art.

Dowsing

To find out if you are a water witch, take a small tree branch with a fork in it — a branch shaped something like a wishbone. Hold the two ends of the forked branch with the palms of your hands facing up. Walk slowly with the branch pointing straight up. When you approach a source of moving water, even through an underground water pipe, you will feel a definite pull on the branch as it begins to move toward the earth. When you are directly over water (if you have the power of a water witch), the branch will insist upon pointing straight downward even though you are trying your best to hold it up.

Part of an old tradition, water witches are still called upon to use their divining rods. Some can even get results by holding the rod over a map of the area. Most water witches say that a forked stick from almost any tree will work if you have the power, but the preferred species are peach, apple, willow, and maple.

Fishing with Herbs

Oil of anise rubbed on bait will attract fish, and so will the juice of smallage or lovage and the steeped root of sweet cicely.

Floral Clock

Certain flowers, called sensitive flowers, have a natural "clock" that causes them to open and close at the same or nearly the same time each day. This effect can be used to create an interesting garden project.

The great Swedish naturalist Karl von Linné (born 1707), better known as Carolus Linnaeus, composed a floral clock. One could determine the time of day by the opening and closing of certain flowers, which folded and unfolded their petals at regular hours. Here are a few of those that served for the construction of his dial:

Dandelion opens from 5 to 6 A.M. and closes between 8 and 9 P.M.; mouse-ear hawkweed opens at 8 A.M. and closes at 2 P.M.; yellow goat's beard opens at sunrise and shuts at noon; smooth sow thistle opens at 5 A.M. and closes at 10 A.M.; white water lily opens between 5 and 6 A.M.; mallow opens at 9 to 10 A.M. and closes at 1 P.M.

Another form of floral clock was popular during the 1800s. Some flower lovers planted sensitive flowers in U-shaped gardens. One point of the U was planted with the spotted cat's-ear flower, which opens at 6 in the morning. Then five more different flowers were planted in the row, each kind opening one hour later than the one before it. The passionflower, opening at noon, was placed at the center of the curve of the U. From this curve to the other point of the U, six other kinds of flowers were planted in a row. Each one closed one hour later than the flower before it. The last flower was the evening primrose, which opened at 6 in the evening. Though not very exact, of course, the flowers' internal clocks made them quite regular and predictable.

Floral Prints

Gather thin, light, colorful flowers (pansies, petunias, columbines, buttercups) just before they come into full bloom. Brush off the pollen and press the blossoms between sheets of absorbent paper (such as paper toweling). Place a heavy object on top. Replace the paper after eight hours, and again after the next eight hours. Then leave the flowers for two to three weeks.

Place your pressed flowers on construction paper in any design you wish. No glue is necessary, as the pressure of the glass will hold them in place after they are framed. Ferns also press well.

Pressed like this, flowers can be used to decorate Easter eggs. Touch them lightly on one side with white glue and gently press them on the egg.

Another method is to press flowers between sheets of plastic wrap and touch them lightly with a warm iron to seal. These make attractive greeting cards between two sheets of folded notepaper.

To make an ink print of dried ferns or flowers, use a blockprint roller. Ink the roller and roll back and forth over the material to be used. Then place in the desired arrangement on construction paper and roll a clean roller over the design. Different colors on the same arrangement give an interesting pattern.

Grocery Plants

Check your grocery bag for some good winter growing projects. While such plants started from seeds cannot be depended upon to produce "true" fruit, or any at all for that matter, they are fun to grow. Lemons, oranges, grapefruit, and other citrus fruits are good for a start, and sweet potatoes make an attractive, interesting vine.

Ivy Tree *(Hedera)*

Many plants change their style of vegetative growth from prostrate to erect at flowering time. This is common among annuals and perennials, but rare in vines. In ivy, the flowering process triggers the formation of erect branches on which the leaves are different from those on other parts of the vine — narrow and lance-shaped.

Ivy vines flower only when about 15 years old. The flower head is a cluster of tiny cream-colored flowers. If cuttings are made of the erect flowering branches before the flowers are produced, the erect form is retained by the plant that develops from the cuttings.

Take the cutting below the tip at the bud on a young woody stem. Insert the cutting into a loose perlite and peat moss mixture; roots will quickly form. After roots have formed, pinch back the stem to produce an interesting form with side branches. The variegated *Hedera canariensis* with dramatic green and white branches is a wonderful subject for this horticultural wizardry. Remove any leaves that revert to the vine habit.

Jack-o'-Lanterns on the Vine

Pumpkins are fun to grow and fun to eat. In pioneer days they were sliced and hung from cabin roofs to dry for winter storage. They were made into soup, stew, pudding, bread, griddle cakes, and a thick sauce, as well as pie.

Pumpkins are pretty in flower and bright in fruit. To decorate them while still on the vine, start with the seeds. Choose your variety for the size you want; small pumpkins are best for small children.

As pumpkins ripen, they turn from green to yellow-orange. While they are still green but have almost reached full size, take a paring knife and carve the jack-o'-lantern face, or a child's name, or any other design, through the rind and into the flesh about ⅛ inch deep.

In a few days a callus will form along the cut lines, and the design will begin to rise up in a distinct pattern, turning light-colored against the orange skin after the pumpkin ripens. No harm comes to the interior of the fruit. Near frost time, harvest the decorated pumpkin as usual.

Jewelry

"Beads" from the garden are a delightful bonus from many colorful flowers and their seeds, such as ornamental corn, sunflowers, and Job's tears plants. But rose-petal beads, with their sweet, mild fragrance, have always been a great favorite. Once these were much in demand for rosaries as well as necklaces, and very lovely examples were produced with contrasting mountings of either gold or silver. Here is how the beads were made.

Rose beads for a rosary. In an enamel pan, heat 1 cup of uniodized salt with one heaping cup of rose petals firmly packed. When this has been mashed together, stir in ½ cup of water. Add a drop of oil paint for any desired color, or omit if natural color is preferred. Reheat over an asbestos plate, stirring constantly until smooth. Roll out to ¼-inch thickness, cut with a thimble, and roll each bead in the palm of the hand until smooth and round. As each bead is rolled, string it on #24 or #26 florist's wire. Hang in a dark place until dry, then string on dental floss. Move the beads occasionally while drying to keep them from sticking.

Rose beads for a necklace. Put 1¾ cups of flour and 4 tablespoons of salt into a bowl and add a little water to make a smooth dough. Into this press 3 cups of rose petals that have been finely chopped. Flour a bread-board and roll the dough to about ¼-inch thickness. Use a thimble to cut the dough. Roll each circle in the palm of the hand to form a smooth bead. Follow above directions for stringing and drying. When stringing, add a crystal, gold, or silver bead after each rose bead.

A drop or two of rose extract or rose oil will add a delightful fragrance to either rosary or necklace.

Plants with Party Tricks

Among the amusing flowers of the plant world is the mouse plant *(Arisarum proboscideum)*. This useful, low-growing ground cover is related to the arum lily. The flower is in the form of a single spathe, which by some freak of nature takes almost exactly the shape of the rounded hindquarters of a tiny mouse with a long curling tail. Hold it in your hand as if it were a mouse; friends will probably reward you with gratifying squeals.

Silene armeria is one of the catchflies, related to the campions. The stems are divided into sections by nodes; below each is a dark, sticky patch. And they do actually catch flies and many other tiny insects.

Gayfeather *(Liatris pycnostachya)* is an upside-down plant. Unlike other flowers that grow in a spike, this herbaceous perennial blooms from the top first, the opening buds gradually working their way down the stem.

An easy perennial to grow is *Gaura lindheimeri,* four feet high, which when in flower looks like a cloud of white butterflies. The flowers, which have pink buds, have only four petals. Each petal spreads out like the wings of a butterfly, while the long stamens resemble antennae.

Dictamnus albus, the gas plant, gives off a volatile gas that on a hot, still day can be ignited by a match held near it. It will flare for a moment without the plant suffering any damage.

Obedient plant *(Physostegia)* demonstrates its obedience when you touch the flowers. They can be moved, up, down, or sideways and will stay where they are put.

Sharing

Gardeners are generous people, and one of their greatest pleasures is sharing — an experience all the more delightful for both giver and receiver if the gift plant is unusual.

An unusual plant should be hard to find in the rank and file of nursery catalogs or garden stores, something not too well known, yet interesting and effective wherever it is planted. If the plant is easily grown and easily separated, so much the better.

Adonis amurensis, a very early-spring perennial, blooming sometimes before the snow has entirely melted, is just such a one. The feathery, much-divided foliage dies to the ground by late June and is forgotten after that; the following spring it peeps through even before the snowdrops with bright yellow, buttercup-like flowers. Divide the long, fibrous roots with a spade so that several buds are left on the clump of roots for starting the new plant.

Another gift possibility is the double-flowered bloodroot, a native American plant not, as yet, too well known. The large, white, double flowers appear in early spring not long after the adonis has bloomed. The plant grows well in shade.

Other good gift plants include *Narcissus asturiensis,* a miniature daffodil that flowers in the very early spring along with the snowdrops. A bulb that flowers in early summer is the golden garlic, *Allium moly.* It has yellow, star-like flowers in clusters up to three inches across. White-flowered scillas and grape hyacinths or truly white violets are also good conversation pieces, and these, too, increase rapidly, making them ideal for sharing.

Terrariums

Terrariums fascinate and are not at all difficult to care for. You can make one in a glass container (almost any size) that closes with a lid.

Mix up soil for the planting base. A good combination for foliage plants and a general woodsy scene is two parts peat moss, one part perlite, two parts reasonably decent garden soil (or potting soil), and one part sand. You can buy a mix from a nursery and adjust according to the kinds of plants you will be growing.

Clean your container thoroughly. Scrub, rinse, and air if it has been used before. Put down the bottom layer of an inch or so of moist perlite (the exact depth depends on the proportions of the container). Sprinkle a thin layer of charcoal on top of the perlite. Add the soil mixture and shape the basic land construction with hills, valleys, or gentle slopes.

Tentatively place the plants in the terrarium to make sure that the living design is effective. Then plant your miniature garden. In large containers, you can sink the pots to their rims. In smaller terrariums, either unpot the new plants and shake their old soil loose, or set them in the new soil and tamp it around to the same level as the pot soil. Or tap the plant loose from its pot and plant the entire earth ball. The choice depends on the quality of the original pot soil and the individual plant's sensitivity to transplanting.

Plant ferns and small evergreen seedlings for the taller growth of the terrarium. Ivy, moss, and lichens are also attractive. For a grasslike "carpet" effect, plant partridgeberry. Place each plant carefully in the soil with enough space between plants to allow for growth. Set the completed terrarium in a light place, but not where sun will strike it. With the glass container closed, this "balanced terrarium" preserves temperature and moisture inside. Open the lid if the glass clouds with moisture.

Victorian Bouquet Plantings

The Victorians were lavish with flowers. They planted large formal bedding gardens for viewing and for cutting, and grew quantities of flowers that they arranged in huge bouquets of many varieties. Many gardeners are now copying the Victorian-bouquet effect with living flowers, by mixing many plants in one planting container for a full summer of floral abundance.

Choose flowers of different shapes, sizes, and forms. Arrange so that tall plants are surrounded by less stately plants. Fill out with varieties that will tumble over the side of the hanging basket or planting container. Flowers growing like this create their own sense of compatibility and usually grow well together.

Choose a container with ample volume for supporting the growth of 10 or 12 plants of four or five varieties at a minimum. To keep the plants growing well, give them plenty of water and fertilizer, or use soluble fertilizer as you water.

A wave of nostalgia is sweeping the country, and this is making Victorian gardens very popular. Victorian flower arrangements, too, are seen more often.

Plants to include in your Victorian bouquet might be: pansies, browallia, *Felicia amelloides,* verbena, lobelia, dianthus, zinnias, begonias, ageratum, marigolds, vinca, torenia, petunia, impatiens, coleus, and cineraria. For height, choose from such winning plants as snapdragons, geraniums, Shasta daisies, and the taller varieties of African marigold.

Victorian Gardens

The Victorian-style garden is again becoming popular. This style provides for a garden of seclusion and natural beauty. Such gardens include lawn shrubbery (including the exotics), terrace walks, and even a conservatory if room permits.

Weather Forecasters

Old sayings or clues from nature often contain truths. Signs of a hard winter include: unusually large crops of nuts or acorns, heavy moss on the north side of trees, sap of maple and sassafras going down early in the fall, leaves of grapes turning yellow early in the season, and thick husks on the ears of corn.

When the flowers of scarlet pimpernel close during the day, it was believed to be a sign of rain. For this reason the plant also became known as poor man's-weatherglass.

Mushrooms and toadstools are said to be more numerous before a rain.

If the down flies off dandelions when there is no wind, it is a sign that rain is on its way.

Scientists are studying plants in areas known to be earthquake-prone, believing that certain plants indicate by their behavior when tremors are impending.

Plants and People

Allergy Sufferers

Linda Alpert developed an allergy-free demonstration garden outside the Tucson Medical Center's Allergic Clinic. Her garden shows that many attractive plants can be grown in desert areas without contributing to the pollen count. In addition, the plants she chose take very little water once established. Recommended trees include desert willow *(Chilopsis linearis)* and the lysiloma, sometimes known as the fern of the desert. Both are lacy-looking with attractive flowers and grow to about 25 feet high.

Cassia, jojoba, and Texas ranger *(Leucophyllum)* are among the shrubs of choice. Flowering ground covers include the desert primrose *(Oenothera* species) and desert verbena *(Verbena wrightii)*. For flowers almost year-round, there is blackfoot daisy *(Melampodium leucanthum)*. As might be expected, there is also an assortment of cacti, agaves, and yuccas, many of which are gorgeous in blossom.

Businesses

Increasingly business offices are making use of green plants. Professional space planners and interior designers are entering the picture. Their first concern is function and efficiency, but they are making very effective use of healthy, thriving plants to soften the lines of functional architecture and, at the same time, subtly direct traffic, diffuse sound, or screen certain areas.

Selecting the wrong plants can be an expensive mistake, so consulting an interior landscape specialist is often money well spent. It may be best to let the specialist not only provide the plants but maintain them as well.

For the small office, the tried-and-true sansevieria, rubber plant, cacti, African violets, and ivies are good choices.

GEORGE WASHINGTON CARVER

Jerry Baker didn't originate the idea of talking to plants; George Washington Carver did, and went him one better. Farmers' wives brought Carver their ailing houseplants. He cared for them tenderly and sang to them. During the day he would take them out to "play in the sun." When he returned them to their owners he would tell them gently, "All flowers talk to me and so do hundreds of little living things in the woods. I learn what I know by watching and loving everything."

As a botanist and chemist, Carver (1864–1943) is best known for the range of uses he found for the peanut, but he has many other achievements to his credit. From the leaves, roots, stems, flowers, and fruits of various plants he coaxed 536 separate dyes that could be used to color wood, cotton, linen, silk, and even leather. Forty-nine of them were produced from the scuppernong grape alone!

Children

Teach your children the principles of gardening. These may well be some of the most important skills they will ever learn. To start, keep things simple. Let children grow the veggies and flowers they like. You might even buy them some started plants to ensure the success that builds confidence in growing things. Counsel and encourage, aid and comfort, but don't do their work. And praise their efforts, especially when vegetables or flowers are brought to the table for the rest of the family to enjoy.

Hospital Patients

Sending cut flowers to hospital patients recovering from surgery is a thoughtful gesture, but, according to a British medical journal, it may lead to possible infection. A concentration of dangerous bacteria may grow in vases within one hour after flowers are put in water. And after three days, some of the bacteria are resistant to commonly used antibiotics. Flowers, the article continues, should be avoided in hospital units dealing with intensive care, burns, neurosurgery, and newborn babies.

Hunters

Some Native American hunters imitated the scent of the deer with roots and herbs. The roots of blue wood aster and others were used to make smoke to attract the deer so that they could be shot with bow and arrow. Other plants used to attract deer were large-leaved wild aster (root smoked);

Canada and Philadelphia fleabane (disk florets smoked); and swamp persicaria (flowers smoked).

To sharpen their powers of observation, some hunters drank a tea made of heal-all root *(Prunella vulgaris)*.

Peoples of the Great Lakes region used botanicals for trapping and fishing. The smell of the root of alternate-leaved dogwood, boiled in water, was used to disguise muskrat traps. Mountain mint was used as a lure on traps to catch mink. Other fur-bearing animals were attracted by a wash made from the roots of kidney liverwort. Traps were boiled in maple bark to deodorize them so the animal would not detect the scent of previous victims.

The roots of wild sarsaparilla, mixed with roots of sweet-scented calamus, were boiled in water to make a lure for fish. Nets were then soaked in this brew; the scent would cling to the nets even after they were immersed for many hours.

Livestock Owners

Botanicals have been used to relieve domesticated animals of insects. Freshly cut pumpkin or squash leaves, a decoction of black walnut leaves soaked overnight, or an infusion of pignut leaves, rubbed on horses or cattle, will repel flies. Sometimes yellow wild indigo is placed on harnesses to keep horses free of flies. Concentrations of potato water rubbed on cattle, and clove on chickens and dogs, will repel lice, and a water solution of wormwood is used to bathe small animals and rid them of fleas. In Brazil, a tincture of cocoa leaves is considered a remedy for poultry lice, while cocoa shells, used as bedding for dogs, are credited with repelling fleas.

Persons under Stress

Gardening gives relief from tension, fears, and worries. Many people with stressful occupations — doctors, pilots, police officers, mothers of small children, teachers, and others — escape to their gardens whenever possible. Stresses disappear in the familiar tasks of preparing soil, planting, cultivating, and harvesting. The garden is a place of healing, not just a "factory" for producing food or flowers.

Persons with Disabilities

Gardening is wonderful therapy for the physically and mentally challenged. Children of all ages, including children with developmental delays, love to "make things grow." And wheelchair gardening can add interest to a life that may often be dull and monotonous. Even a box or raised bed of suitable height in which to grow flowers or vegetables (or both) can brighten the hours as seeds sprout, leaves unfold, and flowers bloom.

Senior Citizens

Some retired persons are born gardeners, some learn gardening after they retire, still others have gardening thrust upon them. Many retirees have moved to places where they must learn about new soils, new climates, and even new types of plants. For born gardeners the new environment presents an interesting challenge.

Those who have never gardened before become gardeners as the result of encouragement by neighbors, friends, and relatives. And then there are those who have had gardening thrust upon them as a way to pass the time, or because social pressure has demanded that they "keep the place looking nice." If you asked these seniors, they would probably say they garden because they like growing things, because it takes them outdoors and gives them exercise, or because it's something pleasant to do.

The handicapped, too, find a way.

Stamp Collectors

One of the most popular design topics for postage stamps the world over is flowers. Switzerland was the first country to bring the beauty of a flower to a postage stamp. For many years Switzerland issued a yearly colorful series showing its native flowers: edelweiss, alpine rose, slipper orchids, and many others. Inspired by the Swiss success, other nations including the United States followed suit; now almost every country that issues stamps has honored flowers on some of them.

Students

A survey has shown that the most popular plants for students are Swedish ivy, coleus, and spider plants.

Therapists

Many professional therapists are advocating gardening to alleviate mental depression. They believe that gardening is a time-proven way to stay "alive and well," both mentally and physically. If you know someone who is lonely or depressed, you might write on their behalf for information from the

American Horticultural Therapy Association (AHTA), 362A Christopher Avenue, Gaithersburg, MD 20879-3660, or call (301) 948-3010.

Travelers

To traveling gardeners: Resist the temptation to dig up unusual plants. Certain plants may not be shipped to certain states, and there is a sound reason for this.

Whenever a nonnative species, plant, animal, or insect is introduced to a new environment where natural controls are not present, big trouble may lie ahead. Given the right conditions, it can spread like wildfire. Just look at the case of the Mediterranean fruit fly, the present worry over fire ants in certain southern states, and the so-called "killer bees." The beautiful water hyacinth, now clogging southern waterways, is another case in point. By bringing plants home and possibly letting them escape from your garden, you may be creating a monster.

Wheelchair Gardeners

Choose easy-to-grow plants that need a minimum of repotting. Terrariums, midget gardens, dish gardens, and bonsai are all practical choices for wheelchair gardening.

FIRST GARDEN BOOK

Published in England in 1563, the first garden book, entitled *A Most Briefe and Pleasaunt Treatyse Teachynge Howe to Dress, Sowe and Set a Garden,* was written by Thomas Hyll of London. "If you want your Parsley to be crinkeld or curled," he writes, "bruise the seed, or when it comes up roll small weights on it, or else jump up and tread it down with your feet." Botany and medicine, which in Hyll's time were identical, were just beginning to free themselves from the influence of superstition and witchcraft — influences that are frequently evident in Hyll's book.

From it we learn much about gardens at the time of Queen Elizabeth I. They were laid out formally with arbors and trellises. Mazes and knot gardens were popular, and often wells were included "for water is a great nourisher of herbs." Beds were raised for drainage, and walks were sanded "lest by rayne or shower the earth should cleave and clogge on thy fete."

Plants of the North

Akpik, Appleberry, Cloudberry, Salmonberry *(Rubus chamaemorus)*
This perennial sends out erect shoots from a creeping rootstock. Its flowers are solitary and its terminal leaves have three to five rounded lobes with toothed edges. The fruit is red when unripe, amber color when mature. In the fall it is collected by native people, who store large quantities for winter use. The berries are eaten like strawberries with sugar and cream or used in pie or shortcake. The berries are very high in vitamin C and if frozen will retain much of their nutrient value.

Anemone, Narcissus-flowered *(Anemone narcissiflora)*
The anemone grows in open meadows, along hillsides, and on alpine tundra. Its flowers appear in clusters at the top of the stem, with the white petals often being tinged with blue on the back. The early-spring growth on the upper end of the root is eaten by Aleutian Island natives and has a waxy, mealy texture and taste. *Note:* Some members of this family contain the alkaloid anemonine, which causes irritation and inflammation in sheep that feed on it.

Asparagus, Beach *(Salicornia pacifica standley)*
The stem is smooth, fleshy, and jointed, with opposite branches. The inconspicuous flowers are usually three, sunk into the fleshy hollow of the thickened upper joints. The plant grows on sea beaches in southeastern Alaska around Prince of Wales Island and Ketchikan. It is available in summer. When young, plants may be used in salads or for pickles.

Brook Saxifrage, Wild Cucumber *(Saxifraga punctata)*

The flowering stalk, 4 to 20 inches high, is hairy and leafless. Small flowers with five white or purplish petals form headlike or flattened open clusters at the top of the stem. Found in moist, rocky, shady places along rivulets, roadsides, rocky cliffs, and gulches throughout southeastern Alaska, the Gulf Coast, and westward on the Alaskan Peninsula, leaves for salad are collected in spring before the plant flowers and are a good source of vitamin C.

Bumblebee Plant, Woolly Lousewort *(Pedicularis lanata)*

This perennial flowers in spikes that are pink to rose, although occasionally they may be white. The entire plant except the lower leaves is densely gray and woolly. It is common on the tundras of the high mountains and in the Bering Sea district. Flowers are collected in June by the natives around Cape Prince of Wales and Shishmaref. Water is added and the flowers allowed to ferment. The root is also edible, and may be gathered in the fall and prepared by boiling or roasting.

Buttercup, Pallas, Kapugachat *(Ranunculus pallasii schlecht)*

This pretty plant, a native of Alaska, is found growing in the saturated sphagnum moss at the shallow edges of tundra lakes and ponds. The natives of the lower Kuskokwim Valley use the young, tender, succulent shoots, which are available in spring and autumn. They must be cooked before eating to drive off the poisonous anemenol contained in the plant.

Chive, Wild *(Allium schoenoprasum)*

This edible perennial reproduces by small bulbs and seeds. The narrow, hollow leaves grow to a foot long. The flowers cluster in a rose-purple umbel, or head, at the top of the stem. Wild chives are found in interior Alaska and southward. Cut leaves are used as a substitute for salad onions.

Coltsfoot *(Petasites frigidus)*

The tawny-colored flowers, appearing before the leaves expand, are not showy. The leaves are palmate or somewhat triangular in shape, green, shiny above and felty beneath, and may become extremely large. Widespread, the plant is usually found on tundra. The young leaves are collected and mixed with other greens. Mature leaves are sometimes used to cover berries and other greens stored in kegs for winter use.

Cowslip, Marsh Marigold (*Caltha palustris*)

The plant is found in marshy places along creek beds and ditches, in swamps and wet meadows. The large plant, *C. asarifolia,* is abundantly found in southeastern Alaska and the coastal areas of the Gulf of Alaska westward to the Aleutians. A much smaller and less leafy plant, *C. artica,* is found throughout the Yukon and Tanana River basins. The bright yellow flower may be borne singly or in clusters. The leaves and thick, fleshy, smooth, slippery stems are best when young and tender before the flowers appear. The raw leaves contain the poison helleborin, which is destroyed in cooking. The roots are long and white. When boiled, the usual method of preparation, they look somewhat like sauerkraut.

Dock, Arctic, Sourdock, Wild Spinach (*Rumex*)

The flowers are green or tinged with purple, numerous, and mostly crowded in panicled racemes. The plant grows in wet, marshy places along riverbanks in Canada and Alaska. Its young tender leaves, an excellent source of vitamins A and C, make an excellent salad green and cooked vegetable.

Etak, Eetaht, Tall Cotton Grass (*Eriophorum augustifolium*)

The flower heads of this perennial develop into 2 to 12 nodding heads of white, silky bristles called cotton by Alaskans. Etak is found on tundra bogs and wet roadsides. In autumn tundra mice cache the underground stem for winter use. Native Alaskans call these underground stems mouse nuts and sometimes eat them with seal oil.

Indian Rice, Chocolate Lily, Kamchatka Lily
(*Fritillaria camchatcensis*)

This perennial plant has a simple stem, one to two feet, arising from bulbs with thick scales. The flowers are one to six, large, nodding, bell-like, dark wine color — often almost black — tinged with greenish yellow outside, and have three petals. The bulb of large scales is subtended by numerous ricelike bulblets. The plant grows in open coastal meadows in southeastern Alaska, the Gulf of Alaska coast, and north to Talkeetna, the Alaska Peninsula, Kodiak Island, the Aleutian Islands, and the Bristol Bay area.

Bulbs are dug in the fall; they are then dried and used in fish and meat stews or pounded into flour. They are used extensively by natives of southeastern Kodiak and the Aleutians.

Garden Plans

In this chapter you will find a number of plans for creating gardens that show-case flowers. Feel free to depart from these plans as much as you wish, to make the garden truly your own inspiration.

The Fragrant Evening Garden

At night, when the moon lights the garden, the gaudy garden colors disappear and leave only brilliant white and pale pastel flowers to attract the eye. Then come the sweet fragrances to refresh us. Gardens are sweetest when the air is mild and moist; in heat and drought fragrant ethers are appreciably lessened. A frost will also set fragrance free, as does a shower of rain. The perfume of a plant is not always in its flowers. It may be in the root, seeds, bark, gum or oils, leaves, or stalks. When we are tired at end of day, it is a real pleasure to enter-tain friends or just sit quietly and enjoy the fragrance of our evening garden.

Cactacea. There are a number of genera among the cacti that have fragrant flowers and one of the sweetest is the night-blooming cereus *(Epiphyllum oxypetalum),* giving unforgettable pleasure on the night that it blooms.

Calonyction aculeatum (**moonflower**). This strong-growing vine is a must for the evening garden. Its fragrant, pearly white, wide-faced, trumpet-shaped blooms are a wonderful conversation piece as they spin open evening after evening, spilling their lemon-scented fragrance on the evening air.

Cestrum nocturnum (**night jasmine**). Hardy in the far South, elsewhere as a greenhouse plant. This 6- to 9-foot West Indian shrub has insignificant flowers in the leaf axils, which produce an evening fragrance out of all pro-portion to their size.

Dianthus **sp.** (**carnation**). The very word carnation or pink connotes fra-grance. It's wonderful for an evening garden as a terrace edging plant.

Hesperus matronalis (**sweet rocket**). Sweetest at night, this common and easily grown plant should be in every evening garden.

Hosta plantaginea (**plantain lily**). This was a delightful feature of our great-grandmothers' gardens. The large white flowers with their distinctive fragrance make it "stand out" literally and figuratively.

Linnaea borealis (**twinflower**). This flower is sweetly fragrant but needs special treatment in acid soil.

Lilium species (**lily**). Fragrant lilies will dramatize your evening garden.

Lippa citriodora (**lemon verbena**). This delightful, lemon-scented shrub has unremarkable flowers but its leaves are lovely to pinch and smell.

Lonicera japonica (**honeysuckle**). There is no aroma lovelier than that of the Japanese honeysuckle at night. It is a rampant grower, however, and may become a pest.

Lychnis alba (vespertina) (**evening or white campion**). This easy-to-grow member of the Catchfly family has a most delightful fragrance.

Mathiola bicornis (**stock**). This night-scented stock is powerfully fragrant at night. It has no floral value, however, and is best sown in patches in open garden spots.

Nicotiana affinis (**flowering tobacco**). This plant has a bold habit of growth, pretty white flowers, and a lovely evening fragrance. Seek the older kinds.

Oenothera species (**evening primrose**). Nearly all members of this family open their flowers at night, but all are not night fragrant. *O. caespitosa* is one that is.

Petunia **hybrids.** Not many realize just how fragrant petunias are at night. The white and pale yellow varieties are attractive in the evening garden.

Polianthes tuberosa (**tuberose**). Grown for centuries in Mexico, and one of the most delightful of all sweet flowers, it needs a long growing season.

Ptelea trifoliata (**hop tree or water ash**). A sweet-scented shrub. It has a cloying sweetness when smelled close by but a nice fragrance if planted at some distance from the evening activity.

Reseda odorata (**sweet mignonette**). Every garden should have a small planting.

Rosa (**rose**). White and yellow roses are especially fragrant at night.

Schizopetalon walkeri. This plant has no common name. It is a low-growing annual with erect racemes of fringed white flowers that emit a delicate, almondlike fragrance in the evening.

We'd love your thoughts . . .

Your reactions, criticisms, things you did or didn't like about this Storey Book. Please use space below (or write a letter if you'd prefer — even send photos!) telling how you've made use of the information . . . how you've put it to work . . . the more details the better!

Thanks in advance for your help in building our library of good Storey Books.

Book Title: _____

Purchased From: _____

Comments: _____

_____

_____

_____

_____

_____

_____

Pamela B. Art

President, Storey Books

Your Name: _____
(Please Print)

Mailing Address: _____

E-mail Address: _____

You have my permission to quote from my comments and use these quotations in ads, brochures, mail, and other promotions used to market Storey Books.

To order this book or any Storey title CALL 800-441-5700 or visit our web site at www.storey.com

Signed _____ Date _____

e-mail: feedback@storey.com   website: www.storey.com   PRINTED IN THE USA

8/02

From: _____

Thymus serphyllum (**creeping thyme**). The creeping, carpeting kinds of thyme provide fragrance underfoot and are especially nice to plant near the barbecue.

Green Aromatica. While most herbs emit odors only when crushed, they are attractive protective plants and are easily grown with night-scented flowers. And they are handy to have nearby to use fresh to season outdoor cookery or salads. Guests enjoy choosing their favorites. Here are some outstanding examples: Apple mint, catmint, costmary, dill, hyssop, lavender, marjoram, peppermint, rosemary, rue, sage, spearmint, summer savory, sweetbrier, sweet geranium, tansy, tarragon, thyme, and winter savory.

Sweet-scented trees include frangipani, honey locust, hop tree, juniper, linden, magnolia, sassafras, and sweet gum.

Plan for a succession of bloom. Honeysuckle blooms first in my area, followed by moonflower. Try out, experiment with various kinds of plants, change the annuals from time to time to find out what you like best and what does well for you. Where plants are placed may make a difference. Hop tree and tuberose may be overpowering close up but enjoyable at a suitable distance.

The Fragrant Evening Garden

The Edible Flower Garden

Plants for the Edible Flower Garden

PLANT	PART USED
Artichoke, globe	flower buds
Borage	flowers, leaves
Broccoli	flower heads
Cabbage, flowering	salad, kraut
Camomile	blossoms
Capers	flower buds
Carnation	blossoms, petals
Cauliflower	flower head
Chives	flower heads, salad, float in soup
Chrysanthemum	petals
Cowslip (American)	buds
Dandelion	buds, leaves
Daylily	buds, leaves, roots
Dill	flower heads, seeds, pickling
Elder	flowers, wine
Honey locust	flowers followed by pods
Garlic	tiny bulbs suitable for flavoring follow flowers in heads
Heliotrope	blossoms
Lavender	blossoms
Lotus	petals, tender young leaves, seeds
Marigold	petals
Mint (spearmint or peppermint)	sprigs used in mint julep
Orange flowers	brandy
Periwinkle	flowers
Plum blossom	buds used for pickling
Primrose	blossoms, petals
Rose geranium	leaves in preserves and canning fruits
Rose	buds, petals, hips, candied petals
Tulip	blossoms used as containers for salads
Violet	blossoms, leaves; candy blossoms

The Butterfly Garden

Unlike bees, butterflies can see the whole spectrum of colors but prefer the brilliantly colored, deep pink, red, scarlet, bright blue, and usually those that are very fragrant.

The butterfly garden is one that must not be tamed. Just place it at the edge of your property in full sunlight, and let it find its own wild, natural look. Most butterfly plants are perennial or self-seeding and will be a permanent sanctuary for butterfly caterpillars.

Key:

Wildflowers

1 Butterfly weed	3 Indigobush	5 Shrubby cinquefoil
2 Milkweed	4 Dogbane	6 Cutleaf coneflower

Garden Flowers

7 Honeysuckle	10 Lantana	13 Columbine (also
8 Verbena	11 Butterfly bush	wild columbine)
9 Hibiscus	12 Violets	14 Larkspur

15 Morning glory
16 Frog-fruit
17 Blue-eyed grass
18 Lemon mint
19 Salvia
20 Verbena (also wild
     verbena)
21 Penstemon
22 Spring beauty

Insect-Repellent Companion Plants
(many are also breeding plants)

23 Ornamental allium
24 Four-o'clock
25 Milkweed
26 Parsley
27 Dill
28 Rue
29 Fennel
30 Anise
31 Flax
32 Wormwood
33 Borage
34 Petunia
35 Larkspur
36 Geranium
37 Nasturtium
38 Feverfew
39 Nettle
40 Tansy
41 Marigold
42 Garlic

Butterfly Breeding Plants

43 Black swallowtail —
     parsley, dill, parsnips
44 Blue swallowtail —
     Dutchman's-pipe,
     wild ginger
45 Tiger swallowtail —
     tulip tree, birch, wild
     cherry, apple, ash,
     poplar
46 Cabbage butterfly
     — cabbage (unde-
     sirable)
47 Gossamer-winged
     orange tip —

     Mustard family
48 The sulphurs —
     wild senna, alfalfa,
     buffalo clover
49 The nymphs — frit-
     illaries, angel-wings,
     and sovereigns —
     elm, willow, poplar,
     nettle
50 The crescent spots
     — snakehead or
     turtlehead (Chelone
     glabra)

51 The emperors —
     goatweed, hack-
     berry, and various
     grasses
52 The heliconians
     (zebra butterflies)
     — passionflowers
53 The milkweed but-
     terflies (monarchs)
     — milkweed
54 The coppers —
     alder leaves

Natural Insecticides for Butterfly Flowers

55 Leaves, stems, and
     spent flowers of
     flowering tobacco
     (Nicotiana)
56 Elderberry tea
     against aphids
57 Wormwood against
     slugs and snails
58 Citrus peels: Chop
     in blender with
     water — good
     against various
     insects
59 Garlic, onions, hot
     pepper: Chop and
     blend with water

Trees and Bushes Used for Breeding

60 Sassafras
61 Spicebush
62 Tulip tree
63 Birch
64 Wild cherry
65 Apple
66 Poplar
67 Ash
68 Pawpaw
69 Alder
70 Peach

The Bee Garden

One of the most charming of old-time gardens combined beauty and utility. Until rather recent times almost everyone who had a bit of land was a beekeeper. The price of honey today may be an incentive to again keep bees to enjoy one of nature's most healthful foods. My husband had kept bees as a boy in New York and when we married and bought our first home we established two hives at the south end of our garden, where they lived happily and prospered.

Bee plants are both beautiful and useful. Beees are not especially attracted to fragrant flowers but have a marked preference for those of blue color. Bee garden flowers should include some for honey and some for pollen, for easily available sources of pollen are second only to an abundant supply of nectar.

It is best to bathe before working with bees; sweat infuriates them.

Bee masters of old recommended drinking a cup of good beer before going among the bees.

Working with the bees should be done gently, calmly, but with decision.

"If by accident," instructs an old beekeeper, "a bee buzzes about your face, thrust your face amongst a passel of Boughs or Herbs, and he will desert you."

In her book *The Fragrant Garden,* Louise Beebe Wilder says, "Indeed, if you go your way among bees anointed with the bitter juices of the Herb o' Grace you will be quite safe, for no bee will come near you."

As previously mentioned, bees are not especially attracted to fragrant flowers but apiarian lore of the ancients lists a number of plants used by bee-keepers to attract bees by rubbing the inside of the hive:

Juniper	Bee balm *(Melissa)*
Fennel	Lime flowers
Hyssop	Anise

Bees seldom notice the sweet-scented blossoms of the lilac, heliotrope, or rose.

Bees like flowers on which they can land and poke around. They have good color vision, preferring blue and yellow. They cannot see red but they can see ultraviolet. Using an ultraviolet filter to photograph bee flowers allows us to see them as the bee sees them. A flower that appears one color to us may have additional markings, nectar guides, in the ultraviolet. Color changes on plants "help" the bees save time by showing them which flowers are older and have probably already had their nectar taken. For instance, the blossoms of the horse chestnut, catalpa, or golden currant turn from yellow to pink as they age. Bees prefer to visit the fresh, yellow-centered flowers.

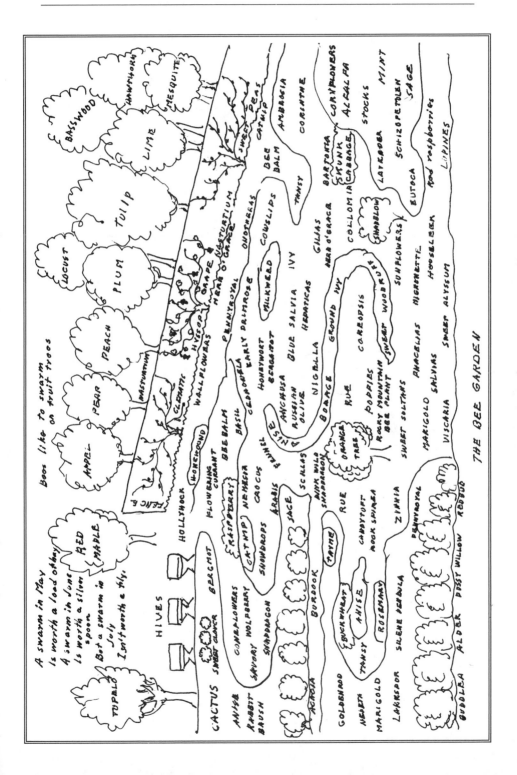

THE BEE GARDEN

- Honey is not "just honey." Depending on the plant variety of the bees' feeding area, it can have many flavors.
- The most prized honey in the United States is clover honey; second is the product of orchards.
- Honey gathered later in the season is usually darker in color and stronger in flavor.
- Orange blossom honey is fragrant and delicious and highly prized.
- Alfalfa honey is mildly spicy.
- Buckwheat honey is very fragrant.
- Mignonette honey has an exquisite bouquet.
- Honey most esteemed by the ancients was made from lime flowers.
- Aromatic nectar comes from the blossoms of thyme, lavender, and rosemary.
- In France, sanfoin honey is preferred and is made from the fodder plant of that name.
- In Spain, rosemary and orange flower honey, along with peach honey, are the favorite flavors.
- Heather honey is a bright, warm amber with an unusual flavor.
- The most prized honey in Germany, called Echter Honig, is harvested from the pine forests to delight epicures. It is nearly black.
- In Portugal the bees feed on the vine flowers, which produce a delicate and fragrant honey.
- The Syrians prize honey made from lavender, wild acacia, cactus, and wild thyme.

Early Plants

Snowdrop	Early primrose	Red maple catkins
Crocus	Cowslip	Redbud
Scilla	Catkins of alder and	Shadblow
Hepatica	pussywillow	

Later-Flowering Trees

Apple	Locust	Orange trees
Pear	Basswood	(California)
Peach	Tulip tree (especially	Palmetto (Florida)
Plum	fine honey)	Tupelo
Hawthorn	Lime tree	

Bee Sting Remedies: Rub the Wound

Bee balm	Hollyhock	Burdock
Marigold	Ivy	Rue

Companion Herbs for Bee Flowers
(many of which are also nectar plants)

Horehound	Lavender	Winter savory
Pennyroyal	Rosemary	Summer savory
Aromatic tansy	Borage	Basil
Mint (all mints)	Sweet woodruff	Anise
Catnip	Bergamot	
Thyme	Sage	

Plants Reputed Poisonous or Undesirable to Bees

Mountain laurel	Andromedes	Flowering tobacco
Snow-on-the-	Pieris	Wild aster
mountain	Rhododendron	Box

Plants of Offensive Odor

Leek	Onion	Garlic

Wild Honey Plants

New Mexico privet	Pink wild snapdragon	Salvia
Mesquite	Bee balm	Rabbitbrush
Wolfberry	Rocky Mountain bee	Skunk cabbage (the
Russian olive	plant	odor does not
Rock spiraea	Phacelias	flavor the honey)

Nectar Flowers

Buckwheat	Cedroneda	Ambrosia
Clover, white	Nepeta	Nemexia
Clover, sweet	Mints	Coreopsis
Basswood	Thymes	Buddleia
Tupelo	Violet	Zinnia
Raspberry	Pinks	Collomia
Milkweed	Broom	Candytuft
Goldenrod	Heather	Viscaria
Alfalfa	Cornflower	Eutoca
Acacia	Nigella	Gilia
Catnip	Blue salvia	Bartonia
Mignonette	Phacelias	Lupine
Lime blossoms	Sweet alyssum	Cerinthe
Labiate tribe	Sweet pea	Flowering currant
Ground ivy	Sweet sultan	Snapdragon
Archangel (angelica)	Arabis	

This small hummingbird garden has a selection of colorful plants and protective herbs.

The Hummingbird Garden

Here's a list of plants hummingbirds love.

Anise
Artemisia
Azalea
Basswood
Bean, scarlet runner
Bearberry
Beardtongue, dwarf
Bee balm
Bellflower
Betony, wood
Bluebell, Virginia
Blueberry, highbush

Blueberry, lowbush
Borage
Bottlebrush
Bouncing Bet
Bridgesii
Buckeye, dwarf
Buckeye, flame
Butterfly bush
Campion, Mexican
Canna
Cardinal flower
Catnip

Century plant
Chestnut, red horse
Columbine
Coralbells
Cornflower
Cotoneaster
Currant, red flowering
Daylily
Eucalyptus
Fennel
Feverfew
Figwort

Firecracker
Fireweed
Flax
Flowering quince
Four-o'clock
Foxglove
Fuchsia
Geranium
Gilia
Gladiolus
Gooseberry, wild
Great Solomon's-seal
Hamelis, scarlet
Hibiscus
Hollyhock
Honeysuckle
Honeysuckle, cape
Hummingbird trumpet
Hyssop, wild
Indian paintbrush — seed
   helped to germinate by
   blue grama grass.
Iris
Jasmine
Jewelweed
Lantana
Larkspur
Lilac
Lily
Loquat

Lupine
Maranta
Matrimony vine
Mexican mint marigold —
   exudes a repellent from
   the root system of
   greater potency than
   other marigold species
Milkweed
Mint
Monkeyflower
Morning glory
Nasturtium
Nettle — increases
   potency and vigor in
   other plants nearby, also
   repels aphids and plant
   lice
Nettle, scarlet
Nettle, scarlet hedge
New Jersey tea
Ocotillo
Onion — ornamental
   alliums, also
Painted cup
Pelargonium
Penstemon
Petunia
Plumbago, cape
Poinciana, flame fence

Poinciana, royal
Poppy, Oriental
Prickly pear
Ragged robin
Rattlesnake root
Red-hot poker
Sage, autumn
Salmonberry
Scabious
Scarlet-bugler
Siberian pea tree
Skyrocket
Snapdragon
Sourwood
Spiderflower
Star-glory, scarlet
Sweet William
Tansy — controls ants
Thimbleberry
Thistle
Tigerlily
Toadflax
Tree tobacco
Trumpet creeper
Waxmallow
Weigelia
Wormwood
Yarrow — helps seeds
   germinate, protective
   against insect pests

Hummingbird enemies are few — no other bird can catch them. They may be occasionally caught in a spiderweb or grabbed by a frog. Weather may sometimes be a danger.

The Witch's Garden of Companion Medicinal Plants

The witch's garden of companion medicinal plants is in the form of a pentagram. The pentagram is believed to be a weapon of power. When one point projects upward, the pentagram may be used to invoke good influences and banish evil ones.

A Garden for the Blind

Recreational gardens for the sight-impaired are being built in many areas where there is a sufficiently large population to enjoy them. But often it is possible for a caregiver to plant just a few fragrant roses, iris, daylilies, and other easily grown plants for just one blind person to enjoy. If the project is to be enjoyed by many, however, thought should be given to providing handrails or ropes, nonslip material for paths, benches for resting, and a drinking fountain.

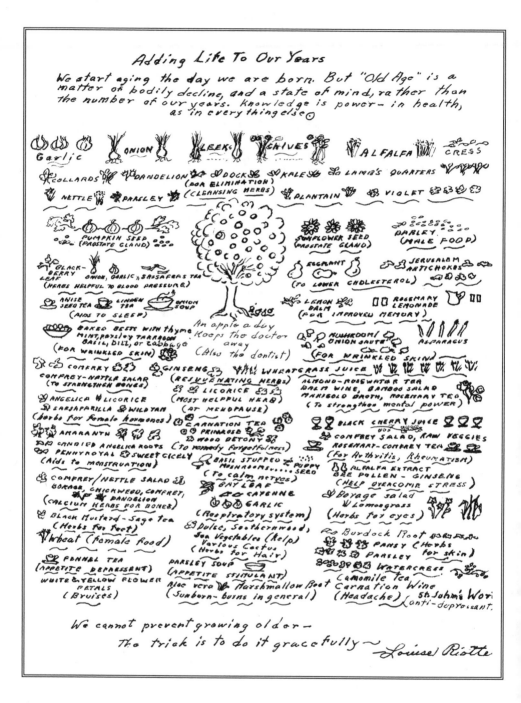

Adding Life To Our Years

We start aging the day we are born. But "Old Age" is a matter of bodily decline, and a state of mind, rather than the number of our years. Knowledge is power – in health, as in everything else⊙

Garlic   ONION   LEEK   CHIVES   ALFALFA   CRESS

COLLARDS   DANDELION   DOCK   KALE   LAMB'S QUARTERS
(FOR ELIMINATION)

NETTLE   PARSLEY   (CLEANSING HERBS)   PLANTAIN   VIOLET

PUMPKIN SEED
(PROSTATE GLAND)

SUNFLOWER SEED
(PROSTATE GLAND)

BARLEY
(MALE FOOD)

BLACK-
BERRY
LEAF   ONION, GARLIC, SASSAFRAS TEA
(HERBS HELPFUL TO BLOOD PRESSURE)

EGGPLANT
(TO LOWER CHOLESTEROL)

JERUSALEM
ARTICHOKES

ANISE
SEED TEA   LINDEN
TEA   ONION
SOUP
(AIDS TO SLEEP)

LEMON
BALM   ROSEMARY
LEMONADE
(FOR IMPROVED MEMORY)

BAKED BEETS WITH THYME
MINT, PARSLEY TARRAGON
BASIL, DILL, or CABBAGE
(FOR WRINKLED SKIN)

An apple a day
Keeps the doctor
away
(Also the dentist)

MUSHROOM/
ONION SAUTÉ   ASPARAGUS
(FOR WRINKLED SKIN)

COMFREY   GINSENG   WHEATGRASS JUICE
COMFREY-NETTLE SALAD   (REJUVENATING HERBS)
(TO STRENGTHEN BONES)   LICORICE
ANGELICA LICORICE   (MOST HELPFUL HERB)
SARSAPARILLA WILD YAM   (AT MENOPAUSE)
(herbs for female hormones)   CARNATION TEA
AMARANTH   PRIMROSE
CANDIED ANGELICA ROOTS   WOOD BETONY
PENNYROYAL SWEET CICELY   (To remedy forgetfulness)
(Aids to menstruation)

ALMOND-ROSEWATER TEA
BALM WINE, BAMBOO SALAD
MARIGOLD BROTH, ROSEMARY TEA
(To strengthen mental power)

BLACK CHERRY JUICE
COMFREY SALAD, RAW VEGGIES
ROSEMARY-COMFREY TEA
(For Arthritis, Rheumatism)

BASIL STUFFED   POPPY
MUSHROOMS..... SEED
(To calm nerves)

COMFREY/NETTLE SALAD
BORAGE, CHICKWEED, COMFREY,
DANDELION
(CALCIUM HERBS FOR BONES)

BAY LEAF
CAYENNE
GARLIC
(Respiratory system)

ALFALFA EXTRACT
BEE POLLEN - GINSENG
(HELP OVERCOME STRESS)

Borage salad
Lemongrass
(Herbs for eyes)

BLACK MUSTARD-SAGE TEA
(Herbs for feet)

Wheat (female food)

Dulse, Southernwood,
Sea Vegetables (help)
Various Cactus
(Herbs for Hair)

Burdock Root
PANSY (Herbs
for skin)
PARSLEY
WATERCRESS

FENNEL TEA
(APPETITE DEPRESSANT)
WHITE & YELLOW FLOWER
PETALS
(Bruises)

PARSLEY SOUP
(APPETITE STIMULANT)
Aloe vera   Marshmallow Root
(Sunburn- burns in general)

Camomile Tea
Carnation Wine
(Headache)   St. John's Wort
(anti-depressant)

We cannot prevent growing older –
The trick is to do it gracefully ~   Louise Riotte

Adding Life to Our Years

Plants for the Elderly

Anti-aging
Asparagus
Beets
Garlic
Mushrooms
Onion

Antidepressant
St.-John's-wort

Appetite depressants
Fennel tea

Appetite stimulant
Parsley soup

Arthritis, rheumatism
Black cherry juice
Comfrey salad
Raw vegetables
Rosemary/comfrey tea

Blood pressure
Blackberry leaf
Garlic soup
Onion soup
Sassafras

Bones
Comfrey/nettle salad
Calcium herbs
  Borage
  Chickweed
  Comfrey
  Dandelion

Brains, to improve
Almond, rose water
Balm wine
Bamboo salad
Marigold broth
Rosemary tea

Bruises
White and yellow
  flower petals

Burns
Aloe vera
Marshmallow root

Cholesterol (to lower)
Eggplant
Jerusalem artichoke

Colds, coughs
Angelica sweetmeats
Cayenne
Elecampane sweet-
  meats
Garlic soup
Garlicked beans
Rose-hip soup

Constipation
Garlic, onion
Leek, chives
Alfalfa, cress
Collards
Dandelion
Dock, kale
Lamb's-quarters
Nettle, parsley

Plantain, violet
Spinach

Dental problems
Apple eaten raw daily

Disease, to protect from
Garlic soup
Mallows

Eyes
Borage salad
Lemongrass

Feet
Black mustard
Mullein leaf

Female foods
Angelica
Wheat

Hair
Lemongrass
Sea vegetables (kelp)
Southernwood
Various cacti

Headache
Carnation wine

Heart, to improve
6 garlic cloves per
  week
9 onions per week

Hormones (female)

Angelica
Licorice
Sarsaparilla
Wild yam

Memory

Lemon balm
Rosemary lemonade

Male food

Barley

Menstrual

Amaranth
Candied angelica root
Pennyroyal
Sweet cicely

Menopause

Licorice

Muscle

Linden tisane
Sage
Wallflower

Nerves

Basil-stuffed mush-
    rooms
Poppyseed

Prostate

Pumpkin seed
Sunflower seed
Garlic soup

Rejuvenatives

Comfrey
Ginseng
Wheatgrass juice

Respiratory system

Bay leaf
Cayenne
Garlic

Sinus

Garlic soup
Steamed zucchini

Skin

Burdock root

Pansy
Parsley
Watercress
Cabbage

Sleep

Aniseed tea
Linden tea
Onion soup

Stress

Alfalfa extract
Bee pollen
Ginseng

Sunburn

Aloe vera
Marshmallow root
    (external use only)

Wrinkled skin

Baked beets
Mushroom/onion
    sauté
Steamed asparagus
Cabbage (Russian)

Use of herbs as alternative medicine is more widespread in England, Germany, and other foreign countries than in the United States. Much of what we use comes from Native Americans.

Adding Life to Our Years

Greetings to my fellow octogenarians — and good wishes to all you younger kids who hope to become one of us! As many of you know, I am 88 years old and confidently looking forward to the 21st century. How have I managed to get this far? For one thing, I picked the right ancestors; my mother lived to be 93. Even so, I could have muffed it if I had not taken care of my health. I enjoy life and eat anything I want to, including all garden vegetables enhanced by herbs, both in growing and in cooking.

Are any herbs especially helpful to the elderly? Yes, and two are at the top of my list — garlic and greens. Garlic is especially helpful to the cardiovascular and digestive systems. It is an anti-aging herb. It is antibacterial, antiseptic, bactericidal, a blood cleanser and purifier, lowers blood pressure, and is helpful in colds and coughs. It protects against many diseases. When I was a hospital volunteer I took a small clove of garlic each day, chopping it fine and swallowing it whole like a vitamin pill, followed by chewing a sprig of parsley or a bit of apple.

Garlic yogurt is helpful in cases of dysentery, herpes, indigestion, and itchy skin.

Greens of all kinds are particularly helpful in cleansing the system, so necessary to the aging body. These include alfalfa, cress, collards, dandelion, dock, kale, lamb's-quarters, nettle, parsley, plantain, and violet. Kelp, containing alginic acid, aids the excretion of lead from our bodies.

Herbs helpful to the prostate include pumpkin seed, sunflower seed, and garlic soup.

Herbs helpful to blood pressure are blackberry leaf, onion soup, garlic soup, and sassafras. The herb most helpful at time of menopause is licorice.

To lower cholesterol, take helpings of eggplant and Jerusalem artichoke.

Aids to sleep include aniseed tea, linden tea, and onion soup.

To improve memory, try lemon balm and rosemary lemonade. For wrinkles, try baked beets, mushroom/onion sauté, and steamed asparagus. Asparagus is also a laxative.

Beets are especially noted as an anti-aging food (they contain potassium good for the heart), boiled and seasoned with mint, parsley, tarragon, basil, or dill. They are good baked with a dressing of oil and lemon juice. Pickled beets are an old-time favorite of our ancestors.

One more thought. Elderly people need light — not direct sunlight, but filtered light. Far too many of us spend too much time indoors. We need to exercise in the cool of the morning or the evening.

Live well. Laugh often. Love much.

Suggested Reading

Clarkson, Rosetta. *Herbs, Their Culture and Uses.* Old Tappan, NJ: The Macmillan Publishing Co., 1990.

Gibbons, Euell. *Stalking the Wild Asparagus.* Chambersburg, PA: Alan C. Hood & Company, Inc., 1988.

— — —. *Stalking the Healthful Herbs.* Chambersburg, PA: Alan C. Hood & Company, Inc., 1989.

Harris, Charles. *Eat the Weeds.* New Canaan, CT: Keats Publishing, Inc., 1995.

Meyer, Clarence. *The Herbalist Almanac: Fifty Years of Herbal Knowledge.* Glenwood, IL: Meyerbooks, 1977.

Riotte, Louise. *Carrots Love Tomatoes.* Pownal, VT: Storey Communications, Inc., 1998.

— — —. *Catfish Ponds and Lily Pads.* Pownal, VT: Storey Communications, Inc., 1997.

— — —. *Successful Small Food Gardens.* Pownal, VT: Storey Communications, Inc., 1993.

Tompkins, Peter, and Christopher Bird. *The Secret Life of Plants.* New York: HarperCollins Publishers, Inc., 1989.

Wilder, Louise Beebe. *The Fragrant Garden.* Mineola, NY: Dover Publications, Inc., 1974.

Sources

Applewood Seed Company
5380 Vivian Street
Arvada, CO 80002
(303) 431-6383

Bluestone Perennials
7211 Middle Ridge Road
Madison, OH 44057
(800) 852-5243

Breck's
5623 N. Galena Road
Peoria, IL 61656
(800) 722-9069

Burgess Seed & Plant Co.
905 Four Seasons Road
Bloomington, IL 61701
(309) 663-9551

W. Atlee Burpee Seed Co.
300 Park Avenue
Warminster, PA 18974
(215) 674-4900

Dutch Gardens, Inc.
P.O. Box 200
Adelphia, NJ 07710
(800) 818-3861

Emlong Nurseries, Inc.
2671 West Marquette
Woods Road
Stevensonville, MI 49127
(616) 429-3431

Farmer Seed & Nursery
616 North Cedar
Owatonna, MN 55060
(507) 451-2363

Henry Field Seed & Nursery Co.
415 North Burnett
Shenandoah, IA 51602
(605) 665-9391

Garden Way Manufacturing Co.
1 Garden Way
Troy, NY 12180
(518) 391-7000
(tillers and composters)

Gurney Seed & Nursery
110 Capital Street
Yankton, SD 57079
(605) 665-1671

H.G. Hastings Nature & Garden Center
3920 Peach Tree Road NE
Atlanta, GA 30319
(404) 869-7447

House of Wesley
1704 Morrissey Drive
Bloomington, IL 61704
(309) 663-9551

J. L. Hudson, Seedsman
PO Box 1058
Redwood City, CA 94064
(mail order only, no phone calls)

Indiana Botanic Gardens
P.O. Box 5
Hammond, IN 46325
(219) 947-4040
(800) 644-8327

Jackson & Perkins
P.O. Box 1028
Medford, OR 97501
(800) 292-4769

Johnny's Selected Seeds
310 Foss Hill Road
Albion, ME 04910
(207) 437-9294

J.W. Jung Seed Company
335 S. High Street
Randolph, WI 53957
(414) 326-3121
(800) 247-5864

Kitazawa Seed Co.
1111 Chapman Street
San Jose, CA 95126
(408) 243-1330

**Lilypons Water
  Gardens**
P.O. Box 10
Buckeystown, MD
 21717-0010
(301) 874-5133

**Mellingers Nursery,
Inc.**
2310 W. South Range
 Road
North Lima, OH 44452
(330) 549-9861

Michigan Bulb Co.
1050 Waldorf NW
Grand Rapids, MI 49550
(616) 771-9500

**J.E. Miller Nurseries,
Inc.**
5060 W. Lake Road
Canandaigua, NY 14424
(716) 395-2674

Musser Forests, Inc.
P.O. Box 340
Indiana, PA 15701
(412) 465-5685

**Nichols Garden
  Nursery**
1190 N. Pacific Highway
 NE
Albany, OR 97321
(541) 928-9280

Novartis Seeds
P.O. Box 959
Minneapolis, MN 55440
(612) 593-7333

Park Seed
P.O. Box 46
Greenwood, SC 29647
(800) 845-3359

Plants of the Southwest
Route 6 Box 11-A
Santa Fe, NM 87501
(505) 471-2212
(800) 788-7333

**R.H. Shumway
  Seedsman**
P.O. Box 1
Graniteville, SC 29829
(803) 663-9771

Spring Hill Nurseries
6523 N. Galena Road
Peoria, IL 61601
(800) 582-8527

Stark Bros. Nurseries
Highway 54 West
Louisiana, MO 63353-
 0010
(800) 325-4180

Stokes Seeds, Inc.
P.O. Box 548
Buffalo, NY 14240
(716) 695-6980

Thompson & Morgan
P.O. Box 1308
Jackson, NJ 08527-0308
(800) 274-7333

Twilley Seed Co.
P.O. Box 65
Trevose, PA 19047
(215) 639-8800

Van Bourgondien Bros.
245 Farmingdale Road
Babylon, NY 11703
(516) 669-3500

**Van Ness Water
  Gardens**
2460 N. Euclid
Upland, CA 91786
(909) 982-2425

**Vermont Bean Seed
  Co.**
Garden Lane
Fair Haven, VT 05743
(802) 273-3400

Wayside Gardens
1 Garden Way
Hodges, SC 29695
(800) 845-1124

White Flower Farm
Route 63
Litchfield, CT 06759
(800) 503-9624

Wolfe Nursery
601 Dallas Drive
Denton, TX 76205
(817) 387-5262

Index

Page references in *italics* indicate illustrations; **bold** indicates charts.

Other Storey Titles You Will Enjoy

The Big Book of Gardening Secrets, by Charles W.G. Smith. Provides scores of professional secrets for growing better vegetables, herbs, fruits, and flowers. 352 pages. Paperback. ISBN 1-58017-000-5.

Bugs, Slugs, & Other Thugs, by Rhonda Massingham Hart. Suggests hundreds of ways to stop pests without risk to the user or the environment. 224 pages. Paperback. ISBN 0-88266-664-9.

Carrots Love Tomatoes, by Louise Riotte. Explains how to put vegetable relationships to work for you in your garden to produce a bountiful crop. Contains hundreds of interesting facts that offer both practical advice and entertaining reading. 244 pages. Paperback. ISBN 1-58017-026-9.

Deer-Proofing Your Yard and Garden, by Rhonda Massingham Hart. Offers valuable advice on landscape features that attract and repel deer. Explains how to identify deer damage and evaluates commercial and homemade deterrents. 160 pages. Paperback. ISBN 0-88266-988-5.

Mulch It! by Stu Campbell. This book shares the secret of healthy, easy, beautiful gardens and landscapes — mulch. 128 pages. Paperback. ISBN 1-58017-316-0.

The Organic Gardener's Home Reference, by Tanya Denckla. Includes complete information for growing, harvesting, and storing 62 of the most popular vegetables, fruits, nuts, and herbs. 304 pages. Hardcover. ISBN 0-88266-839-0.

Secrets to Great Soil, by Elizabeth P. Stell. Shows how soil health affects gardens, and how to evaluate your soil's texture, structure, pH, and general fertility. 224 pages. Paperback. ISBN 1-58017-008-0. Hardcover. ISBN 1-58017-009-9.

These books and other Storey books are available at your bookstore, farm store, garden center, or directly from Storey Books, 210 MASS MoCA Way, North Adams, MA 01247, or by calling 1-800-441-5700. Visit our Web site www.storey.com